DEVELOPING
A STRATEGY
FOR MISSIONS

A. Scott Moreau, *series editor*

Also in the series:

DEVELOPING A STRATEGY FOR MISSIONS

A Biblical, Historical, and Cultural Introduction

JOHN MARK TERRY
J. D. PAYNE

Baker Academic

a division of Baker Publishing Group
Grand Rapids, Michigan

Published by Baker Academic
a division of Baker Publishing Group
P.O. Box 6287, Grand Rapids, MI 49516-6287
www.bakeracademic.com

Printed in the United States of America

Library of Congress Cataloging-in-Publication Data
Terry, John Mark, 1949–
    Developing a strategy for missions : a biblical, historical, and cultural introduction / John Mark Terry and J. D. Payne.
        pages cm. — (Encountering Mission)
    Includes bibliographical references and index.
    ISBN 978-0-8010-3953-9 (pbk.)
    1. Missions—Theory. I. Payne, J. D. (Julius D.) II. Title.
BV2063.T335 2013
266—dc23   2013014498

13   14   15   16   17   18   19   7   6   5   4   3   2   1

Contents

Preface

If you are reading this book, then you are probably serving as a missionary or preparing to serve. Though you probably are not aware of it, this makes you part of the Modern Missions Movement. William Carey, pastor of a tiny church in England, launched the Modern Missions Movement with the publication of his pamphlet "An Enquiry into the Obligations of Christians to Use Means for the Conversion of the Heathens" in 1792. He argued that Christians have a God-given responsibility to bring the gospel to the peoples of the world.

In this book we aim to continue William Carey's work. Another book in the Encountering Mission series presents the biblical mandate for missions. In this book we focus on explaining Carey's view of "Means." Some believe that strategic planning is unnecessary; after all, the Holy Spirit will guide the missionaries to do what is necessary. Certainly, we believe that the Holy Spirit does guide Christians today; however, we fervently believe that the Holy Spirit can guide our planning as well as our work.

In Carey's day some pastors rejected his pleas for the church to engage in missions. They insisted that God would bring people to salvation without human activity. Andrew Fuller, Carey's mentor, wrote convincingly to show that God works through human instruments to accomplish his will and work in the world. Fuller and Carey persuaded most Christians in Europe and North America that God's plan for world redemption involves human actions.

In this book we show you how to develop strategies to reach the people groups of the world for Christ. To do this, we define *strategy* and explain the difference between *strategy* and *methods*. From there we sketch the development of missions strategy over two thousand years of church history. Finally, we explain how you can prayerfully develop a strategy that will take you from no believers to a vibrant cluster of churches.

I am delighted that I could collaborate on this book with J. D. Payne. For many years I have taught a doctoral-level seminar on missions strategy. Some years ago, J. D. was my student in that seminar. I also had the privilege of serving on his doctoral committee. He was an excellent student, and he has become an outstanding professor, missiologist, and author. He has surpassed his professor in many ways. He is an example of why I am thankful to my doctoral students over the years. They have taught me much about missions strategy, and this book reflects their careful scholarship and edifying writing.

J. D.'S COMMENTS . . .

In my heart this book actually began well over a decade ago. As a doctoral student, I had the privilege of being in one of Mark Terry's seminars on world evangelization strategies. I recall him commenting on the lack of good literature on missionary strategy. Unknown to him, it was at that moment that I began to consider writing such a book. And many years later, the thought of writing a book on strategy continued to haunt me. However, I clearly could not complete a satisfactory work by myself, and there was no kindred spirit with whom I could shoulder the load other than Mark Terry. He not only has a great missiological mind, a heart for the Great Commission, a wealth of missionary experience, and has been studying and teaching strategy for many years, but he is also a great friend who has significantly influenced my life and ministry. By then, however, Mark and his wife had returned to the field as missionaries, and he was teaching at a seminary in Asia. I contacted him and shared the idea for such a book. We took almost two years to discuss, pray, and begin working on this project. This book would not have been written without the influence of Mark and his willingness to share his life with his students. That said, it is truly an honor to have worked with him on this project.

Though in the past few years a handful of books have been written on developing strategy, we have to return to 1980 (or 1990 with the revised edition) to find a comprehensive work on missionary strategy, namely, Edward R. Dayton and David A. Fraser's massive *Planning Strategies for World Evangelization*. We have been greatly influenced by their work, and in this book hope to follow their leadership by attempting to provide a comprehensive work for a new generation.

While numerous matters of strategic planning today are the same as those thirty years ago, one of the topics on the minds of many in the West is the developing of missionary strategy in relation to majority world Christians. Though I began this book while serving as a seminary professor, I am now the pastor of church multiplication with The Church at Brook Hills (Birmingham, Alabama). Each year we send missionaries across the globe for short-, mid-, and long-term service. We also have partnerships with like-minded believers and churches in other countries. One topic that is on the hearts of our global disciple-making pastor and myself is: "What does healthy missions partnership look like between a church in the West and a church in the majority world?" We don't have the definitive answer. Other churches, missionaries, and agencies are asking variations on this question today. This area of strategy development is a brave new world for many of us, and resources on the topic are few at this time. As case studies and guidelines are developed and shared broadly, Mark and I hope future authors will do a better job developing this important matter than we have done in this book.

Throughout this work we periodically draw attention to the importance of understanding and working with majority world churches on strategy development. However, even with the reality that missions today is no longer "from the West to the rest," it is important to keep some matters in mind. First, in order to work with others on strategy development, you need to understand the foundations and mechanics of strategic planning. A failure to understand this process is likely to result in numerous unnecessary problems when working with others of different cultural backgrounds. Therefore, much of the foundational and practical components of this book are written with the Western individual and local church in mind. When doing strategic planning with a team composed of majority world believers, you will need to think through how some of the linear thought and values translate across cultural lines. Such is not an easy task in some contexts.

Second, in areas of the world where the unreached and unengaged remain, there are no majority world believers among such peoples with whom Western Christians can partner. Churches are yet to be planted. Most of this book is written with such contexts in mind, where partnerships are not possible.

We are extremely grateful to the Lord, who has allowed us to complete this project and commit this work to him, praying that he will use it to advance the gospel across the world for his glory. We are also thankful for the willingness of Baker Academic to publish this book. Jim Kinney and his team are to be commended for their hard work, gracious spirit, and desire to see good missiological writings come to the public. We have truly enjoyed working with them. Thank you, Jim. Also, this project would not have been possible without the labors of Scott Moreau, the editor of the Encountering Mission series. We have known Scott for many years. He is a true friend, one of the world's leading missiologists, and an outstanding educator. He believed in this project and provided excellent guidance along the journey. Thank you, Scott.

Of course, we must also thank our families for their encouragement, prayers, and support during the writing of this book. While they did not spend the time researching and writing as we did, their influence is found throughout these pages. Without them, we would not be where we are today, and the book before you would not exist.

Strategy Defined

ave you ever been in a conversation with someone, thinking that you
knew what the person was talking about when you realized that, even
though you were both using the same terminology, your definitions
differed? Such situations are frustrating and sometimes even embarrassing. For
that reason, rather than assuming that you already know the definitions we
have in mind, we begin with a chapter that focuses on the question, "What is
strategy?" In order to answer this question, we will define important foundational concepts and ground the discussion by touching on several important
historical matters.

The notion of strategy has its roots in the fields of military science and
marketing. An internet or library catalog search using the word *strategy* is
likely to yield a list of resources related to warfare and how to succeed in
the corporate world. While such fields do not directly relate to the missionary labors of the church, as will be noted, these fields still offer some helpful
insights for understanding missionary strategy.

One of the earliest writings on the topic of strategy was specifically related
to military tactics. *The Art of War*, written in China by Sun Tzu, is believed
to have been written 2,500 years ago. Over the centuries the notion of strategy became coupled to warfare. It is not uncommon to find definitions of
strategy related to knowing how to take the offensive against an enemy or

to defend against an enemy's incursion on the battlefield. While a wealth of information exists about military strategy, we are not addressing strategy from this perspective. Granted, being engaged in missionary activity is a spiritual battle, but we war not against flesh and blood but "against the rulers, against the authorities, against the powers of this dark world and against the spiritual forces of evil in the heavenly realms" (Eph. 6:12). And, yes, since all truth is God's truth wherever it can be found, we can learn from military strategy.

The second major area related to strategy is that of the business world. While the realm of business has its own way of conceptualizing and operationalizing strategy, its foundations are never far removed from military science. For example, Richard Luecke notes this historic connection: "Businesspeople have always liked military analogies, so it is not surprising that they have embraced the notion of strategy. They too began to think of strategy as a plan for controlling and utilizing their resources (human, physical, and financial) with the goal of promoting and securing their vital interests" (2005, xii).

While the corporate world did not begin writing books on this topic until 1971 with the publication of Kenneth Andrews's *The Concept of Corporate Strategy*, today a plethora of books exist on marketing strategy (Luecke 2005, xii). As I (J. D.) write this chapter, in my study are titles such as *Choosing the Future: The Power of Strategic Thinking* (Wells 1998); *Thinking Strategically: The Competitive Edge in Business, Politics, and Everyday Life* (Dixit and Nalebuff 1993); *Good to Great: Why Some Companies Make the Leap . . . and Others Don't* (Collins 2001); *Blue Ocean Strategy: How to Create Uncontested Market Space and Make the Competition Irrelevant* (Kim and Mauborgne 2005); and *Strategy: Create and Implement the Best Strategy for Your Business* (Harvard Business School 2005), just to mention a few. As with military science, while there are certain truths found in the world of business strategy that the church can take captive for the sake of kingdom advancement, that is not our focus.

The church is not selling a product, marketing a commodity, or launching a new service for the consumer. The church is not in competition or at war with another church, for there is only one church. The church is not a corporation but rather a family. It is not a nonprofit organization but a body of priests on mission until Jesus returns.

Over the past thirty years, within American evangelical circles, the church has been guilty of embracing the world of corporate America and drinking too deeply from the well of business strategy. We have marketed worship services, children's programs, Bible studies, and sermons—just like businesses do in promoting their jeans, soft drinks, or hamburgers. While we reference writers whose primary audience is not the church, we want to be clear that we are not writing from the perspective of Wall Street, Madison Avenue, or a five-star general. Rather, we write from the perspective of kingdom citizens seeking to make disciples of all nations (Matt. 28:18–20) by calling people to repentance and faith in Jesus (Acts 20:21) and to serve him through local churches.

WHAT IS STRATEGY?

It is helpful to start by listing a few common definitions of strategy, without getting distracted by each definition's military, marketing, or missional emphasis:

- "Strategy is a plan that aims to give the enterprise a competitive advantage over rivals through differentiation" (Luecke 2005, xiv).
- "The overall planning and conduct of large-scale military operations" ("Strategy" 1983, 672).
- "A plan of action" (ibid.).
- "Strategy is simply the means agreed upon to reach a certain goal" (Wagner 1983, 106).
- "A strategy is an overview of how we will go about something" (Dayton and Engstrom 1979, 100).
- "The process that determines how your ministry will accomplish its mission" (Malphurs 2005, 167).
- "Strategy is basically betting the farm on who the company is and what it intends to become" (Wells 1998, 65).

All these definitions have in common the notions of a *future orientation* and a *plan for process*. To understand strategy, it is important that these two commonalities are kept in mind. While wise strategy development involves a healthy understanding of the past and present, it moves us beyond history to future actions and results.

Future Orientation

Strategy involves the future. Although a team learns from the past and recognizes what it is in the present (e.g., its talents, gifts, passions, resources), strategy belongs to the future. Strategy is about how to accomplish something desired. If it is the Lord's will that tomorrow arrive (James 4:13–16), the team will plan to do this or that. Dayton and Fraser note this future orientation: "If we are going to get on with the business of world evangelization we need to have a way of thinking about the future. Since we cannot predict it in any

3

SIDEBAR 1.1
RIGHT STRATEGY

In the following excerpt Donald McGavran writes about some of the components of healthy strategy.

Right strategy tailors mission to fit each of the thousands of separate communities, so that in it the Church may grow. There is no one humanity in which the Church grows. The one world we often speak of is made up of numerous ethnic units, suddenly brought close together but not yet fused into one race. . . .

Right strategy will also take church growth with life-and-death seriousness. Right strategy will not so focus attention on "many good things to do" that church growth is not desired. . . .

The continual checking of every aspect of Christian mission against the church growth achieved is the *esse* of right strategy. Methods of church and mission work, systems of training missionaries, forms of ministerial and pastoral training, ways of producing tens of thousands of unpaid leaders, church mergers and co-operative enterprises of various kinds, institutional expressions of the faith—all these must be checked against the growth of the Church. . . .

Right strategy will devise hard, bold plans for planting churches, and will put them into execution. . . .

Right strategy recognizes that church growth is an exceedingly

---

detail, we can only consider the future and our actions in it in broad terms. But think of them we must" (1990, 24).

Strategy includes an attempt to discern what the Lord would desire to be accomplished among a particular people, population segment, village, tribe, or city. The focus of strategy is not on the present realities but rather on future possibilities. Strategy allows the team to look down the corridor of time, asking, "Lord willing, what will become of these people?" Strategy forces the team to think in terms of the practical outworking of the power of the gospel to transform an individual, family, tribe, or society. Strategy helps the team members discern where to go in their efforts.

Plan for Process

Strategy involves making plans. The future orientation component of strategy is a dream or a vision—but not the process of getting to the vision. Strategy therefore includes not only prayerfully discerning future realities but also developing a plan of action to reach them. Strategy assists in putting feet on future desire. It helps move a team from where it is to where it believes the Lord would have it go.

The plan to reach a vision involves a process. A strategy is typically not a complex process and cannot be commanded. . . .

The Church can develop right strategy in mission. All she has to do is to observe what has taken place in the hundreds of matchless laboratories which a hundred and sixty years of modern missions have provided. By amassing knowledge, by pooling the common experience of missions and churches, by assembling the evidences of instances where the Church was planted, where it grew, where it stopped growing, and where it never even started, she can discern which processes in which specific circumstances receive God's blessing and which do not. Right strategy will spend large sums of money and the lives of some of its best men and women in intensive research into the most effective ways and means of reconciling men to God and of multiplying churches. . . .

Right strategy can be discerned, learned, taught and executed. When it is, the enormous potential in today's missions will be realized. When it is, the confusion and frustration that mark so much mission today will happily become a thing of the past. (1965, 457, 458, 459, 460, 461)

REFLECTION AND DISCUSSION

- What aspects of McGavran's understanding of "right strategy" were surprising to you? Why?
- What are the dangers of a strategy focusing attention on "many good things to do"?
- Do you agree that right strategy can be "discerned, learned, taught and executed"? Explain.

single-step event that results in the fulfillment of the vision. Strategy involves a process of major steps as the team climbs the stairs to reach the desired end. And along the climb each major step taken will consist of several smaller, minor—yet important—steps along the journey. While this journey may not be a linear one (e.g., many times several steps will happen simultaneously), the outworking of a strategy involves a procession, and movement from point A to point B, and so on, until the team reaches the vision on the horizon.

Our working definition of strategy throughout this book is the following:

Mission strategy is the overall process describing what we believe the Lord would have us accomplish to make disciples of all nations.

While this book is not the place to address the debate revolving around the definition of "mission," we need to explain the term and its relationship to strategy. We understand mission first and foremost as related to making worshipers for the Creator and, therefore, mission strategy as related to the process of seeing such disciples made.

First, mission is derived from a conversionistic theology. From Genesis to Revelation, the metanarrative of the Scriptures is that all creation has been affected by the fall. While God will create a new heaven and a new earth (Isa.

65:17), the redemption of people through the atoning work of Jesus on the cross is primary in his mission. The promise to crush the head of the serpent via the seed of the woman (Gen. 3:15) was fulfilled with the death and resurrection of Jesus. From the promises made in the garden, and more clearly defined with Abram (Gen. 17), to the wedding of the Lamb (Rev. 19:7), the Creator is glorifying himself by building his church (Eph. 2:19–22) as men, women, boys, and girls repent, confessing Jesus as Lord (Phil. 2:11).

Second, the Father's means of redeeming fallen humanity is through the gospel being proclaimed (1 Cor. 1:21). As the Spirit works his regenerative process in the lives of people who come face-to-face with the exclusive truth of Jesus, they leave the kingdom of darkness and enter into the kingdom of God (Col. 1:13). And while this proclamation is the means by which God works, the medium that brings this good news to people is his church (Acts 13:47). The redeemed have not been made into kingdom citizens to be disengaged from the rest of creation. Rather, as priests they are called to proclaim his truth (1 Pet. 2:9), make disciples of all peoples (Matt. 28:19), and be his witnesses (Matt. 5:14–16). Such are the primary responsibilities of kingdom citizens.

Third, while there are many excellent activities that kingdom citizens can be involved in to bring glory to God, the primary New Testament teaching is that the mission of God is first and foremost to do evangelism that results in the birth and growth of churches. The kingdom advances and Jesus builds his church numerically as people are converted. We recognize that the mission of God includes matters such as healing, casting out demons, caring for the poor, and issues of justice. But we would add that such matters either follow conversion, with newly planted churches carrying out such tasks, or are done to open doors for the calling of others to repentance and faith in Jesus, as observed throughout the Gospels and Acts. Service and conducting social ministry are both necessary and extremely important but should be carried out in the world so that the peoples of the world may come to declare the greatness of God's name (Ps. 47).

TYPES OF STRATEGIES

Not all strategies are created equal. Although many missionary strategies share similar visions, goals, and action steps, diversity exists regarding the philosophies on which such strategies are conceived. It is these philosophies that influence the strategy from planning to execution.

Henry Mintzberg notes that a 1962 *Harvard Business Review* article "offered literally hundreds of models of a process by which strategy could supposedly be formally developed and operationalized." Despite these numerous approaches, Mintzberg concludes, "with some specific exceptions . . . these built on a single conceptual framework, or basic model, differ less in fundamentals than in levels of detail" (1994, 35).

So, although there are a multitude of paradigms for strategy development, many of them can be reduced to a few ideal types. In 1980 Dayton and Fraser developed a taxonomy of strategy that differentiates strategy based on the underlying philosophy. They categorized strategies into four types: (1) Standard Solution, (2) Being-in-the-Way, (3) Plan-So-Far, and (4) Unique Solution (Dayton and Fraser 1980, 17–18).

Standard Solution

The Standard Solution strategy is an approach to strategy development that holds a particular strategy constant. The rationale for this strategy is that the means we used to accomplish the task worked well in the past, so they will continue to work in the future.

While people using this philosophy of strategy development attempt to eliminate the unexpected and make strategic planning into a science, the reality is that the Standard Solution paradigm falls short on many levels. Past successes are no guarantee of future successes, and we may note several reasons for this.

First, this approach assumes that the ways of the Lord are constant. Though this is certainly true in certain matters regarding God's character and nature, it is not always the case with the working of the Spirit. For example, the apostle Paul attempted to enter Asia Minor and Bithynia, and the Spirit interrupted his plans (Acts 16:6–7). Based on what is known of the apostle's work in the book of Acts until this point, few people would contend that the apostle was attempting to work outside the Spirit's will. Rather, for some unknown reason the Spirit interrupted Paul's plans to take him to Philippi to plant the church in that city.

An example of this paradigm would include taking a tract-distribution strategy that the Lord used greatly in a highly literate part of the world and applying it in a predominately oral setting. Although the gospel message contained in the booklets is God's Word, relevant for everyone, the strategy would not be as effective when applied to a society primarily composed of oral learners.

Second, the Standard Solution strategy fails to take humanity and society into consideration. Missionary strategy is about reaching people with the gospel. While people can be predictable, that does not mean that they are constants. People are sentient creatures. They receive stimuli, process them, and react. They are not robots and do not always respond in the same manner.

Finally, the Standard Solution strategy fails to take culture into consideration. No one can become culturally neutral during the strategy development process. In their attempt to engage peoples with the gospel, missionaries must recognize that the cultures of those peoples are often different from their own. Whenever they work with different peoples and population segments, they encounter different contexts, worldviews, communication and lifestyle patterns, family dynamics, social and political influences, and religious diversity. When a strategy works well in one context, there is no guarantee that it will work just as well in a different context—even one that is only marginally different.

Being-in-the-Way

Strategists who use a Being-in-the-Way philosophy advocate that those making plans get in the way of the Holy Spirit. Proponents aver that the Spirit, like the wind, blows with no one knowing where he comes from and where he is going. Advocates often use Isaiah to support this perspective:

> "For my thoughts are not your thoughts,
>   neither are your ways my ways,"
> declares the LORD.
> "As the heavens are higher than the earth,
>   so are my ways higher than your ways
>   and my thoughts than your thoughts." (Isa. 55:8–9)

While this concept and passage might be used to proof text an argument against making any plans, the biblical picture is far richer than a simple declaration to make no plans and has much to say about the need to make plans for the future.

Dayton and Fraser note that the Being-in-the-Way philosophy allows missionaries to succeed every time, since they take no responsibility for their actions: "The net effect of this approach eliminates failure. Whatever happens is God's responsibility. Anything that happens is God's will. . . . A hidden assumption of this approach is that proper spirituality cuts out the need for human forethought" (Dayton and Fraser 1990, 15).

The Being-in-the-Way philosophy can easily devolve into supporting a strategic antinomianism, offering missionaries a license for laziness. Missionary activity, by its very definition, is engaging. There is no room for a laissez-faire approach to making disciples of all nations.

Plan-So-Far

While this paradigm, for no disclosed reason, was omitted from Dayton and Fraser's revised edition of *Planning Strategies for World Evangelization*, it was addressed in the original version. Those who follow this philosophy of strategic planning advocate making plans to get the work started but leaving the process and results to the Lord.

This model could be visualized with the image of missionaries standing at the top of a hill with a large boulder. They begin to push and shove to get the rock moving, but little more. Once the stone is rolling down the hill, they step out of the way and have no further involvement. Dayton and Fraser illustrate: "An example would be the agency that after negotiations with a local government received permission to begin a craft industry in a country. However, the agency made no specific plans as to how it would relate to the Christian churches that were already in the country, churches that in their view were a mixture of Christianity and animism" (Dayton and Fraser 1980, 18).

Unique Solution

The final paradigm offered by Dayton and Fraser is the one that they (and we as well) advocate. Those who advocate the Unique Solution philosophy recognize both the science and the art of strategy development. Rather than supporting a model for strategy development that treats peoples as automatons and social change as predictable and known, those using this approach offer strategists both parameters to guide planning and freedom for the work of the Spirit.

SIDEBAR 1.2
WINNING STRATEGY

Judith M. Bardwick, founder of Bardwick and Associates, a management consulting firm, describes some of the elements for a healthy business strategy.

For strategy to succeed it must anticipate, create, and guide change and create commitment in the organization's members. It should be so plausible, clever, bold, and achievable that in itself it generates a conviction that even if the journey is hard, it is worth taking because the strategy has created a major competitive advantage. Defining the business of the business shrewdly and wisely and creating a convincing strategy for winning are critical in terms of persuading people that they have real leaders and that success will be achieved. (1996, 136)

REFLECTION AND DISCUSSION

- What elements (if any) of Bardwick's recommendations are applicable to the development of mission strategy?
- Do you disagree with any of her recommendations for use in missions? Why?
- What is the importance of *success* in relation to strategy? What is success when it comes to mission strategy?

The Unique Solution approach offers a middle way between the Standard Solution and the Being-in-the-Way. This paradigm allows for the wisdom and knowledge that come from knowing what has worked throughout history in reaching people, while allowing for the Spirit to work as we labor to innovate and contextualize our strategy to the world of the people, both today and tomorrow.

CONCLUSION

We hope that as you read this book you recognize that while there are important routine and predictable aspects of mission strategy, reaching the world with the gospel is built on a principle Paul Eshleman, chairman of the Lausanne Strategy Working Group, notes: "What has become clear in many strategic discussions is that world evangelization is not so much about materials, tools and techniques. It is about love, compassion, prayer, holiness and obedience" (Eshleman 2007).

Apart from our obedience to Christ, we can do nothing of any significance for the kingdom (John 15:5). Apart from our faithful service to him, the components of strategy development are of little value. It is our prayer that in the process of developing mission strategies you will become more conformed to the image of Christ (Rom. 8:29), relying on him as you assess your situation, make your plans, and implement your action steps.

2

The Crafting of Mission Strategy

The development of mission strategy is a process that involves obtaining a vision from the Lord for reaching a people, understanding the missionary team's present realities, and developing the steps to move the team from where it is to where it believes it needs to go. In chapter 1, we described strategic planning as both a science and an art. Before proceeding any further, we need to address some of the fundamental matters related to crafting strategy. In this chapter, then, we explain how strategy development is both science and art, offer our definition of strategic planning, and address some paradoxes related to planning mission strategy.

CRAFTING STRATEGY

Recently the concept of strategic planning has developed a reputation for being a task that occurs in the sterile environment of the boardroom, with no option for change once the strategy is brought to the place of service. Some understand strategic planning as rigid, scientific, structured, bureaucratic, and linear in its application. They view it as based on research that is divorced from reality.

To provide a better image to communicate the planning of strategy, Henry Mintzberg advocates the notion of "crafting" a strategy. While we agree that crafting probably suggests a better image, it should be understood that whenever we refer to strategic planning or planning strategy we do not advocate what Mintzberg fears. Throughout this book we use the terms "crafting" and "planning" interchangeably. Provided we are able to explain our understandings of these concepts, we see no difference between the two when it comes to developing mission strategy.

Mintzberg notes, "Smart strategists appreciate that they cannot always be smart enough to think through everything in advance" (1987, 69). Circumstances change. What was once a predictable situation transitions to another reality. Of course, this situation should not be a surprise to the mission strategist since strategy in particular involves people, who are not always predictable.

Following his conviction regarding smart strategists, Mintzberg reveals the significance of the artistic side of planning by drawing on the image of a craftsperson. This is where the necessity for fluidity and flexibility come into the strategy development process. This side of planning is necessary to deal with and respond to the challenges posed when we attempt to reach peoples and societies. Mintzberg writes:

> At work, the potter sits before a lump of clay on the wheel. Her mind is on the clay, but she is also aware of sitting between her past experiences and her future prospects. She knows exactly what has and has not worked for her in the past. She has an intimate knowledge of her work, her capabilities, and her markets. As a craftsman, she senses rather than analyzes these things; her knowledge is "tacit." All these things are working in her mind as her hands are working the clay. The product that emerges on the wheel is likely to be in the tradition of her past work, but she may break away and embark on a new direction. Even so, the past is no less present, projecting itself into the future.
>
> In my metaphor, managers are craftsmen and strategy is their clay. Like the potter, they sit between a past of corporate capabilities and a future of market opportunities. And if they are truly craftsmen, they bring to their work an equally intimate knowledge of the materials at hand. That is the essence of crafting strategy. (1987, 66)

It is this metaphor of crafting that we believe is the most beneficial for developing mission strategies, for contained within Mintzberg's model is the reality that strategists must have knowledge of the past and the present as they anticipate the future.

Past knowledge of the working of the Spirit among the people, in the church, the team, or the organization is important. Since the past influences and guides future behavior, strategists need to know history. This includes knowledge of the significant historical matters that presently affect a group's receptivity to the gospel. Past knowledge allows team members to recall their individual pasts and reflect on how their pasts will affect the present and future outworking of the strategy.

Present knowledge of what the Spirit is doing is also important. Where is the Lord at work, so that the team can join him? What are the major socio-cultural issues affecting life and decision making among the people at this very moment? Is the team serving in an area where the largest employer in the town is threatening to move to another country for cheaper labor? How do the people in the community view decision making? Does the city encourage diversity or fear change? What are the gifts, talents, passions, and interests of the team members? There are a multitude of questions that a team can ask about the present to assist it in crafting strategy.

From a humanistic perspective the future is uncertain. And even from a theological perspective, while we know that the Lord holds the future in his hands, we do not know all the details of tomorrow—or even if time will continue. The mission strategist is like a sailor with a telescope. Although the telescope provides the sailor with a different perspective, it will not allow him or her to see around the curve of the earth's surface. The boat on the horizon will come into view mast first, and then only as the boat sails closer will the hull be observed. Similarly, the strategist cannot predict what will happen tomorrow, let alone next month or the following year. Because of this reality, there is always a major element of uncertainty in strategic planning.

STRATEGIC PLANNING

Without planning, strategy is forever locked in the ironclad cage of theory. While planning is no guarantee that action steps will be taken to implement the strategy, without it strategy remains within missionary hearts and on computer files. Aubrey Malphurs notes that strategic planning is a process involving both thinking and acting (2005, 30). And here, within this under-standing, we see the wedding of the theoretical (thinking) and the practical (acting). Dayton comments, "Planning is seeing *things as they are* and then trying to describe *things as we want them to be*" (1980b, 17, emphasis in original).

Throughout this book our understanding of strategic planning, or strategy development, is the following:

> Strategic planning is a prayerfully discerned, Spirit-guided process of preparation, development, implementation, and evaluation of the necessary steps involved for missionary endeavors.

Before we continue, each of the phrases in this definition needs to be explained. These concepts will be clarified throughout this book; for now it is important to have a basic understanding of this definition.

Prayerfully Discerned

The development of mission strategy is a supernatural process. While resources abound on the development of military and business strategies, mission strategy is dynamically related to the Father of mission. Before a team begins to think through and develop a strategy, it needs to pray. Prayer must precede and remain an essential part of strategic planning. The Lord of the harvest works through the prayers of his people to guide in strategy development. If strategy is from the Lord, then prayer is a part of the process of knowing, understanding, and accomplishing what the Father has in mind in making disciples of the people.

SIDEBAR 2.1
PEOPLE BLINDNESS

The following passage is taken from Ralph Winter's famous 1974 presentation at the Lausanne Congress on World Evangelization:

> I'm afraid that all our exultation about the fact that every *country* of the world has been penetrated has allowed many to suppose that every *culture* has by now been penetrated. This misunderstanding is a malady so widespread that it deserves a special name. Let us call it "people blindness," that is, blindness to the existence of separate *peoples* within *countries*; a blindness, I might add, which seems more prevalent in the U.S. and among U.S. missionaries than anywhere else. The Bible rightly translated could have made this plain to us. The "nations" to which Jesus often referred were mainly ethnic groups within the single political structure of the Roman government. The various nations represented on the day of Pentecost were for the most part not *countries* but *peoples.* In the Great Commission as it is found in Matthew, the phrase "make disciples of all *ethne* (peoples)" does not let us off the hook once we have a church in every country—God wants a strong church within every people!

> "People blindness" is what prevents us from noticing the sub-groups within a country which are significant to development of effective evangelistic strategy. Society will be seen as a complex mosaic, to use McGavran's phrase, once we recover from "people blindness." (1975, 221)

REFLECTION AND DISCUSSION

- How does Winter's notion of people blindness affect the crafting of mission strategy?

- What are the advantages and disadvantages—as related to the development of strategy—of seeing society as a complex mosaic?

Spirit-Guided

The Spirit of God is living and active. He is at work in the lives of the missionaries even before they arrive where he has called them to serve. He provides leadership. For example, Philip was led by the Spirit to the Ethiopian (Acts 8:29). We must also remember that the Scriptures note: "In their hearts humans plan their course, but the LORD establishes their steps" (Prov. 16:9). Those laboring to develop mission strategy must understand the importance of walking in fellowship with the Spirit. Unconfessed sin that grieves (Eph. 4:30) and quenches the Spirit (1 Thess. 5:19) interferes with the development of strategy. The development and implementation of mission strategy are supernatural endeavors.

Process

Strategy involves movement. Teams wish to progress from where they are to where they believe their ministries should go. The development and implementation of a strategy do not occur instantaneously. Even the simplest of strategies requires an action step or two before the end vision is accomplished.

Preparation

It is important that strategists do their homework before developing a strategy. All the important elements of knowing oneself, the team, and the context are found in the area of preparation. Matters such as knowing the vision to be accomplished, the theological and missiological values of the team, and understanding the targeted people geographically, demographically, culturally, spiritually, historically, politically, and linguistically are part of preparation.

Development

Development involves thinking through the major and minor steps necessary to see the vision fulfilled. Although this element of strategic planning is still a theoretical construct in the beginning, it is nevertheless important to consider how the team will practically move from point A to point B. Teams consider the realities that must occur in order for each particular step to be taken and the desired vision achieved.

Implementation

Strategy is not meant to remain in a notebook on a shelf or in a document on a computer. It is intended to be implemented. Failure to implement the strategy will result in failure in accomplishing what the team set out to do. Larry Bossidy and Ram Charan refer to this act as *execution*. According to them this matter is vital to the outworking of a strategy. They note, "You can't craft a worthwhile strategy if you don't at the same time make sure your organization has or can get what's required to execute it, including the right resources and the right people" (Bossidy and Charan 2002, 7). The plans must be applied on location.

Evaluation

While the word *evaluation* occurs at the end of the definition of strategy, in reality it is a part of the overall process. It must engulf everything the team does, even before it arrives at its place of service. Evaluation begins when the vision to be accomplished comes onto the horizon. It continues through the establishing of goals. Evaluation occurs as action steps are taken to accomplish those goals. From start to finish, mission strategy must be immersed in the sea of evaluation. Strategists must be good stewards of the Lord's resources. They want to know what is working well and not so well to reach people with the gospel and multiply churches. Evaluation helps in the process of making adjustments along the journey of implementing strategy.

THE BIG FIVE

In light of our definition, the planning involved in the crafting and implementing of missionary strategy can be summarized in five important practices. Some of these are evident in the definition above:

- Asking good questions
- Responding with healthy answers
- Applying wise action steps
- Evaluating everything
- Praying with diligence

Asking Good Questions

Strategists have inquiring minds. They want to know answers. They ask questions such as: Are we being faithful to the Lord? Is what we are doing the most Christ-honoring thing? What is working well in our strategy? What is not working very well? What do we need to change? How can we do a better job? Are we being wise stewards with all the resources and opportunities the

Lord has entrusted to us? What do we need to do first? What do we need to do next?

Strategists must also take the following questions into consideration whenever they begin the strategic planning process: What do we know about the context and people? What is the purpose of our team? What is the best way to reach these people with the gospel and plant churches? What are the barriers for evangelization? Does our team have the callings, resources, gifts, and abilities to execute the strategy? What are our immediate, short-term, and long-term goals?

Responding with Healthy Answers

Along with asking good questions, strategists must respond with healthy answers. Not just any answers will do, but only those that are true to the biblical and theological foundations for Great Commission activity, in agreement with missiological principles supporting healthy missionary practices, and efficient and relevant to the context. Here is where the theoretical begins to meet the reality of the field. According to Dayton and Fraser, "Planning should be thought of as a bridge between where we are now and the future we believe God desires for us" (1990, 293). Finding healthy answers will require intense research.

Applying Wise Action Steps

The application work is mainly done on location. Action steps involve the team's movement from goal to goal on the upward stairway toward accomplishing the overarching vision (i.e., end vision). The application of the steps is obviously done in conjunction with knowing oneself, the team, and the context, for it is out of the knowledge of these three areas that the strategist is best poised to make wise practical decisions regarding the outworking of the strategy.

Evaluating Everything

Evaluation was included in our definition; it is also the fourth major component in strategic planning. The evaluation of everything is an ongoing process. Strategic planners never rest from this component of planning. Such evaluation is necessary if planners are to stay focused on what the Spirit is doing. It also is a matter of proper stewardship. The strategist wants to be the faithful and wise servant (Matt. 25:14–30). Constant evaluation is not done to justify a critical spirit but rather to reveal a desire to make the best decisions under the circumstances.

Praying with Diligence

Prayer must be a natural part of the strategist's life. Strategy development should be bathed in prayer. The practice of strategy development should be a supernatural event, requiring time with the Lord. Throughout this book we often make reference to the place of prayer in the development and implementation of missionary strategies. This repetition may appear to be

---

SIDEBAR 2.2
THE ROAD AHEAD

In the 1970s William R. Read wrote about his reflections on the development of a trans-Brazilian road system and its impact on the churches in the country. With five-year plans to settle five hundred thousand people in different villages along the four-thousand-kilometer road, Read recognized that such growth would provide many unique opportunities. He noted:

> The magnitude of the church planting task among the new settlers and the problems that such an effort along this road will face in the next two decades is breath taking. Many of the foreign missions that are now working in Brazil are pursuing the policy, from a distance, of watchful waiting, taking time to examine carefully this highly fluid opportunity. At the same time, some mission leaders are making definite plans for exploratory survey trips into the Amazon Basin areas. These surveys will become the means by which these missions will be able to gather the information they need that will permit them to formulate a strategy for their church planting effort in this vast hinterland area. National church leaders are anxiously following the latest reports that come out of this advancing road system. Some of these leaders are trying to determine what resources should be set aside for some adequate type of evangelistic endeavor that their churches can initiate in some of the more strategic centers. It takes time for many of the fast growing centers to be spotted in time for favorable consideration as "strategic" locations. Familiarity with the entire road system in all of its extension and vastness is a necessity in order to make many of these important decisions. (1973, 174)

REFLECTION AND DISCUSSION

- Do you agree or disagree with Read that the development of a road is a critical matter as related to crafting strategy? Why?

- How important were the responses of the different mission leaders to the development of strategy in this part of Brazil? Explain.

- If you were a strategist for this area, would you have responded similarly or differently than the mission leaders? Explain.

an accidental redundancy on our part; however, we are intentionally repetitive. We are convinced that the prayer of a righteous person has great power (James 5:16), and such power is needed for the development and outworking of strategy.

THE PARADOXES OF STRATEGIC PLANNING

The notion of paradox is ever present in the development of missionary strategy. There are at least eight seemingly contradictory elements of strategic planning that need to be addressed. Having an awareness of these components will assist the strategist in wrestling through the process of developing appropriate strategy.

God Is Sovereign but Works through Our Planning

While more is stated about this paradox in chapter 4, it must be noted here that crafting strategy is not an unbiblical act. Although God is in control of his universe and the outworking of his story of the redemption of creation, he works through the means of his church to make known his wisdom (Eph. 3:10). Throughout the Bible many of God's people developed plans: Abram, Moses, Joseph, David, Solomon, Nehemiah, Peter, Paul, and so on. Even God sent forth his Son at just the right time (Gal. 4:4). Strategists commit all their plans to the Lord, allowing him to guide the process from beginning to end. Proverbs notes, "Plans are established by seeking advice; so if you wage war, obtain guidance" (20:18), and "A person's steps are directed by the LORD. How then can anyone understand their own way?" (20:24).

Strategic Planning Is Both a Linear and Nonlinear Process

Models for strategy development are typically presented in linear fashion. The reason for this is twofold. First, it is difficult to convey a nonlinear process in a written format such as a book, just as it is difficult to draw a three-dimensional object on a piece of paper. The task can be accomplished but comes with challenges. Similarly, when describing strategic planning, it is much easier to explain: "first you do this . . . second you do that . . . third you do this," than it is to describe a process that involves simultaneous or other nonlinear events. Second, many elements of strategy development require a linear approach. Certain steps in the overall process cannot be envisioned and planned for by a team until previous steps occur; sequential steps are a necessary part of the entire process.

19

Strategic Planning Involves Both Rigidity and Fluidity

Daniel J. Isenberg correctly notes that strategy development requires "the ability to remain focused on long-term objectives while staying flexible enough to solve day-to-day problems and recognize new opportunities" (1987, 92). Strategy development is both a *determined* process and an *emerging* process, involving both certainty and uncertainty. Therefore, crafting strategy is a messy process. On the one hand, teams will be able to make decisions through God-given wisdom knowing the likely outcome in advance. On the other hand, teams will often have to take action with little knowledge of the future. While all strategy development involves faith, it is in the times of uncertainty that faith is stretched.

Mintzberg found that some of the most effective strategies involved both control and flexibility (1987, 70). Some elements of a strategy will remain constant, while others will demand that a team readjust as it makes progress. There will be times when a team will be able to apply its action steps exactly as it developed them, but there will be times that will call for "experimentation" with the action steps. Like the person who uses a long stick to strike the ice on a frozen pond to see if it is safe to walk across, strategists will more often than not have to develop their strategies in reaction to the circumstances around them as they take their steps toward their goals.

Mintzberg makes another important observation related to the necessity of fluidity in the strategy development process. Strategists need to be students of their context and fight hard against the familiarity that breeds contempt. Though they have the Spirit and wisdom, they still must recognize the responsibility to be vigilant and aware of the times. Strategists must not grow complacent as they move from goal to goal on the path toward accomplishing the vision. Although the changes that demand radical strategic shifts are easily observed, a subtle challenge occurs during the times of normalcy. And this challenge comes from familiarity with that norm. Mintzberg exhorts:

> The real challenge in crafting strategy lies in detecting the subtle and developing discontinuities that may eventually undermine the organization, or provide it with a special opportunity. And for this, there is no technique, no program, just sharp minds in touch with the situation. Unfortunately, this form of strategic thinking tends to atrophy during the long periods of stability that most organizations experience. So the trick is to manage for long within a given strategic orientation yet be able to pick out the occasional discontinuity that really matters. (2007, 378)

20

Strategic Planning Involves Both History and Future

It is incorrect to assume that crafting strategy is an exclusively future-oriented activity. While the future is a major aspect of planning strategy, it is not divorced from the past or the present. Excellent strategy development requires that the strategist know what the Lord has used in the past to reach the particular people with the gospel. If the team is pioneering a new work, then knowledge of how the Lord has moved among similar peoples in similar situations is helpful.

Strategic Planning Is Both Art and Science

Sometimes strategy is referred to as both an art and a science. What does this mean? Consider, for example, the chef who describes cooking this way. The "art" of cooking is knowing which seasonings and spices complement one another, knowing by intuition and experience what types of chocolates to use with certain ingredients, and, of course, understanding the visual presentation of the food on the plate. The art of cooking involves wisdom gained over the years, discernment, impressions, and knowledge of one's kitchen appliances and ingredients. The art is not always predictable.

The "science" of cooking, however, can be found in the knowledge of the chemical reactions that occur as starches and sugars break down at certain temperatures, the reason for blanching vegetables, and the functions of butter when used at different temperatures. The science of cooking involves the empirical knowledge gained from knowing about measurements, temperature, catalysts, and reactions. The science is generally predictable.

The development of strategy involves principles to guide and skills to be applied. Certain aspects of the process are conducted in a controlled environment (e.g., on a computer, in an office), but much of strategic planning revolves around the evaluation and revising of one's strategy when the winds of change blow as the strategy is applied. Although there are mechanics of strategy such as articulating a vision, developing goals, and planning action steps, the work of the artist is also involved—hence, our previous discussion on the crafting of strategy.

Strategic Planning Is a Simple Process but Difficult to Execute

The process of strategic planning is not a difficult process. As already mentioned, much of it involves asking and answering the right questions. Strategic planning is not extremely complicated. The paradox is found in the execution. Strategy is meant to be applied, to be executed. The challenge of

21

progressing through the action steps necessary to achieve a goal is the real difficulty. Developing the strategy has some challenges, but the difficulty lies in implementing the strategy where the missionary serves.

Strategic Planning Involves Commonality and Customization

While all strategies have certain characteristics in common, each must be customized to the specific context and people. Dayton and Fraser were aware of this reality as they described the Unique Solution philosophy (see chap. 1), noting, "Strategies must be as unique as the peoples to whom they apply" (1990, 15). In other words, a one-size-fits-all approach to strategy development and implementation is unhealthy and unwise.

Consider an example from daily life. My (J. D.) oldest child is now riding a bicycle that she was not able to ride several years ago. I remember when she first started out on a very small bicycle with training wheels, not much larger than a tricycle. After she developed her riding skills and was physically able to touch the ground, my wife and I removed the training wheels. Shortly after that time she was able to ride a much larger bicycle. While she is physically not able to ride an adult's bicycle yet, she is getting there.

It is important to note the parallel in this situation with strategy development. Just as my wife and I realized that our daughter had to have a customized bicycle appropriate for her physical and mental development, the development of strategy requires some flexibility on behalf of missionaries to the people. While the truths of the Scriptures never change from people to people, the strategic approaches must be customized to the contexts.

Strategic Planning Involves the Known and the Unknown

The church has two thousand years of missions history to draw from when it comes to understanding how the gospel spread and churches multiplied. Over the centuries numerous strategies have been used to advance the kingdom, with some working better than others. Biblical and missiological principles are also in place to assist in developing strategy. Yet even with the wisdom of the ages, every generation and context creates unique and unknown challenges to building the church.

In the United States the letter X has become a symbol for uncertainty. I (J. D.) am a part of Generation X, the generation that followed the baby boomers. My generation obtained this appellation from the title of a novel by Douglas Coupland (1991), with X representing a generation that has not figured out life, is in hiding, or is very uncertain. In the late twentieth and early twenty-first centuries, The X-Files was a science-fiction television series, with the X-files representing unsolved cases involving paranormal activity. So when we address the X factors in relation to missionary strategy, we are referencing that which is an unknown or uncertain factor.

Over the years I (J. D.) have invited church planters to speak to my classes about their ministries. On more than one occasion, I have asked them to discuss issues related to strategy, and on more than one occasion, I have heard the following statement: "Prior to going to the field, I had my strategy put together in a nice binder. However, shortly after arriving on the field, I realized that none of it would work. I had to discard all my plans and start over."

While I do think that such is the case for some church planters, scrapping one's entire strategy plan is rare. I also think that some church planters use hyperbole to shock students. My point is that strategies can be developed, but once the team begins putting those strategies into practice, the strategies will have to change. And here is the challenge: A team cannot constantly and accurately predict the factors that will lead to change in its strategy. They are an unknown. The only thing that a team can know for certain about the X factors is that they will force the team to make adjustments in its strategy.

Individuals, families, villages, towns, and cities are not static but rather dynamic. People are social beings, able to make decisions and act and react to the changes in their environments. Thankfully, for the mission strategist, the changes that normally occur are not to such a degree that a radical strategic shift has to occur often.

CONCLUSION

In this chapter we have provided an overview of the components involved in crafting strategy. Much of the rest of this book relates to and amplifies the contents of this chapter. In the next chapter we turn to some of the contemporary arguments against the development of mission strategy.

3

Contemporary Objections to Missionary Strategy

The notion of the church making plans to reach others with the gospel has not always been looked on with favor. The development of strategies has at times been misunderstood as something unspiritual, atheological, and too secular. William Carey faced such challenges whenever he advocated the use of "means" to reach others with the gospel. Donald McGavran, the father of the contemporary Church Growth Movement, encountered misunderstandings when he advocated the development of strategies to plant and grow churches. To better understand missionary strategy, it is necessary to discuss a few possible objections to strategy development. Though the following two chapters will address the biblical foundations and missiological principles for strategy, thinking through these objections will better prepare us for the development of a theological and missiological framework regarding such an important aspect of the advancement of the kingdom.

OBJECTION 1: STRATEGIC PLANNING ATTEMPTS TO REPLACE GOD'S SOVEREIGNTY

"Since God is sovereign, developing missionary strategies is a waste of time," according to one popular objection. Of course, such an argument is not new; in fact, it is a variation on the same objection raised when William Carey made a plea to evangelize the unbelievers on the other side of the world over two centuries ago. When Carey's biblical conviction was challenged by those believing that God will reach the heathen when he desires, Carey wrote his famous little book *An Enquiry into the Obligations of Christians to Use Means for the Conversion of the Heathens* (1792). Carey's point was that though God is sovereign in working out his plan of salvation history, he has mandated the use of means through his church to reach the world with the gospel.

In his sovereignty and throughout history, God has worked through plans to accomplish his purposes for salvation (e.g., Eph. 1:7–10). God had specific blueprints for Noah's ark (Gen. 6:14–16). He revealed a few brief details to Abram regarding the plan he had for Abram's descendants to obtain the land (Gen. 15:12–16). While in the days of famine, Joseph clearly recognized God's plan after Joseph's rise to power (Gen. 45:4–8), telling his brothers, "So then, it was not you who sent me here, but God" (Gen. 45:8). God told Moses a plan for the design of the tabernacle (Exod. 26:30). Though God had a plan for his people to enter the promised land, they nevertheless rejected his plan and wandered for forty years (Num. 13–14). God worked through the plan of the bronze serpent to bring healing to the children of Israel (Num. 21:4–9). Much of the book of Deuteronomy addresses God's detailed plan for how his people were to relate to him, one another, and the alien after they arrived in the promised land. Gideon and Joshua drew up battle plans, even after God told them that he was going to use them to carry out his purposes. The Lord worked through the cultural practices of Boaz to become the kinsman-redeemer for Ruth. He worked through the strategy of Esther and Mordecai to deliver his people. He worked through the plans that David gave to Solomon for the temple (1 Chron. 28:11–12). He worked through Nehemiah's particular strategy to rebuild the wall around the city. Throughout the prophetic writings God revealed elements of his plans to his prophets and people, at times giving them specific directions about how to live in light of his plans. Isaiah was told of the plan that God had for the Assyrians (Isa. 14:24–27). Jeremiah shared God's plan against Edom (Jer. 49:20). It was revealed to Habakkuk that God's plan involved using the Babylonians as a means of judgment on his people (Hab. 1:6).

In the New Testament God used the magi's deception to send Herod into a diabolical rage; Herod ordered the murdering of the male children in Bethlehem, in the process of bringing about the fulfillment of Old Testament prophecy (Matt. 2:16–18). Paul writes that it was at the right moment in God's plan that Jesus was born (Gal. 4:4). Matthew's Gospel tells us that Jesus is on his way to the cross, just as it had been planned (Matt. 26:24). Peter shared with the people in Jerusalem that Jesus's death was a part of God's plan (Acts 2:22–23). A reading of the missionary travels of the apostle Paul throughout Acts shows a general pattern of entering into a significant city, beginning at the synagogue if one existed, doing evangelism, gathering together the new believers into churches, and returning to appoint elders in those churches (Acts 13–14). When speaking to the Ephesian elders, Paul noted his Spirit-led plans to go to Jerusalem (Acts 20:22). He wrote to the Roman believers that he was planning to go to Jerusalem to help those in need and then to stop to visit the Romans on his way to Spain (Rom. 15:22–25). Though his plans changed, Jude was originally hoping to write to the believers about their common salvation (Jude 3). A reading of the book of Revelation clearly reveals that God has a plan for the establishment of his kingdom in the new heaven and the new earth and is actively engaged in the outworking of that strategy.

Though God is sovereign over his creation, he chooses to work through means to bring about his glory. He has promised to build his church (Matt. 16:18) but does so through the church's use of the kingdom's keys (Matt. 16:19). Jesus sent out the Twelve and the Seventy-Two with respective strategic plans (Luke 9:1–6; 10:1–12). His followers are to be strategic with their Master's resources, making wise decisions (Luke 19:11–27). The church is commanded to make disciples of all nations (Matt. 28:19), to preach the gospel to all nations (Luke 24:45–47), and to be the Lord's witnesses beginning in Jerusalem and extending to the ends of the earth (Acts 1:8). With these Great Commission passages revealing a divine strategy for kingdom advancement, it is difficult to read the Scriptures and miss the value of planning even in relation to God's sovereignty.

OBJECTION 2: STRATEGIC PLANNING IS CONTRARY TO SOME BIBLICAL PASSAGES

The writer of Proverbs notes, "The heart of a man plans his way, but the LORD establishes his steps" (16:9 ESV). What about this and other passages that appear to speak against strategic planning? Do they offer support for the notion that missionaries should not develop strategies? If missionaries attempt to develop strategies apart from seeking the face of the Lord for guidance or failing to understand that he is sovereign, then such is a violation of the spirit behind this proverb. But it is proper for an individual to recognize that he or she can prayerfully develop biblically based, missiologically grounded strategies, all the while allowing for the interference of the Lord. He or she must remember that "many plans are in a man's heart, but the counsel of the LORD will stand" (Prov. 19:21 NASB) and the warning, "Do you see a man wise in his own eyes? There is more hope for a fool than for him" (Prov. 26:12 NASB).

Another passage that could be misconstrued as offering contrary evidence against strategic development is from the book of James: "Come now, you who say, 'Today or tomorrow we shall go to such and such a city, and spend a year there and engage in business and make a profit.' Yet you do not know what your life will be like tomorrow. You are *just* a vapor that appears for a little while and then vanishes away" (James 4:13–14 NASB).

Clearly, James's warning is one that missionaries must heed. James, addressing some people who believed that they had all the time in the world, reminded his readers that they are not guaranteed the completion of their plans.

When some people think about the development of strategies, they believe that such a process is tantamount to the prediction and manipulation of the future. Books such as Stuart Wells's *Choosing the Future: The Power of Strategic Thinking* contain great principles and insights beneficial for strategy development but may cause some followers of Christ to cringe after reading the title (Wells 1998). The development of missionary strategies, however, should not cause believers to fear that they are going against James's declaration.

With this passage in James's letter, however, we must remember to include James's command, "Instead, *you ought* to say, 'If the Lord wills, we shall live and also do this or that'" (James 4:15 NASB). In other words, James is prohibiting not the making of plans but rather the making of plans without the will of the Lord included in the strategy's development.

OBJECTION 3: STRATEGIC PLANNING HINDERS THE SPIRIT

Healthy strategic planning does not hinder the work of the Spirit but rather works in cooperation with the Spirit, even submitting to his lordship to overrule any strategy. C. Peter Wagner was correct to note, "Missionary strategy is never intended to be a substitute for the Holy Spirit. Proper strategy is Spirit-inspired and Spirit-governed. Rather than competing with the Holy Spirit, strategy is to be used by the Holy Spirit" (1971, 15). The Spirit of God is sovereign. Missionaries who keep this biblical truth in mind will not be guilty of allowing their strategy development to grieve or quench the Spirit.

SIDEBAR 3.1
OVERCOMING OBJECTIONS

The following account is taken from one of the most famous writings in mission history, William Carey's *An Enquiry*. In this passage Carey is responding to some of the objections to missionary activity during his day.

Our Lord Jesus Christ, a little before his departure, commissioned his apostles to *Go, and teach all nations*; or, as another evangelist expresses it, *Go into all the world, and preach the gospel to every creature.* This commission was as extensive as possible, and laid them under obligation to disperse themselves into every country of the habitable globe, and preach to all the inhabitants, without exception, or limitation. They accordingly went forth in obedience to the command, and the power of God evidently wrought with them. Many attempts of the same kind have been made since their day, and which have been attended with various success; but the work has not been taken up, or prosecuted of late years (except by a few individuals) with that zeal and perseverance with which the primitive Christians went about it. It seems as if many thought the commission was sufficiently put in execution by what the apostle and others have done; that we have enough to do to attend to the salvation of our own countrymen; and that, if God intends the salvation of the heathen, he will some way or other bring them to the gospel, or the gospel to them. It is thus that multitudes sit at ease, and give themselves no concern about the far greater part of their fellow-sinners, who to this day, are lost in ignorance and idolatry. There seems also to be an opinion existing

in the minds of some, that because the apostles were extraordinary officers and have no proper successors, and because many things which were right for them to do would be utterly unwarrantable for us, therefore it may not be immediately binding on us to execute the commission, though it was so upon them. To the consideration of such persons I would offer the following observations.

First, if the command of Christ to teach all nations be restricted to the apostles, or those under the immediate inspiration of the Holy Ghost, then that of baptizing should be so too; and every denomination of Christians, except the Quakers, do wrong in baptizing with water at all.

Secondly, if the command of Christ to teach all nations be confined to the apostle, then all such ordinary ministers who have endeavoured to carry the gospel to the heathens, have acted without warrant, and run before they were sent. . . .

Thirdly, if the command of Christ to teach all nations extend only to the apostles, then, doubtless, the promise of the divine presence in this work must be so limited; but this is worded in such a manner as expressly precludes such an idea. *Lo, I am with you always, to the end of the world.* (1792, 8–9)

REFLECTION AND DISCUSSION

- Do you anticipate any objections to developing your strategy? If so, what are those likely objections?
- How can you properly respond to those objections?

The apostle Paul did not have any problem making his plans in light of the rule of the Holy Spirit over his life and ministry. On his second missionary journey, he traveled through the Phrygian and Galatian region, having been forbidden by the Spirit to preach the gospel in Asia Minor (Acts 16:6). Assuming that Paul and his team were making plans to travel into this region, here we have evidence of the interruption of the Spirit. Immediately following this interference the team made plans to enter Bithynia, but Luke records that the Holy Spirit interrupted this aspect of his strategy (Acts 16:7). Shortly after this change in strategy, Paul received the vision of the Macedonian man, which resulted in the team eventually arriving in Philippi and the birth of the Philippian church (Acts 16:9–15).

OBJECTION 4: STRATEGIC PLANNING IS TOO LINEAR A PROCESS FOR A RAPIDLY CHANGING WORLD

Some may argue that because the development of strategies is a modernistic linear process requiring step 1 to occur before step 2, after which step 3 can happen, and so on, it is inappropriate for a diverse and rapidly changing context. Though missionary strategies can be developed in such a sequential manner, healthy strategies involve some tasks happening sequentially *and* simultaneously.

For example, a linear approach for church multiplication could be described as:

- Step 1: Do evangelism.
- Step 2: Gather the new believers together and constitute as a church.
- Step 3: Train the new church in evangelism.
- Step 4: Send a team from the new church to another city to plant a church.

Obviously a church-planting strategy requires that evangelism (step 1) occur before disciples will be made and gathered together as new churches (step 2). However, it is possible that following step 1, those new believers should be trained in evangelism skills, even before they are officially constituted as a new church, and begin doing evangelism in another city to plant other churches. In other words, some of the steps can happen simultaneously. While the church is being planted in the first city, the missionary is working with new believers to evangelize a second city.

OBJECTION 5: STRATEGIC PLANNING DOES NOT TAKE THE CONTEXT INTO CONSIDERATION

Some may be resistant to the notion of developing strategies because they have been involved in many "boardroom" discussions where much ink was placed on whiteboards, a gazillion sticky notes were scattered across the room, and a multitude of flow charts existed all in the name of strategic development. Afterward they spent hours in front of a computer putting together a nice, neat strategy proposal only to have it be radically changed or even discarded once they arrived on location.

Missionary strategies cannot be developed divorced from working in our place of service. Certainly, teams can develop, to a degree, strategies in the sterile laboratory environment of a conference room, but they *absolutely must* recognize that the context will require adjustments to be made to their proposals. Again, Wagner is correct in his observations on the significance of the environment. He notes:

> Many choices have to be made in planning strategy. When you have discovered an appropriate strategy for one situation you cannot assume it will always work in another situation, although some strategies can be transferred, if the goal and circumstances are nearly identical. For example, certain situations in a baseball game indicate that the best strategy is clearly for the batter to bunt, and almost invariably a bunt will be attempted. But change the circumstances slightly and the decision on whether to bunt becomes much more difficult. Likewise, some evangelistic methods may work very well in a given situation, but they may be next to useless when circumstances are different. (1989, 27)

Though more will be noted about this issue in a later chapter, missionary strategies must be flexible and adjust to the contexts in which such strategies are applied. Ministry is about people, and people change. If no flexibility for the context is allowed in the strategy, then the strategy will be next to useless when the winds of contextual change blow.

OBJECTION 6: STRATEGIC PLANNING IS PRAGMATISM

In the 1970s and 1980s the Church Growth Movement elevated the notions of methods and strategies for church growth to a level that caused many people to label inaccurately the entire movement as being concerned with little more than pragmatism. Granted, there were many voices within the movement that provided much evidence for such an appellation.

Possibly due to such recent history, some individuals believe that strategic planning is little more than pragmatism, the notion that the end always justifies the means. We are in complete agreement with those who oppose strategic planning when such strategies deviate from biblical guidelines, even if great results are the outcome. In the economy of the kingdom, the end does not justify the means.

Although his assessment of North American strategies appears to lack fairness because it is based on a sweeping generalization for all strategies from this part of the world, Valdir Steuernagel makes several excellent points about the problems with embracing unhealthy Western strategy in Latin America:

> This strategy was established on the basis of pragmatism: you choose an area and/or challenge, you establish a goal and an achievement timetable, and you seek to fulfill both.
>
> The problem is that not only does our culture not operate that way, but this philosophy runs counter to the biblical pattern and mandate which says that the person is more important than the goal. In the biblical pattern strategy is constantly interrupted and held in check by the blind man who cries out alongside the road to Jericho. (2008, n.p.)

And yet, while strategists are to avoid the mistakes mentioned by Steuernagel, they are to be good stewards with the opportunities and resources of the King (Matt. 25:14–30). Kingdom citizens are told to bear fruit (John 15:8) and make disciples (Matt. 28:19). Though believers are not to follow the philosophy of pragmatism, they are called to be pragmatic (practical), for such is a matter of stewardship. The church should desire to know what means the Spirit is using to bring people to faith and birth churches throughout the world.

OBJECTION 7: STRATEGIC PLANNING IS NOT IN THE SCRIPTURES

Although it is true to a point that detailed strategic planning is not found in the Scriptures, one must be careful to avoid overstating the matter. For example, in his 1974 address to the Lausanne Congress on World Evangelization, Michael Green noted: "There does not seem to have been anything very remarkable about the strategy and tactics of the early Christian mission. Indeed, it is doubtful if they had one. I do not believe they set out with any blueprint. They had an unquenchable conviction that Jesus was the key to life and death, happiness and purpose, and they simply could not keep quiet about him. The spirit of Jesus within them drove them into mission" (quoted in Douglas 1975, 165–66).

While it is true that the apostolic church did not possess a "remarkable" plan in the sense of contemporary strategies, Green appears to overstate his case.

Obviously, the Bible does not provide us with a reason to believe that the church met for an extended period of time in the upper room, huddled around a whiteboard, developing a detailed ten-page document on the evangelization of Asia Minor. However, to state that it is doubtful that the church had a strategy appears to overlook the obvious.

We can give Green the benefit of the doubt and consider his reference to the church having a "blueprint" as his attempt to discourage modern strategists from being anachronistic by reading contemporary strategic development back into the text.

Eckhard J. Schnabel helps to clarify matters for those who question the legitimacy of strategy in the Bible. He notes that "irrespective of the details of definitions of strategy and method, it is obvious that Paul planned his missionary initiatives in the context of a general strategy that shaped specific decisions" (2008, 257). Even more specific, J. Herbert Kane writes: "Did Paul have a missionary strategy? Some say yes; others say no. Much depends on one's definition of strategy. If by strategy is meant a deliberate, well-formulated, duly executed plan of action based on human observation and experience, then Paul had little or no strategy; but if we take the word to mean a flexible *modus operandi* developed under the guidance of the Holy Spirit and subject to His direction and control, then Paul did have a strategy" (1976, 73).

OBJECTION 8: STRATEGIC PLANNING REQUIRES ACCOUNTABILITY

This objection is one of two that would never be stated aloud as a reason for abstaining from developing missionary strategies, since raising it would reveal the speaker's character flaws.

Inherent within any strategy is the demand for accountability. This is one of the reasons that strategic planning is needed. If a team develops a strategy that is designed to result in the planting of twenty churches in the next five years, then at the end of those five years, someone will ask, "Were twenty churches planted?" If not, then the immediate question will be, "Why not?" By definition strategies create accountability. If someone wants to *not* be accountable to anyone, he or she should refrain from developing strategies.

OBJECTION 9: STRATEGIC PLANNING INTERRUPTS LAZINESS

The second objection that would never be stated publicly is that the process of developing strategies is hard work. If one is slothful when it comes to his or her work, then strategic planning will not be a desired venture. Many hours of prayer and fasting, research, time in service with the people, team discussions, evaluations, and reflection are required.

CONCLUSION

The task of developing missionary strategies is extremely important for global missionary work. Rather than being a process devoid of theological substance and missiological integrity, strategic planning is part of being a wise steward with the Lord's resources given to the church. When founded on a healthy theological and missiological foundation (the subjects of the next two chapters), the development of strategy is part of the process that Jesus uses to build his church. Rather than being something that attempts to hijack the sovereignty of God and straitjacket the Holy Spirit, strategy development and the use of strategies should bring glory to the Lord of the harvest. Strategic planning should not be a linear process that does not adjust with the leading of the Spirit or the changing contextual winds but rather a flexible tool to be used in making disciples of all nations.

4

Strategic Planning
in Biblical Perspective

Anyone seeking to develop missionary strategy must do so with great humility and complete dependence on the Master Strategist. Arthur F. Glasser notes how such planning should be done with a holy fear:

> Our task is to define a relevant missionary strategy for the church of Jesus Christ in today's world. Humanly speaking this is an impossible, even dangerous task, chiefly because no human strategy can ever suffice for a divine enterprise. "God's thoughts are not our thoughts." Although intensely desirous of being alert to contemporary political, social, economic, intellectual, and spiritual tides, we must resist the temptation to draw a strategy from our understanding of our world. It must be drawn from God's thoughts about the significance of his kingdom in its penetration of the present world order and the unfolding of his redemptive activity in Christ among the nations. (1968, 178)

Glasser's sobering reminder of the realities facing the strategist gives one cause to pause and consider first the notion of strategic planning in light of the Scriptures. If the truth of God's Word is not the foundation on which all strategy is built, then the practical outworking of any missionary strategy is truly "an impossible, even dangerous task." The purpose of this chapter is to provide a biblical and theological foundation for healthy missionary strategy.

We note at the outset the two constraints in addressing the components of this foundation. First, we assume that the reader already has a solid understanding of the theology of mission. Second, space limitations require that we delineate the major components for a foundation for strategy rather than examine an exhaustive list of all components.

ON FUTURE MATTERS

The act of strategy development is a futuristic endeavor. The very thought of devising a strategy requires an attempt to see into the future. Strategists set goals with the full expectation that they will be able to see the fulfillment of those future dreams.

A theology of the future is a necessity before strategists can begin to develop God-honoring approaches to reaching others with the gospel. An examination of the Scriptures reveals that while God is eternal, he created time. Creation came into existence at a moment in time. God established morning and evening on day one (Gen. 1:5), and established seasons and years on the fourth day (Gen. 1:14–19). After the fall the Scriptures begin to reveal that a day is coming when time will not exist. This event will herald a new heaven and a new earth (2 Pet. 3:13). Also, we learn that Jesus has promised to return (Matt. 24:3–51; Acts 1:11).

James adds perspective on the future for the strategist:

> Now listen, you who say, "Today or tomorrow we will go to this or that city, spend a year there, carry on business and make money." Why, you do not even know what will happen tomorrow. What is your life? You are a mist that appears for a little while and then vanishes. Instead, you ought to say, "If it is the Lord's will, we will live and do this or that." As it is, you boast in your arrogant schemes. All such boasting is evil. (James 4:13–16)

As mentioned previously the problem with the merchants in James's day was not the sin of making future plans. Rather, they failed to include the Lord in their profit-making strategies. They had become arrogant and self-sufficient and took time for granted. The strategist must understand that while it is not wrong to make plans, the will of the Lord must govern all thoughts and strategies.

The Scriptures are clear that the mission of the church is future-oriented. The church is to continue making disciples until the end of time (Matt. 28:18–20), bearing witness until the Lord returns in the same manner in which he went

(Acts 1:8, 11). The gospel is to be proclaimed to all peoples before the end will come (Matt. 24:14), which is a promise to be fulfilled based on future evangelistic activities of the church. On numerous occasions throughout the book of Acts and in his epistles, Paul made future plans. For example, he prepared to provide relief for those in Judea (Acts 11:29–30), to return to visit newly planted churches (Acts 15:36), to go to Macedonia to make disciples (Acts 16:10), and to go to Spain (Rom. 15:24).

Even the act of goal setting is a futuristic endeavor with biblical support. Dayton and Fraser explain the theological support for planning strategies for world evangelization:

SIDEBAR 4.1
INVIOLABLE PRINCIPLES

Melvin L. Hodges shares the following from a Pentecostal perspective on some of the essentials for healthy missions strategy:

> Pentecostals would agree with Dr. McGavran that the strategy for missions must be kept flexible. Even so, certain principles are inviolable. The message we preach, the spiritual new birth of individuals, the control of the Holy Spirit in the believer's life and in the activities of the Church, the responsibility of Christians to form themselves into churches and to multiply themselves—all of these things are basic and must not be modified. The approach, however, must vary with the widely differing opportunities. If a particular tribe or section of society is "ripe for the harvest," the Church must be sufficiently flexible to find the means for taking advantage of the occasion. The Pentecostal's deep conviction that the guidance of the Holy Spirit must be sought for each situation makes for flexibility and ensures variety in method.
>
> In one place an evangelistic campaign may be the means for opening the area to the Gospel. Elsewhere the beginning will be made by opening a small out-station in a home, following up with literature saturation. Again the healing of a paralytic, or the restoring of sight to a blind person through the prayer of faith may be the means of stirring interest and founding the church. Pentecostal believers pray for their sick neighbors and lead them to Christ. The deliverance of an alcoholic or a narcotic addict may open the door in a community. Admittedly, all this may seem foreign to those who are accustomed to an institutional approach to the mission of the Church, but to Pentecostals such happenings are to be expected and are entirely in accord with the New Testament concept of the Church's mission. (1968, 307–8)

REFLECTION AND DISCUSSION

- Are there any other "inviolable" principles from the Scriptures that you can identify?

- Do you agree or disagree with Hodges's inviolable principles? Why?

Since all statements about tomorrow are statements of faith, a Christian response to the future ought to begin with what we imagine is the kind of future God desires for mankind. . . . Once we understand what God desires for the future of mankind, then we are responsible for taking both individual and corporate action that will move mankind toward that future. This should cause us to make individual statements (or goals and plans) about what we, in faith, believe the future should be like, and what we and others should do about it. And even as we make these statements, we need to be ready to modify them as we acquire new understanding. (1980, 12)

In light of our knowledge of God, his mission for the church, and the outworking of his salvation history on the way to the restoration of the broken creation, the church must walk by faith when it comes to setting goals and strategic planning.

STEWARDSHIP

The issue of missionary strategy is also a matter of stewardship. While stewardship involves the use of finances, it is certainly much more than that. It involves our use of people, time, talents, gifts, and opportunities that the Lord provides. Developing strategy is based on a theology that advocates that kingdom citizens are to be good stewards of all that has been entrusted into their care to reach the nations for Christ.

Several times throughout the Gospels we read about our Lord's desire to find good and faithful servants (Matt. 24:45; 25:21, 23; Luke 19:17). Such faithfulness is related to their proper use of all that they were entrusted with for the King. Strategists should remember that stewards must be trustworthy (1 Cor. 4:1–2).

For example, it is worth noting that in the parable of the wise servant it appears that though the servant did not know when the master was going to return, he remained faithful to the original task that the master gave to him before his departure:

Who then is the faithful and wise servant, whom the master has put in charge of the servants in his household to give them their food at the proper time? It will be good for that servant whose master finds him doing so when he returns. Truly I tell you, he will put him in charge of all his possessions. But suppose that servant is wicked and says to himself, "My master is staying away a long time," and he then begins to beat his fellow servants and to eat and drink with drunkards. The master of that servant will come on a day when he does not expect him and at an hour he is not aware of. He will cut him to pieces and assign him a place with the hypocrites, where there will be weeping and gnashing of teeth. (Matt. 24:45–51)

37

In other words, the servant was commended because he did not become lazy but rather was the one who made the plans to provide food for the household. He was faithful with what he had received and planned accordingly.

In light of the billions of unbelievers who live in the world today, the wise steward makes the very best plans to take the gospel to them and multiply churches among them. Missionary strategy involves being the best steward with all that one is and has until the Master returns. Therefore, the strategist operates from the theology of stewardship with the perspective that he will work diligently and plan accordingly whether Jesus returns later today or one thousand years from now.

SUCCESS

If not understood properly, the notion of success is a dangerous concept when applied to missionary strategy. This is especially true whenever cultural expectations and definitions of success do not equate with the biblical framing of success. For example, the capitalist mind-set that my worth and success are determined by the quota of widgets that I can produce by the end of any given day on the assembly line cannot be brought to where I serve. Just because we work hard today, there is no guarantee that we will have the desired quantifiable results by the end of the day (or month, for that matter).

It is true that our strategies must be pragmatic to some degree. We need to be involved in seeing the gospel advance across a people group. We are to be involved in using biblical means to reach people. Christ's commands to us come with the expectation of results. We are told to bear much fruit (John 15:1–8) and make disciples (Matt. 28:19). Because of these and other expectations of the Lord, strategists who constantly miss their goals should have their strategy and methods questioned. We should question whether a missionary administrator who is always overspending his or her budget should be serving in that role. A missionary veterinarian who cannot treat any animals successfully should be questioned regarding his or her role as a vet. A missionary teacher whose students cannot read or pass their exams should be questioned regarding his service as a teacher, and a missionary surgeon whose patients always need corrective surgery by another surgeon should be questioned about her medical skills. While all these people may be devout followers of Jesus, in their assignments they would be considered failures for not living up to the expectations that are a natural part of their roles.

Those serving on location should be engaged in what is working to reach people with the gospel, teaching them obedience and planting churches among them. If something is clearly not working, then the wise, faithful missionary will make adjustments in his or her strategy in an attempt to achieve success for the kingdom. Sometimes such changes will be a shift to different methods. And sometimes it will be determined that the people are so resistant to the gospel that the missionary needs to shake off the dust (Acts 18:6–7) and move on to a more receptive group.

Rick Cruse raises some very important matters regarding missionary success: "In missions (as in local church ministry), much of what we do is 'spiritual.' Almost by definition, it proves difficult to know when we have done well, when we have done enough, when we have really finished a task. When have enough people come to Christ? When are believers mature enough? When are the leaders adequately trained? And what about our colleagues who labor faithfully in less responsive or nonresponsive areas? How do they measure effectiveness and success?" (1999, 50).

This dilemma can lead to confusion, frustration, and sometimes disillusionment. What are the right measuring sticks for determining effectiveness and fruitfulness in a calling such as missions?

Whether we work with faith goals or with measurable objectives, we need to be especially clear and biblical in how we ultimately assess missionary effectiveness. We—the missionaries, agencies, and boards; the sponsoring, sending, and supporting churches; and the sacrificially giving believers—must exercise great caution. We should all fear the paradigm shift that places supreme value on getting the most return for our missionary dollars ("getting the most ministry bang for your missionary buck"). This attitude puts significant and at times inappropriate pressure on the missionary to "produce" in terms more suitable to a corporate venture than to a spiritual undertaking.

The art of strategy development will require the strategists to develop standards of measuring effectiveness based on matters such as the context and the individual's/team's gifts, personalities, and talents (see chap. 27).

A DISCLAIMER

Because all mission strategists must be pragmatic to some degree in relation to Jesus's commands, we need to make a disclaimer to prevent misunderstanding. Obedience to the call of God on one's life trumps this reality. There will be and *must* be men and women who will serve the Lord in "hard-soil" contexts. Such is not only necessary for today, but also has historical and biblical precedent. For example, was Jeremiah successful? How about Ezekiel? William Carey? These faithful saints, along with many others, would likely not be considered successful in their ministries according to contemporary definitions of success. However, if successful strategy involves being faithful to the Lord's calling on one's life, even in a resistant area, then such activity is successful. A healthy strategy will reflect such contexts. Unrealistic goals, not based on what the Spirit has been doing, are unwise and in the end make the missionary appear to be unsuccessful.

GOD PLANS

God is the great strategist. He has made plans in eternity past that have been worked out and are continuing to be worked out in the present and the future. He revealed his plans for the tabernacle (Exod. 26:30). The plans of his heart last for all generations (Ps. 33:11). Our plans will be established whenever we commit them to the Lord (Prov. 16:3). Isaiah praised God for his planning (Isa. 25:1). The Lord planned a disaster against Judah (Jer. 18:11). The Lord made plans against Edom and Babylon (Jer. 49:20; 50:45). The Lord makes plans for his people's welfare (Jer. 29:11). The numerous prophetic passages throughout the Scriptures are also examples of divine planning.

Joshua acknowledged that all God's plans for his people to receive the promised land had come to pass (Josh. 23:14). Even though the Israelites wandered for forty years in the wilderness, God's plans still were accomplished. God planned to pour out his Spirit on his people and announced this plan to Joel (Joel 2:28). Many years later the church experienced the fulfillment of this goal at Pentecost (Acts 2:16–21).

Paul reminds his readers that God planned the salvation of the elect from before the creation of the world (Eph. 1:3–14). And when the right moment in time occurred, God sent a Savior to provide salvation (Gal. 4:4). Jesus was delivered over to death, according to the plan and foreknowledge of God (Acts 2:23). And this gospel that he preached was the "plan of the mystery hidden for ages in God" (Eph. 3:9 ESV).

The ability of people to make plans is an extension of being created in the image of God. Numerous times throughout the Scriptures, God's people make plans. David provided Solomon with plans for the temple (1 Chron. 28:11). Esther and Mordecai worked together to make plans to save their people (Esther 4). The psalmist desires a blessing on God's people with the hope that God will fulfill all their plans (Ps. 20:4). The diligent planner is to be emulated (Prov. 21:5). Nehemiah made plans to return and build the wall around Jerusalem (Neh. 2:1–8). The noble person makes good plans (Isa. 32:8).

GOD IS SOVEREIGN

Although God's people have the ability to make plans for the future, all plans must be made in light of God's sovereignty. The apostolic church

SIDEBAR 4.2
REACHING A NATION

Jim Montgomery shares his strategy for world evangelization. During his time in the Philippines, he developed the DAWN strategy, described here:

DAWN is an acronym flowing from Matthew 28:19 and 20 that stands for "Discipling a Whole Nation." It is the name of a strategy for world evangelization that is gaining acceptance around the world by many leaders. . . .

DAWN aims at mobilizing the whole body of Christ in whole countries in a determined effort to complete the Great Commission in that country by working toward the goal of providing an evangelical congregation for every village and neighborhood of every class, kind and condition of people in the whole country.

It is concerned that Jesus Christ become incarnate in all his beauty, compassion, power and message in the midst of every small group of people—400 or so to 1,000 or more in number—in a whole country including all its people groups.

When this is accomplished, it is *not* assumed the Great Commission for a country has been completed, but that the last practical and measurable goal has been reached toward making a disciple of that country and all the "nations" within it.

With a witnessing congregation in every small community of people, it is now possible to communicate the gospel in the most direct, contextualized and productive way to every person in that land.

Every person now has a reasonable opportunity to make an informed, intelligent decision for or against Jesus Christ.

Everyone now has a church within easy access both in a practical as well as cultural sense where he or she can attend and be further trained in discipleship should he or she become a believer.

The penultimate step for making a disciple of every "nation" in a country has been reached. (1989, 11–12)

REFLECTION AND DISCUSSION

- Do you think it is possible to complete the Great Commission in a country? If so, what would that practically look like? If not, then why not?

- What do you think are the strengths and limitations of the DAWN strategy?

acknowledged this sovereignty (Acts 4:24) and made plans to speak the gospel to others (Acts 4:31), not holding on to its plans too tightly. While Paul acknowledged the Lord's sovereign control over everything (1 Tim. 6:15), he made plans (Acts 21:13–15) and encouraged Timothy to make plans (2 Tim. 4:9–13).

Although we may plan our steps, the Lord is the one who establishes those steps (Prov. 16:9). It is vital for the church to walk in step with the heart of the Lord. For while we make plans, the purposes of the Lord stand (Prov. 19:21).

41

As already mentioned, we should make godly plans but always recognize that if the Lord is willing, our plans will be accomplished (James 4:15).

GOD WORKS THROUGH HIS CHURCH

Basil Clutterbuck was correct to note, "At the heart of Christian obedience and Christian enterprise, lies this paradox: God is the supreme Strategist, and it is He who does His work in the world; yet He does not do it without us. He uses us as His workmen; He also calls us to intelligent planning under His own direction" (1957, 30). Part of the sovereign plan is that the gospel of the kingdom is meant to be spread through the ministry of the church. Although the Lord promises to build his church (Matt. 16:18), it is through the evangelistic work of kingdom citizens that he has determined to work out his salvation history. While the Lord is in control over his universe, he has determined the means by which his mission goes forth. And this means is through the local expressions (i.e., churches) of his body. Strategies that involve partnerships between Western and majority world churches can be a powerful testimony to the gospel and how God works through his church in all its diversity.

Because the church has been given a great commission (Matt. 28:18–20), we now plan diligently to be as faithful as possible to this task. Being a kingdom citizen involves the honor of being an ambassador for the King (2 Cor. 5:20). And along with this great mission is the requirement that the church make the best possible decisions about how to communicate this great love of God to the multitudes across the world. The mission strategist, therefore, seeks to make plans recognizing that part of the sovereign plan of God involves his people going to all nations.

GIFT OF WISDOM

If the Lord used wisdom to establish creation, how much more do we need wisdom for mission (Prov. 8:22–31)? Wisdom is a gift from God and should be desired more than gold or jewels (Prov. 8:10–11). Those who attempt to develop strategy must be men and women of wisdom. Wisdom provides insight (Prov. 8:14). It is assumed that wisdom from many counselors enables one's plans to succeed (Prov. 15:22). Wisdom helps the strategist to know the heart of God for the people. It provides understanding in knowing how the mission team can work best together. It enables the strategist to think clearly about how the various components of the strategy fit together. It provides the ability to understand matters that cannot be comprehended by the natural mind. Strategy development is an exercise of wisdom.

GREAT COMMISSION GROUNDING

Strategy development is to be rooted unashamedly in the Great Commission of the church, which demands a conversionistic theology of mission. While mission strategy should seek justice and the betterment of society, even a casual reading of the Scriptures reveals that true, long-standing societal transformation *begins* with the regeneration of the heart. Also, the example set forth in the New Testament reveals that Jesus and the apostolic church went about preaching the gospel of the kingdom *as first priority*. As they encountered the poor, the demon-possessed, and the sick, they ministered to them accordingly but never to the neglect of calling people to salvation in Christ. For the church to provide the entire world to an individual, yet never call him or her to repentance and faith in Jesus, is contrary to the mission of God (Matt. 16:26). Mission strategy must reflect this fundamental issue.

SPIRIT-GUIDED

While God has chosen to work through his church to take the gospel to the ends of the earth, he has not left us alone to accomplish this process (John 14:15–26). His Spirit teaches (John 14:26) and guides (Acts 8:29) our steps. Although some strategists have surely developed plans apart from trust in the Holy Spirit, this is not God's desire. Dayton simply notes, "Planning strategies for evangelization is no substitute for the powerful presence and action of the Holy Spirit" (1981, 595).

So, although strategies must be prayerfully developed, we recognize that the Holy Spirit's guidance will sometimes lead us to change our plans. While such change may be minute, we must also be open to radical adjustments that may appear to the human mind as unachievable and even foolish. For example, Bruce Nicholls warns, "The wisdom of men is not to be compared with the wisdom of God. Mission Boards would never have approved of the rashness of Philip's leaving the revival in Samaria for the deserts of Gaza, or the foolishness of Paul returning to Jerusalem to certain imprisonment, yet these acts of obedience to the Holy Spirit achieved more for the Kingdom of God than would have any strategy of missions" (1962, 1).

CONCLUSION

While maintaining a biblical foundation for mission strategy is no guarantee that unhealthy strategies will cease to be developed, failing to begin with such a foundation is a sure guarantee for kingdom failure. In a world where strategy is heavily influenced by business philosophies, marketing techniques, and military tactics, there is always a real and present danger that missionary strategy will develop into another secular approach to Christian activity. By grounding all the steps in the development of mission strategy in deep biblical and theological foundations, the church is best poised for healthy gospel advancement in the days to come.

In *Strategy to Multiply Rural Churches: A Central Thailand Case Study*, Alex G. Smith reminds us that "the Church must carefully relate its goals and plans to the redemptive purposes of God for all peoples. This is defined in the biblical mandate of mission. Under a sovereign God the chosen instrument of the Church of Jesus Christ must accept responsibility to fulfill its stewardship faithfully and to complete its explicit duty to make disciples of all the ethnic peoples of the earth" (1977, 188).

Apart from relating everything back to God's purposes, strategies run the risk of fostering unhealthy missionary practices that stand in opposition to the Scriptures. While there are numerous principles of strategy development that produce results, we must make certain that the desired results toward which we labor are those pleasing to God.

5

Missiological Principles
for Strategy Development

Over a century ago Robert E. Speer wrote the massive *Missionary Principles and Practice* in which he noted the missionary activities of his day. Concerning principles for missions in his contemporary setting, he penned: "The despondent objection is made by some that no common body of mission principles can be agreed upon. There are doubtless some points on which as yet many could not agree. But on the main principles of missions, or on most of them, at least, missionaries are agreed" (1902, 48).

We also recognize that such divergent opinions continue to exist today when it comes to missionary principles. It may even be a matter of debate whether most missionaries today would agree on—or even be able to identify—"the main principles of missions."

The difficulty of unanimity lies in the fact that different groups have not only different theologies and definitions of mission but also different interests, purposes, and desires. Speer was also aware of this matter during his day and shared his concern about the differences:

> It is to be regretted that this, which is necessarily first, will suggest divergence of opinion. What is the aim of missions? Everything else will depend on this.

First, it is to preach the gospel. We are all agreed here. But it is preaching not merely as superficial announcers, but with a view to the salvation of souls, the establishment of the Church, and the evangelization of the world. So far we are all agreed. But what is meant by the establishment of the Church? The usual reply is "a self-supporting, self-governing, self-propagating native church." And here, obviously, there is difference of practice and opinion; for while some are working toward the erection of independent national Churches in the different countries, others are building up Churches organically related to the American Churches and designed to remain so attached, and to be self-governing only in some such sense as shall not destroy their attachment. (1902, 49–50)

While we recognize that such differences continue to exist, even among evangelicals, we believe that missionary strategy must work primarily for the multiplication of disciples, leaders, and churches throughout the world. Edmund Davison Soper is correct when he writes, "The strategy of the world mission calls for well-understood principles which shall determine the program as the church faces the task lying before it in the future" (1943, 281). While there are numerous principles of mission that we could address in this chapter, we have chosen to mention those that are the most pertinent to missionary

---

SIDEBAR 5.1
PHILIPPE AND MARY

Philippe and Mary arrived on-site eager to get started. Both had studied at seminary and graduated with high honors. They knew that God had called them to plant churches among their own people. After a month of living in the community and getting to know their neighbors, Philippe came home one day and shared with Mary, "We have been here for a month, and I have no idea what to do. Where do we start? How do we get started? I know we are to share the gospel and plant churches, but how do we do that here?"

They found it difficult to connect with their neighbors beyond casual conversations. Most people were not very open to entering into a relationship with them. The culture of the people was not like what Philippe and Mary had known from back home. The people were always very busy with little time for activities beyond work and school, which was not like the culture that Philippe and Mary had known since they were children. They were both very surprised with their struggles. They believed the Bible and could even read it in the original languages. They had taken all the courses they were told to take but quickly realized that the "tests" in actual ministry were not the same as the tests they had taken in class.

REFLECTION AND DISCUSSION

- How could Philippe and Mary have benefited from study in the area of missiological principles?
- If Philippe and Mary came to you for advice, what would you tell them?

strategy as it relates to the redemptive purposes of God and the multiplication of disciples, leaders, and churches throughout the nations.

NEED AND RECEPTIVITY

Although in reality need and receptivity are two separate principles that should govern strategy development, both must be wed together for proper steward-ship of kingdom resources. This marriage allows strategists to reach a better understanding of those areas in need of the gospel that are not receptive and those areas in need of the gospel that are receptive. Therefore, the principles of need and receptivity help us to better understand where we should begin. Since the world is a very big place, where should the wise steward begin in developing strategy? Because of the significance of these principles, we devote a chapter to each (see chap. 20 on need and chap. 19 on receptivity).

The church is called to preach the gospel to all peoples, regardless of their receptivity to the message. While strategy must not include the withholding of the gospel from anyone, strategy does force the church to be a wise steward with our limited resources by asking the question, "Where are the most receptive peoples to the gospel message in our area, so we will know where to begin?" *Unless a team is specifically called by God to a resistant people, it should begin where the Holy Spirit has been working, ripening the field for the harvest.*

Although all peoples of the world are in need of the gospel, in this book *need* refers to the overall percentage of the population of evangelicals present among the people. Of course, simply because someone is an evangelical does not make him or her a follower of Jesus; by classic definition an evangelical is someone who has had a regenerative experience with the Holy Spirit and is constrained to tell others about this gospel. Also, while there are born-again individuals present among nonevangelical groups, we use evangelicals as the easiest benchmark to estimate the percentage of believers present who can evangelize their people group or population segment.

So, the principles of receptivity and need assist in strategically thinking about prioritization of the work. The strategist must assume that the aim of missionary strategy is to make disciples of all nations. Therefore, if the Lord has not extended a specific calling to a hard-soil area, then the wise strategist seeks to prayerfully determine the most receptive *and* most needy field.

EVANGELISM

Mission is about seeing people in the kingdom of darkness come into the kingdom of light. In his postresurrection appearance Jesus made clear that his followers were to continue his apostolic ministry of laboring to bring about the redemption of people: "Again Jesus said, 'Peace be with you! As the Father has sent me, I am sending you.' And with that he breathed on them and said, 'Receive the Holy Spirit. If you forgive anyone's sins, their sins are forgiven; if you do not forgive them, they are not forgiven'" (John 20:21–23).

While strategy can be developed to carry out many wonderful tasks for the kingdom, nothing is more important than communicating the good news of Jesus. Strategy that is not guided by the principle of evangelism is not a missionary strategy.

Missionary strategies that fail to include the preaching of the gospel are no different from those found in the world of business. The church is the means by which the Lord has chosen to carry out his strategy of making disciples of all nations. Therefore, missionary strategy is a strategy of divine purpose. It is not a strategy that seeks to dig wells for remote villages simply for the sake of providing clean water for people. Mission strategy involves providing clean water so that the living water (John 4:10) can be communicated to the people. It is not a strategy that seeks to provide bread for the hungry so that people will have food to eat. Rather, mission strategy is one that provides bread for the stomach so that the bread of life (John 6:35) can be shared with the people.

Any humanitarian organization with a strategy can work to provide assistance to those in need. Mission strategy is of a much higher calling. While it may include such benevolent work, it involves assistance with a purpose. And this purpose involves an evangelistic focus.

SOCIAL NETWORKS

Closely connected to the principle of evangelism is the guiding principle of social networks. Mission strategy is guided by the reality that the gospel is designed to travel across social networks that God has sovereignly established among the peoples of the world. Strategy must take into consideration that such social networks, whether found among highly individualistic societies or among those with high levels of group consciousness, must not be severed by extracting new believers from their networks; rather, missionaries must work through those preexisting relationships to see the gospel disseminated across them.

This forces strategists to think in terms of working through initial converts to begin the process of propagating the gospel across the people. Because missionaries come from outside the society, their relationships among the people are few. As the Spirit brings people into the kingdom, good strategic planning will take into account the need to begin working along local social networks rather than finding people in different networks among whom the missionaries must start the evangelization process over again. Donald McGavran calls these social networks "the bridges of God" (1955).

CONTEXTUALIZATION

While much more will be noted regarding contextualization in a later chapter (see chap. 15), it is necessary to note here that all healthy strategy development must take place with correct cultural knowledge of the people (this includes cultural knowledge of the unbelievers and that of the national believers with whom you may partner). I (J. D.) recall being in a church planting training event in which the participants were asked to develop an elaborate strategy to plant a church. I personally struggled with this activity, knowing that I was being asked to accomplish a task with little knowledge of the people. Another individual in the group with similar limited knowledge devised an elaborate and impressive

---

SIDEBAR 5.2
CONSIDERING MORAVIAN PRINCIPLES

Ruth A. Tucker shares the following information regarding the mission practices of the early Moravians and their leader, Count Nikolaus von Zinzendorf:

As a missionary statesman, Zinzendorf spent thirty-three years as the overseer of a worldwide network of missionaries who looked to him for leadership. His methods were simple and practical and ones that endured the test of time. All of his missionaries were laypeople who were trained as evangelists, not as theologians. As self-supporting artisans and laborers, they were expected to work alongside their prospective converts, witnessing their faith by the spoken word and by their living example—always seeking to identify themselves as equals, not as superiors. Their task was solely evangelism, strictly avoiding any involvement in local political or economic affairs. Their message was the love of Christ—a very simple gospel message—with intentional disregard for doctrinal truths until after conversion; and even then, an emotional mysticism took precedence over theological teaching. Above all else, the Moravian missionaries were single-minded. Their ministry came before anything else. Wives and families were abandoned for the cause of evangelism. Young men were encouraged to remain single, and when marriage was allowed, the spouse was often chosen by lot. (2004, 102)

REFLECTION AND DISCUSSION

- What do you think were some of the missiological principles that established the parameters for the missionary strategy and methods of the early Moravians?

- Do you agree or disagree with the methods described above? Why?

strategy. As he shared his approach with everyone, I could not help but think of how detailed his strategy was, yet he had not even arrived on location. Personally, I felt that the activity, under the guidelines provided, was a waste of time. As for the church planter who developed the complicated strategy, after four years on location he returned home without planting a church.

Strategists must understand that strategy cannot be developed in a boardroom or in front of a computer away from the field. All strategic planning must take into consideration the principle of contextualization. Strategists need a good familiarity with a people's geography, demography, culture, spirituality, history, politics, and language. Such knowledge will assist in the process of setting goals and developing action steps that relate well to the people.

REPRODUCIBILITY

At the time of this writing there are over four billion people on the planet who do not have a relationship with their Creator. Just the simple declaration of this reality reveals that the task is overwhelming. Mission strategists who labor to develop strategies without this reality in mind fail to have Great Commission eyes for the nations. Of course, from a human perspective the only way the church can be poised to reach such a number of people is for our missionary methods to be highly reproducible by the people whom we reach. Because methods are the means for applying our strategies in reality, our strategies must be based on methods that foster the rapid dissemination of the gospel and church planting. Generally, there is a negative association between the complexity of our methods and the people's ability to use those methods to reach others in their social networks.

In *Discovering Church Planting: An Introduction to the Whats, Whys, and Hows of Global Church Planting*, J. D. Payne provides what he calls the Reproducibility-Potential Guide (see fig. 5.1).

The guide notes that while all methods used to implement our strategies can be reproduced by the people to some degree, the more complex those methods are, the less likely they will be able to reproduce what was modeled before them. Simplicity, not complexity, should guide our methods and strategies.

A danger with the Reproducibility-Potential Guide is that we fail to understand the people whom we are strategizing to reach. Methods that are not very complex for us may be extremely complex to them, and vice versa. The importance of cultural research is noted elsewhere in this book, but for now we must recognize that the principle of reproducibility must guide our strategy development, and this principle assumes a familiarity with the people.

FIGURE 5.1: REPRODUCIBILITY-POTENTIAL GUIDE
(ADAPTED FROM PAYNE 2009, 412)

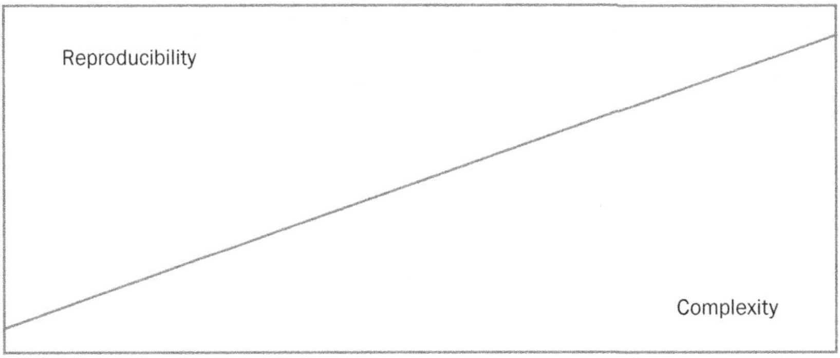

While mission strategy may involve many ministerial tasks, it must be guided by the principle of reproduction. The strategist must consider the multiplication of disciples, leaders, and churches in the planning process. Donald A. McGavran recognized the importance of this principle when he wrote, "Thus today's paramount task, opportunity, and imperative in missions is to multiply churches in the increasing numbers of receptive peoples of the earth" (1970, 62–63). McGavran's assertion remains just as true for us in the twenty-first century. The world will not be reached through the addition of believers but rather through exponential increases of such kingdom citizens.

Although the church cannot create movement, even with the best of strategies, we can hinder the multiplication of the gospel across a people group or a population segment. While movement is a sovereign act of the Spirit, missionaries can certainly hinder it. Strategic plans not based on the principle of reproduction run the risk of making missionary methods so complicated that new believers and churches cannot reproduce what has been modeled for them.

Although we cannot *create* multiplication, mission strategists can make strategic plans with multiplication in mind by keeping matters simple. While we cannot create the wind to move sailboats, we can hoist the sails to receive the wind when it blows. Mission strategies do not manipulate the Spirit, but they do ensure that the sails are unfurled when the time is right.

DEVELOPMENT OF LOCAL LEADERSHIP

Healthy strategy needs to be designed to raise up leaders to work the harvest fields. If missionary strategy does not consider the development of local leaders, then the result will likely be new believers and churches that are overly dependent on the missionaries. When colonialism engulfed missionary strategy, the concept of paternalism permeated the work in majority world countries. Those who accepted the colonial view imagined local believers incapable of leading churches. Control remained in the hand of the Western missionaries, which hindered the advancement of the gospel. Wise strategists take into consideration the development of healthy church leaders. Also, when working with majority world church leaders who have already been in a place of service for years, strategic partnerships must avoid paternalism as well.

PHASE-OUT

Strategists also need to incorporate a plan for the missionaries to remove themselves from the field. Missionaries should work themselves out of their jobs rather than create permanent positions. Missionaries should function as a scaffold on a construction site. The scaffold remains in place until the building is constructed. Afterward it is removed, having served its purpose.

Mission strategy is guided by the principle of phase-out. This concept was popularized by Tom Steffen in his book *Passing the Baton: Church Planting that Empowers* (1993). Steffen argues that missionaries are to strategize for their departure *before* they enter their place of service. Over the course of time, the strategy calls for the missionaries to progress through planned role changes as unbelievers come into the kingdom, begin growing in their faith while using their gifts, and start taking on more and more leadership responsibilities. The principle of phase-out requires that what the strategist desires ultimately to be accomplished be planned (as much as possible) from the beginning. Although details concerning how this will happen are

FIGURE 5.2: STRATEGY PYRAMID

Strategy

Research

Missiological Principles

Biblical and Theological Foundations

impossible to foresee, we nevertheless need to have a vision in place that involves the people progressing from being unbelievers to faithfully serving as missionaries to others.

CONCLUSION

The place of missionary principles is significant to the development of missionary strategy. As shown in figure 5.2, such principles are to be derived from the biblical and theological foundations for mission strategy. Apart from this proper foundation, strategies run the risk of propagating unhealthy practices in the field. Wise strategists allow principles related to need, receptivity, evangelism, social networks, contextualization, reproducibility, and local leadership to guide their strategy planning.

6

The Apostle Paul's Missionary Strategy

Bible scholars and missiologists would surely vote for Paul as the greatest missionary of all time. He established a number of churches in the Roman Empire and wrote a significant part of the New Testament. Most writers on missions strategy base their strategies on the New Testament accounts of Paul's ministry. You cannot understand or evaluate strategies derived from Paul's ministry unless you understand his approach to missionary work.

DID THE APOSTLE PAUL HAVE A MISSIONARY STRATEGY?

Missiologists have debated whether Paul followed an overarching strategy. Michael Green rejects the idea: "It would be a gross mistake to suppose that the apostle sat down and worked out a plan of campaign: the spread of Christianity was . . . largely accomplished by informal missionaries, and must have been to a large extent haphazard and spontaneous" (1970, 256). Roger Hedlund agrees: "Paul did not have a static method. His plans were flexible, his program open, so that he was able to move as the Spirit led and according to response and need" (1985, 217).

We have no evidence that Paul and Barnabas sat down and developed a detailed strategy before departing on their first missionary journey. However, it is clear that over time Paul developed a pattern of ministry that could be described as a strategy. In other words, he developed a set of principles that characterized his ministry.

This is hardly surprising. Most veteran missionaries develop a pattern that they employ in their work. Those who study the pattern would describe it as a strategy, even though the missionary probably did not begin with that pattern in mind. What, then, was Paul's strategy or modus operandi?

FACTORS AFFECTING MISSIONS STRATEGY

No missionary works in a cultural vacuum, and that was certainly true for Paul and his missionary team. Several factors positively aided Paul's missionary efforts. Perhaps the most important factor was the excellent Roman road system. The Romans built roads to improve commerce and to enhance the mobility of their legions. These roads were a great help to early missionaries.

The *pax Romana* (peace of Rome) also aided missionary travel. The Roman army suppressed banditry, and the Roman navy cleared the sea of pirates so that sea travel was less dangerous. All these factors positively affected missionary travel.

The early missionaries could communicate freely within the Roman Empire using the Greek language. While modern missionaries must study language for months or years, Paul and his companions could go almost anywhere in the empire and communicate using Greek, the trade language of the empire.

Greek philosophy was widely taught and admired throughout the empire. This helped the Christian mission because it inculcated a love for truth in educated people. The Jews of the Diaspora established synagogues in most cities of the empire. Through their synagogues the Jews promulgated a belief in monotheism. This was a novel concept to most people. The Jews also taught that God was personal and that people could have a personal relationship with him. The Jews proselytized actively, and in many cities they won a good number of "God-fearers" (gentile inquirers) who attended the synagogues. These "God-fearers" responded readily to Paul's preaching. In fact, the opposition of the Jews to Christianity in Asia Minor and Greece was perhaps due in part to jealousy at the loss of their gentile adherents.

The factors that made the time right for the birth of Jesus also prepared the way for the apostles. Paul writes, "But when the set time had fully come, God sent his Son" (Gal. 4:4). This was the "fullness of time" (Gal. 4:4 ESV) not only for the incarnation but also for missionary efforts.

PAUL'S STRATEGY

Paul testified before King Agrippa, "I was not disobedient to the vision from heaven" (Acts 26:19). How did Paul perceive his calling? What did he aim to do? He reveals one aspect of his personal strategy in Romans 1, when he writes that the Lord had given him "grace and apostleship to call all the Gentiles to the obedience that comes from faith for his name's sake" (Rom. 1:5). Clearly, Paul understood his mission to be reaching the gentiles for Christ (Rom. 15:16) in a wide-ranging sphere of missionary work: "From Jerusalem all the way around to Illyricum, I have fully proclaimed the gospel of Christ. It has always been my ambition to preach the gospel where Christ was not known, so that I would not be building on someone else's foundation" (Rom. 15:19–20). It is clear that Paul viewed himself as a pioneer missionary who emphasized the preaching of the gospel to the gentiles.

In his missionary work Paul made church planting a priority. Wherever he spent a significant amount of time, he planted a church. David Hesselgrave emphasizes this:

> The biblical record leaves no room for thinking that either Paul or the members of his team were basically engaged in raising living standards, ameliorating social conditions, imparting secular knowledge, ministering to medical needs, or dispensing aid from previously established churches. There can be little doubt that allegiance to Christ on the part of converts in the churches entailed these effects as by-products of faith even to the sending of needed aid back to the Jerusalem church (a kind of reverse flow). That the missionaries were concerned about social relationships, and about minds and bodies as well as souls, is patently true. But Paul's primary mission was accomplished when the gospel was preached, people were converted, and churches established. (2000, 24)

Not only did he plant churches, but he nurtured them, seen most clearly during his second and third missionary journeys. As Paul Bowers explains, "Paul's missionary vocation finds its sense of fulfillment in the presence of firmly established churches. What lies, in effect, within the compass of Paul's familiar formula 'proclaiming the gospel' is, I suggest, not simply an initial preaching mission but the full sequence of activities resulting in settled churches" (1987, 198).

Paul also gave attention to church leadership. He did not leave the new churches leaderless; he and Barnabas "appointed elders for them in each church and, with prayer and fasting, committed them to the Lord, in whom they had put their trust" (Acts 14:23). This concern for adequate church leadership continued throughout Paul's ministry. He instructed Titus to "appoint elders in every town" in Crete (Titus 1:5), and he advised Timothy on church leadership in his letters. We wish we knew more about how Paul trained leaders, but it is clear that church leadership was a priority in his ministry. It is also clear that Paul found church leaders within the congregations he established.

Kane lists nine principles that can be discerned in Paul's missionary approach (1976, 73–85):

1. Paul maintained close contact with his home church. As narrated in Acts 13:1–3, the church at Antioch commissioned and dispatched Paul and Barnabas on their first missionary journey. When they returned, they visited the church to report on the marvelous work of God among the gentiles (Acts 14:27).

2. Paul concentrated his work primarily in four Roman provinces (Galatia, Asia, Macedonia, and Achaia). He confined his work to a relatively small area so that he could provide guidance and supervision for the new churches.

3. Paul focused his evangelistic and church planting efforts on urban centers. He and his team planted seedbed or mother churches from which the gospel could be spread to the surrounding towns and villages. Ephesus provides a good example of this principle—"all the Jews and Greeks who lived in the

---

SIDEBAR 6.1
CONCENTRATION VERSUS DIFFUSION

All missionary strategists face the question of choosing a concentration strategy or a diffusion strategy. Paul and his missionary team chose a concentration strategy. Paul primarily confined his work to four Roman provinces in Asia Minor and Greece. He remained in a city long enough to establish a church. In Corinth he stayed about eighteen months, and he evangelized in Ephesus for about three years.

Contrast Paul's approach with that of Hudson Taylor and the China Inland Mission. In its early years especially the China Inland Mission followed a diffusion approach. This is how Kenneth Scott Latourette describes Taylor's strategy: "The main purpose of the China Inland Mission was not to win converts or to build a Chinese church, but to spread a knowledge of the Christian gospel throughout the empire as quickly as might be" (1970, 329). The approach of the China Inland Mission has been described this way: no one should hear twice until everyone has heard once.

In modern missions missionary broadcasting and literature distribution are good examples of diffusion strategy. The work of church planting teams exemplifies concentration strategy.

REFLECTION AND DISCUSSION

- Money is always scarce in missions. Should missionaries spend available funds primarily on diffusion strategies, like mass media, or should they use their money for concentration activities?

province of Asia [i.e., the Roman province called Asia] heard the word of the Lord" (Acts 19:10).

4. Paul usually initiated his work in the local synagogue if one existed. Paul knew that when he visited a synagogue for the first time, he would be invited to read from the Old Testament and give a short sermon. The synagogue worshipers already believed in one God, and they awaited the birth of the Messiah. In the synagogue he could share the gospel with Jews, proselytes (gentile converts to Judaism), and God-fearers. Even though the synagogue leaders typically expelled Paul not too long after he began his work, he *began* his new ministry settings in the synagogue, believing the gospel was for the Jews first (Rom. 1:16).

5. Paul preferred to preach to responsive people. He desired to be both faithful and fruitful. So he preached where the people showed interest and he could achieve good results (Acts 18:6).

6. Paul baptized converts when they professed faith in Christ. He and his team did not require the converts to endure a long probationary period before receiving baptism (Acts 9:18; 16:33).

7. Paul remained in one place long enough to plant a church. He did not evangelize people and then leave them without instruction or encouragement.

8. Paul employed a team ministry. Many think of missionary teams as a modern innovation, but Paul used the team approach consistently in his missionary work. He knew that a team provided better security while traveling. Having more workers made the ministry more fruitful, and it gave Paul the opportunity to train new missionaries.

9. Paul became all things to all people. He did not change the gospel or the doctrines he taught; however, he was flexible in his communication methods. Moreover, he sought to adapt to the cultures in which he worked (1 Cor. 9:19–23).

In *Planting Churches Cross-Culturally*, Hesselgrave explains what he calls the "Pauline Cycle." Hesselgrave identified ten features in Paul's missionary approach. He does not claim that Paul followed these ten steps in every city, but he believes this cycle describes Paul's approach to church planting:

1. The Missionaries Commissioned (Acts 13:1–4; 15:39–40)
2. The Audience Contacted (Acts 13:14–16; 14:1; 16:13–15)
3. The Gospel Communicated (Acts 13:17–41)
4. The Hearers Converted (Acts 13:48; 16:14–15)
5. The Believers Congregated (Acts 13:43)
6. The Faith Confirmed (Acts 14:21–22; 15:41)
7. The Leaders Consecrated (Acts 14:23)
8. The Believers Commended (Acts 14:23; 16:40)

9. Relationships Continued (Acts 15:36; 18:23)
10. The Sending Churches Convened (Acts 14:26–27; 15:1–4) (1980, 47–48)

FACTORS IN PAUL'S SUCCESS

A number of factors contributed to Paul's success as a missionary. First, Paul believed without doubt that God had called him as an apostle to the gentiles. He mentions this again and again in his letters (Rom. 1:1; 1 Cor. 1:1; Gal. 1:15). His certainty of a call from God enabled him to endure hardships and persecutions during his ministry.

SIDEBAR 6.2
IS PAUL'S STRATEGY DEFINITIVE FOR MISSIONARIES TODAY?

Should modern missionaries make Paul their missionary model? Or, to put it another way, are modern missionaries obliged to employ Paul's strategy? Roland Allen believed they should. In his 1912 book *Missionary Methods: St. Paul's or Ours?*, he criticizes the missionaries of his day for not imitating Paul. He insists that following Paul's strategy and methods would lead to greater evangelistic results and healthier churches on the mission field. Many other writers have agreed with Allen, writing articles and books to explain Paul's approach.*

Not all agree that missionaries should follow Paul's example, at least in regard to strategy. For instance, Kenneth Scott Latourette, the great missions historian, writes:

> We do well to be cautious in seeking to draw lessons from any one period of the spread of the Faith and to apply them dogmatically to the current situation. Many factors enter into the spread of the Gospel and the emergence of churches. Each method must be judged by its own merits as tested by experience in the particular time and environment in which it has operated. (1953, 143)

Latourette does not mean that there is nothing to learn from Paul's example. Rather, he means a strategy that worked well in the first century might not work well in the twenty-first century.

What should a modern missionary do? We can derive principles from the Bible that are applicable to all eras and environments. Contemporary missionaries need not travel by donkey or sailing ship in order to imitate Paul, but they do well to follow his example in many respects. Hesselgrave, for example, emphasizes three reasons for this: (1) "Paul is the model missionary of the New Testament." (2) "The gospel that Paul preached is normative in Christian missions." (3) "Paul's mission and methodology are exemplary in carrying Christian missions forward." (2011, n.p.)

REFLECTION AND DISCUSSION

- Do you agree with Roland Allen or Kenneth Scott Latourette? Explain your answer.

* *Hodges [1953] 1976 and Gilliland 1983 are good examples.*

Second, Paul dedicated himself to fulfilling the will of God. He expresses this eloquently in his letter to the church at Philippi—"For to me, to live is Christ and to die is gain. If I am to go on living in the body, this will mean fruitful labor for me. Yet what shall I choose? I do not know! I am torn between the two: I desire to depart and be with Christ, which is better by far" (Phil. 1:21–23). Writing from prison in Rome, Paul describes his complete surrender to doing the will of God, no matter what that entailed.

Third, Paul depended on the Holy Spirit to carry out his missionary labors. Paul understood that he could function only in and through the power of the Holy Spirit. He explained this to the church in Corinth: "My message and my preaching were not with wise and persuasive words, but with a demonstration of the Spirit's power, so that your faith might not rest on human wisdom, but on God's power" (1 Cor. 2:4–5).

Paul also depended on the Holy Spirit for guidance. Acts 16 tells how Paul and his missionary team sought to go to Asia (toward Ephesus), but the Holy Spirit prevented them. Then they tried to go north into Bithynia, but the Spirit of Jesus again thwarted them. Finally, they traveled to Troas, and there Paul received his Macedonian vision. The missionary team immediately responded to the Spirit's leading and departed for Macedonia. Of course, in Philippi they planted a strong church.

Paul also performed miracles through the power of the Spirit (Acts 19:12; 20:10). According to the traditions of the ancient church, Paul was a small man who struggled with eye problems. Also, he was not a dynamic preacher. Still, he accomplished great things for God through the power of the Holy Spirit, proving Paul's declaration that God's "power is made perfect in weakness" (2 Cor. 12:9).

CASE STUDY:
PAUL AND RESPONSIVE PEOPLE

Martin, a young missionary working in a predominantly Muslim area, found the work quite hard. In fact, he won few Muslims to Christ. In moving about the city, though, he encountered a group of foreign workers from the Philippines. He befriended the Filipinos and invited them to come to his home to study the Bible. Soon, he established a house church that was growing and dynamic. His team leader did not want to denigrate work with Filipinos, but he reminded Martin that his primary assignment was to evangelize Muslims.

Martin argued that in abandoning Muslim work and evangelizing the

Filipinos he was following Paul's example. He pointed to Acts 18:6 as his justification. At Corinth Paul began by evangelizing in the synagogue, "but when they [the Jews] opposed Paul and became abusive, he shook out his clothes in protest and said to them, 'Your blood be on your own heads! I am innocent of it. From now on I will go to the Gentiles'" (Acts 18:6).

REFLECTION AND DISCUSSION

- If you were Martin's team leader, how would you respond?

7

Missions Strategy
in the Early Church

How did the Christian church grow from the small group that met in an upper-floor room in Jerusalem to become the dominant religion in the Roman Empire by AD 500? Understanding the church's early strategy can help us develop more effective strategies for the twenty-first century. One can understand the development of the church today only by studying its past strategies. The successes and failures of Christianity's former strategies should inform our future ministry.

Church historians usually divide the period from 100 to 500 into two parts, separated by the Council of Nicea in 325. The period before Nicea is called the ante-Nicene, and the period afterward is called the post-Nicene. This chapter focuses primarily on the methods employed by the ante-Nicene church because the strategies employed did not change much in the latter period. Our hope is that when you finish reading this chapter you will better understand the church's missions strategies during this formative period in its history.

THE CHURCH AT THE END OF THE APOSTOLIC ERA

The end of the apostolic era coincided with the death of John at Ephesus (AD 95–100). What was the state of the church at that time? The Acts and the

Epistles tell of clusters of house churches in Palestine, Asia Minor, Greece, Cyprus, Crete, and Rome. Paul and his associates planted many if not most of them. Traditions of the early church hold that Thaddeus preached in Edessa, Mark founded the church at Alexandria, and Peter preached in Bithynia and Cappadocia. There are also ancient traditions that Paul went to Spain and Thomas went to India. Even if one accepts these traditions, it is clear that there were few churches scattered across a broad geographic domain. Additionally, the size of individual churches was limited. Those at Jerusalem, Antioch, Ephesus, and Rome seem to have had large memberships, but most of the churches were rather small. The New Testament indicates that most of the churches met in homes of believers such as Philemon (Philem. 2). This practice continued until the time of Constantine (Guy 2004, 24). Rodney Stark estimates the number of Christians in AD 100 at 7,530 (1996, 7). For the most part they were urban Christians because Paul preached primarily in the cities of the empire. While this was clearly his pattern, it is unclear whether it was a conscious strategy.

In the beginning the church reflected a strong Jewish influence. However, as the number of gentile churches increased, the churches became more and more Hellenistic. This trend greatly accelerated when Jerusalem was destroyed in AD 70, and the Jewish Christians of Jerusalem were scattered. Thus the New Testament was written in Greek as were the majority of Christian documents during the second century. Therefore, it is fair to say that at the end of the apostolic age the church was limited in size (perhaps no more than one hundred congregations or clusters of house churches), mainly urban, and primarily Greek speaking.

General Factors Affecting Expansion

The missionaries of the early church possessed several advantages that contemporary missionaries do not typically enjoy. The widespread use of Greek in the Roman Empire certainly facilitated the expansion of the church. The missionaries and evangelists did not need to spend a year or more in language study before beginning their work. Many of the early missionaries were natives of the multicultural cities of the eastern Roman Empire. This meant that they could speak Greek, and they had interacted with Jews, Romans, Greeks, and others. A multilingual and multicultural background proved to be valuable preparation for missionary work.

Another factor that enhanced the work of the early missionaries was the openness provided by the Roman Empire, which stretched from Syria to Spain. The early missionaries could travel through the lands between Spain and

Syria without crossing a border. Surely, missionaries today would be glad to be relieved of visa restrictions and issues.

The Illegal Church

During the church's first years the Roman authorities viewed Christianity as a sect of Judaism. Because Judaism was a *religio licita* (legal religion), Christians enjoyed protection under Roman law. After 100, Christianity lost that status. The Roman government considered Christianity a secret society and a threat to the stability of the empire. Roman officials persecuted Christians because they refused to bow to statues of Caesar and say, "Caesar is lord." The authorities interpreted the believers' refusal as disloyalty or even treason. Also, many pagans accused the Christians of atheism because they refused to worship idols, of incest because the Christians practiced "the kiss of peace," and of cannibalism because visitors misunderstood the words of the Lord's Supper—"This is my body" (Cairns 1996, 87).

Before 250 most persecutions of Christians were localized and brief; however, in 249 Decius became emperor, and he targeted Christians in his campaign to return Rome to its classic culture and glory. He decreed that all the people should make an annual sacrifice to the Roman gods and to the emperor. Those who refused were subject to torture or death. The famous Christian theologian Origen refused to sacrifice and suffered terrible torture. Thankfully, this persecution lasted only about one year, ending with the death of Decius. A more intense empire-wide persecution began in 303. Emperor Diocletian ordered that Christian worship cease, churches be destroyed, and the Scriptures be burned; Christians who refused to recant were to be arrested and imprisoned. Christians found guilty were subject to exile, loss of property, torture, service in the salt mines, or execution. This persecution continued until Emperor Constantine issued the Edict of Milan in 313, which granted toleration to Christianity (Cairns 1996, 91–93). In spite of persecution, or perhaps because of it, the church grew steadily during the ante-Nicene period.

GROWTH IN THE SECOND CENTURY

Christianity spread naturally along the main roads and rivers of the Roman Empire. It spread eastward by way of Damascus and Edessa into Mesopotamia; southward through Bostra and Petra into Arabia; westward through Alexandria and Carthage into North Africa; and northward through Antioch into Armenia, Pontus, and Bithynia. Somewhat later it spread even farther to Spain, Gaul, and Britain (Kane 1975, 10).

Egypt and North Africa became strongholds of Christianity during the second century. Tradition has it that Mark founded the church at Alexandria. The early church in Egypt was originally limited to those who spoke Greek, though a strong Coptic church developed later. Probably Christians from Egypt carried the gospel into North Africa (Neill 1986, 34).

North Africa produced the first Latin-speaking churches. In the early years, these churches seem to have appealed more to the upper classes, the Latin-speaking people. Then, too, the churches were planted primarily in the cities and towns. During this period the villages remained largely untouched (Neill 1986, 34).

Paul, Peter, and John had all evangelized in Asia Minor, and that region contained many churches that grew steadily. Pliny, a Roman official, complained to Emperor Trajan in 112 concerning the Christians in Bithynia, "There are so many people involved in the danger. . . . For the contagion of this superstition has spread not only through the free cities, but into the villages and rural districts." He added that "many persons of all ages and both sexes" were involved (Kidd 1920, 1:39). Obviously, the churches in Bithynia were growing and multiplying, and this seems to have been true in and around Ephesus as well.

Many scholars believe that the church at Rome was founded by "Jews and proselytes" who were converted on the day of Pentecost (Acts 2:10 NASB). While this is just a theory, it is a fact that the Roman church grew in size and prestige year by year. For the first one hundred years of its existence, the church members used Greek in their services. This shows that the church drew its members from the poorer classes of society. There are no records of the size of the Roman congregation until the time of the Novatian controversy in 251. Eusebius quotes from a letter written by Bishop Cornelius of Rome in which he states that there were forty-six presbyters; seven deacons; seven subdeacons; forty-two clerks; fifty-two exorcists, readers, and janitors; and fifteen hundred widows and needy in the church (Eusebius 1984, 265). Some scholars have calculated the total church membership at that time at around thirty thousand.

Latourette estimates that by the end of the second century Christians were active in all the provinces of the Roman Empire as well as in Mesopotamia (1937, 85). This seems to be a fair estimation in light of a passage from Tertullian. Writing in about AD 200, he reported that many had become Christians including "different races of the Gaetuli, many tribes of the Mauri, all the confines of Spain, and various tribes of Gaul, with places in Britain, which, though inaccessible to Rome, have yielded to Christ. Add the Sarmatae, the Daci, the Germans, the Scythians, and many remote peoples, provinces, and islands unknown to us" (Roberts and Donaldson 1951, 3:44).

Elsewhere Tertullian boasts to the pagans: "We have filled every place belonging to you, cities, islands, castles, towns, assemblies, your very camp, your tribes, companies, palace, senate, forum! We leave you your temples only" (Kidd 1920, 1:143). Tertullian may have employed hyperbole, but it does seem clear that the church had penetrated, at least to some extent, every part of Roman society by AD 200.

GROWTH IN THE THIRD CENTURY

Christianity grew steadily but not dramatically from AD 200 until 260. Then, beginning in about 260, the church grew very rapidly until Emperor Diocletian's edict of persecution in 303. Up until 260 the church had remained a mainly urban institution, but the mass movement in the latter third century was primarily a rural phenomenon. Several factors affected this remarkable growth. First, this was a period of civil strife in the empire. It was the era of the "barrack emperors," when the Roman Empire was threatened externally with invasion by Germanic tribes and internally with chaos in Rome itself. Second, there was great economic dislocation. Inflation made survival very difficult for rural folk, who found it challenging to market their produce. Even the shipment of produce became risky as peace and order began to break down (Frend 1982, 110–11).

As usually happens, the rural folk began to question their traditional cults as the hard times continued. In contrast, the Christians presented a simple gospel that offered both social justice and assurance of power over demonic forces. Thousands, perhaps millions, rejected their old gods and accepted Christ. This was the greatest period of growth in the ante-Nicene period.

The great growth was possible because the church was free of persecution during these forty years. The government was so preoccupied with other problems that it left the church alone. This respite from persecution continued during the early years of Diocletian's reign.

The era of peace and progress ended when Emperor Diocletian issued his edict of persecution in 303. This terrible period of persecution lasted until Constantine assumed control in 311. During the persecution fifteen hundred Christians died as martyrs, and many more suffered lesser persecutions. Many Christians recanted under torture or the threat of it, including the bishop of Rome. Lasting peace came when Constantine issued his edict of toleration in 311 and his famous Edict of Milan in 313 (Kane 1975, 32).

THE EXPANSION OF THE CHURCH BY AD 325

By 300 the gospel had been preached in every city and province of the empire. However, the distribution of the churches was very uneven. The church had grown more rapidly in Syria, Asia Minor, Egypt, and North Africa, including significant centers in Rome and Lyons. Growth in other areas—Gaul, for example—had been slow. Adolf von Harnack believed that in one or two provinces at least half the people were Christians, and in several cities Christians were in the majority. He estimated the number of Christians in the empire at three or four million at the time of Constantine (Harnack 1908, 2:325). Under Constantine's rule the number of Christians increased rapidly because it became advantageous to be a Christian. When Christianity became the favored religion, church member-ships swelled, although the quality may have declined in proportion. Still, the ante-Nicene church had made remarkable progress and withstood tremendous onslaughts. The question remains: *how* did the church grow?

MISSIONARIES IN THE ANTE-NICENE CHURCH

From its inception Christianity has been a missionary religion. The missionar-ies of the second and third centuries followed the example set by the apostles. Eusebius says of them: "The holy apostles and disciples of our Saviour, being scattered over the whole world, Thomas, according to tradition, received Par-thia as his allotted region; Andrew received Scythia, and John, Asia, where . . . he died at Ephesus. Peter appears to have preached through Pontus, Galatia, Bithynia, Cappadocia, and Asia, to the Jews . . . finally coming to Rome" (1984, 82). According to Eusebius, the twelve apostles took deliberate steps to evangelize the world they knew.

It seems that there were itinerant missionaries in the second century who followed the Pauline model in their ministry. Eusebius tells of their work in his church history. The *Didache* from the second century also speaks of itinerant "apostles and prophets" in need of hospitality (Bettenson 1956, 71). So it seems there were full-time missionaries in the second century. Origen testifies to their continuation in the third century: "Some of them have made it their business to itinerate, not only through cities, but even villages and country houses, that they might make converts to God" (Roberts and Donaldson 1951, 4:468). In fact, Pantaenus, the predecessor of Clement and Origen, left Alexandria and went into Asia as a missionary; and Eusebius believed he traveled as far as India (Eusebius 1984, 190). This brief review of the source material indicates that the office of missionary continued in the church after the first century.

Missionary Bishops

During the ante-Nicene period bishops continued the missionary activity of the apostles. The bishops of large urban centers led in the evangelization of the adjacent rural areas. Further, existing churches consecrated bishops and sent them into new areas to organize the Christians into churches. Also, a bishop or bishops living near a group of Christians would gather and instruct the believers until they could elect their own bishop (Conner 1971, 208).

Irenaeus and Gregory Thaumaturgus exemplify missionary bishops. Irenaeus (AD 130–200) was bishop of Lyons. In one of his books he speaks of preaching in the Celtic language to the tribes around Lyons (Neill 1986, 31). Gregory was won to Christ by Origen. In about 240 he was chosen bishop of his hometown in Pontus. According to tradition, when he became bishop, he had a congregation of seventeen, but when he died, there were only seventeen pagans left in the city. The numbers may be exaggerated, but clearly Gregory evangelized successfully. He exposed pagan miracles as frauds and performed so many wonders himself that he became known as Gregory Thaumaturgus (worker of wonders). He also substituted festivals in honor of the martyrs for pagan feasts. He thus sought to ease the transition from paganism to Christianity (Latourette 1937, 89–90).

Lay Missionaries

Though missionaries and bishops set an example in evangelism, laypeople spread the gospel for the most part. They shared the gospel while engaged in their daily activities. It is easy to imagine laypersons conversing with their acquaintances in their homes, at the market, and on the street corners (Green 1970, 173).

Christians also shared the gospel as they moved about. Christian traders evangelized as they traveled through the empire, much as did the Christians dispersed from Jerusalem (Acts 8:4). Christians serving in the Roman army, though relatively few in the early years, carried the gospel as well. They witnessed wherever they were stationed. Some scholars believe that Roman soldiers first brought the gospel to Britain. Further, the government pensioned retiring soldiers by giving them a plot of land in a new territory. These retired soldiers sometimes established churches in those remote places. This was definitely the case in southeastern Europe (Carver 1932, 51).

Women played a major part in the expansion of the church. Harnack writes: "No one who reads the New Testament attentively, as well as those writings which immediately succeeded it, can fail to notice that in the apostolic and sub-apostolic age women played an important role in the propaganda of Christianity and throughout the Christian communities. The equalizing of men and women in grace and salvation (Gal. 3:28) produced a religious independence among women, which aided the Christian mission" (1908, 2:64). Because the

SIDEBAR 7.1
PERPETUA

The ancient church rightly regarded Perpetua as a great hero of the church. Vibia Perpetua and her slave, Felicitas, became Christians at the same time. The Roman authorities in Carthage arrested both of them during the persecution of Christians decreed by Emperor Septimus Severus. Though her family pleaded with her to consider their feelings and the welfare of her infant child, Perpetua remained true to her faith. Before she was led into the arena to die, Perpetua shared her faith with the crowd. As she entered the arena, Perpetua encouraged the weeping Christians: "Give out the Word to the brothers and sisters; stand fast in the faith, love one another, and don't let our suffering become a stumbling block to you." (Tucker 2004, 33–34)

REFLECTION AND DISCUSSION

• How did the early Christians respond to persecution? Should their response be a model for persecuted believers in the 10/40 Window?

early churches met in homes, many women were able to make their homes into house churches. Also, many women died bravely as martyrs and thus gave a testimony for Christ.

MISSIONARY METHODS

Paul and Peter often preached in public, and this practice continued in the second and third centuries when conditions permitted. Eusebius records that Thaddeus preached publicly at Edessa. Eusebius reports Thaddeus saying, "Since I was sent to preach the word, summon for me tomorrow an assembly of all your citizens, and I will preach before them and sow in them the word of life" (1984, 47). The early evangelists were fervent in their preaching. J. G. Davies says that they preached so as to "bring the hearers to repentance and belief . . . [and] to force upon them the crisis of decision" (1967, 19). The steady growth of the church testifies to their efforts.

W. O. Carver believes that teaching was another important method. The early catechetical schools developed into training schools for presbyters (pastors) in Antioch, Alexandria, Edessa, Caesarea, and elsewhere (Carver 1932, 47–50). All these schools sent people into missions. Sometimes teachers, like Pantaenus of Alexandria, set an example in this undertaking. They worked as evangelists inside and outside their schools. Pagans as well as catechumens attended their schools and heard their teaching. The great missionary bishop Gregory Thaumaturgus was won to Christ by Origen at the school in Alexandria (Harnack 1908, 2:362).

The early Christians often spread the gospel through the use of their homes. Because there were no church buildings until about 250, the congregations met in one or several homes. The home setting provided a relaxed, nonthreatening atmosphere. The warm hospitality afforded by Christian homes surely influenced many. Whole households were sometimes converted (such as the Philippian jailer; Acts 16). The New Testament contains many references to house or home churches, and the ante-Nicene church followed this model (Green 1970, 207).

Oral witness through preaching and personal testimony was the main method of evangelism, but literature also became an increasingly effective means of propagating the gospel. Literature evangelism included apologies, letters, polemics, and the distribution of the Scriptures. Carver says that all the ante-Nicene fathers "were in varying degrees missionaries of the pen" (1932, 49).

The early church spread the gospel primarily through personal contact and example. This was much the same as in apostolic times. The church established no elaborate missionary societies or organizations; instead, Christians shared and demonstrated the gospel in their daily lives. Justin Martyr tells about this is his *Apology*: "He has urged us . . . to convert all . . . and this I can show to have taken place with many that have come in contact with us, who were overcome, and changed from violent and tyrannical characters, either from having watched the constancy of their neighbor's lives or from having observed the wonderful patience of fellow travelers under unjust exactions, or from the trial they made of those with whom they were concerned in business" (Kidd 1920, 1:74).

Christians also maintained a public witness by their conduct at their trials and martyrdoms. Though some recanted under pressure or torture, many gave a wonderful testimony for Christ. When threatened with death if he did not recant, Polycarp of Smyrna said: "Eighty and six years have I served him, and he never did me wrong; and how can I now blaspheme my King that has saved me?" (Eusebius 1984, 147). Roman persecution did not destroy Christianity; rather, it strengthened it. The blood of the martyrs really did prove to be the seed of the church, as Tertullian wrote. Many pagans accepted Christ because of Christians' testimonies.

The early Christians won others through social service. Harnack lists ten ministries performed by the Christians: giving alms in general, supporting teachers and officials, supporting widows and orphans, supporting the sick and infirm, caring for prisoners and convicts in the mines, burying paupers, caring for slaves, providing disaster relief, furnishing employment, and extending hospitality (1908, 1:153).

It seems that the benevolent activities affected evangelism positively because the pagan emperor Julian the Apostate (AD 332–363), complained about it: "Atheism [i.e., Christianity] has been especially advanced through the loving service rendered to strangers, and through their care for the burial of the dead. . . . The godless Galileans care not only for their own poor but for ours as well" (Neill 1986, 37–38). Thus in the early church there was no dichotomy between social service and evangelism. Both were natural activities integral to the church's mission.

FACTORS THAT AFFECTED THE CHURCH'S EXPANSION

Based on the information provided thus far about the expansion of the early church and especially the methods used by the church, we now turn to the question, "Why did the church grow?" We can identify at least seven factors.

1. The church grew because of divine blessing. It was God's will for the church to grow, and God blessed the efforts of the early Christians. The early church was the instrument of the Holy Spirit in fulfilling the redemptive purpose of God. Origen says, "Christianity . . . in spite of the small number of its teachers was preached everywhere in the world. . . . We cannot hesitate to say that the result is beyond any human power" (Roberts and Donaldson 1951, 4:350).

2. The church grew because of the zeal of the Christians. They gave of themselves sacrificially for the faith. The early Christians possessed a burning conviction that expressed itself in missionary activity.

3. The appealing message of the church was another important factor. Latourette says that the uniqueness of Jesus was the key. The love of God and the offer of forgiveness and eternal life through Christ appealed to the people of the Roman Empire (Latourette 1937, 168).

4. The organization and discipline of the church aided its growth also. Walter Hyde believes that the organization of the church on the imperial pattern was a positive factor (1946, 187). Certainly, the faithfulness of the bishops enabled the church to persevere in the face of persecution. Also, the strict discipline of the church presented a marked contrast to the licentious pagan cults.

5. The church grew because of its inclusiveness. It attracted people of all classes and races. It became a universal religion. It burst the bonds of restrictive Judaism to become a religion for the world.

6. Christianity prospered because of the ethical standards of the early church. This is not to say that the churches or believers were perfect, but their lives were so different from their pagan neighbors' that they attracted notice. Their morality and works of charity commended the faith to many.

7. Christianity grew, in part, because Christians valued babies. They produced more children than did other population groups in the empire. Over time, their higher birthrate proved significant (Feddes 2007).

CONCLUSION

By 325 the church existed in every part of the Roman Empire. Stephen Neill estimates the number of Christians as at least five million, and Rodney Stark has suggested six million (Neill 1986, 7). By 500 the vast majority of people in the empire called themselves Christians, and missionaries had carried the gospel to many lands outside the empire. The church did not employ secret formulas to achieve growth. Rather, the church followed the example of the apostles in their preaching and teaching. The main innovation of the postapostolic church was literature evangelism, particularly the apologies. Still, the key remained, as it does today, the lives and witness of individual believers. The great missionary itinerants and bishops carried the banner of Christ, but it remained for rank-and-file Christians to make most of the contacts and conversions.

8

Roman Catholic Strategy

In this chapter we focus on Roman Catholic missions strategy from AD 500 to 1600. During this period, the Roman Catholic Church dominated the West and, apart from some small dissenting groups, was the only church in Western Europe, at least until the Protestant Reformation. How did the Catholic Church come to exercise so much power? What missions strategy was employed? We start by examining the strategy of Pope Gregory the Great.

POPE GREGORY'S MISSION STRATEGY

Pope Gregory the Great influenced the Roman Catholic Church for one thousand years. He held the papal office only from 590 to 604, but he established the pattern for the Roman Catholic Church throughout the Middle Ages. First, he set the order of the Catholic Mass, even writing some chants to be used by choirs. Second, he reorganized the Roman Catholic Church. Third, he developed a strategy for Christianizing Europe, which was his dream.

Pope Gregory envisioned all of Europe under the beneficent rule of the Vatican. To accomplish his goal, he sent missionaries into Gaul (France), Sardinia, and England. Of course, there were already some Christians in England, but they were Celtic Christians. Gregory wanted to bring the Celtic Christians into the Roman Catholic Church, and he also wanted to win the

---

SIDEBAR 8.1
SACRAMENTALISM

In New Testament times missionaries sought to save souls by persuading people to believe in Jesus Christ and trust him for forgiveness and salvation from sin. During the Middle Ages missionaries sought to save people by uniting them with the Roman Catholic Church. The missionary monks believed that salvation comes through the sacraments of the church, especially baptism and the holy Eucharist (Lord's Supper). According to the theology of sacramentalism, by his death on the cross and resurrection from the grave Jesus Christ established a treasury of grace in heaven. The Roman Catholic Church is the steward of this treasury of grace. Therefore, the Catholic Church can dispense that grace to people through the seven sacraments of the church: baptism, penance (confession), confirmation, the Eucharist (Holy Communion), matrimony, holy orders (ordination), and the last rites. Thus, medieval missionaries sought to persuade people to accept baptism, thinking that baptism saved them. The forced conversions mentioned in this chapter certainly affected negatively the practice of Christianity practiced in Europe. Of course, most of those who submitted to baptism had no idea what it meant. Also, they continued in their pagan worldview and rituals. (J. M. Terry 1994, 54–55)

REFLECTION AND DISCUSSION

- How can sinful people receive God's grace? Who dispenses grace?

---

pagan majority in England. Pope Gregory implemented a fourfold strategy to Christianize Europe. First, he deployed missionary monks to baptize the people of Europe and establish churches. Second, he exhorted kings and rulers to force all their subjects to accept baptism (Pope Gregory taught that salvation comes through the sacrament of baptism; see sidebar 8.1). Third, he encouraged the bishops to evangelize the people in their areas. And fourth, he established accommodation (see sidebar 8.2) as the Roman Catholic Church's approach to new cultures. While evangelical missionaries more often use the terms *indigenization* and *contextualization*, Roman Catholic writers use *accommodation*. *Accommodation* refers to the changes that the church must make when it encounters a new culture and the adjustments the culture makes when the church enters.

MONASTICISM

Monks represented the main missionary force for the Catholic Church during the Middle Ages. Benedict of Nursia was the chief organizer of monasticism. He established a monastery at Monte Cassino, near Rome, in 529. He wrote a manual, called *The Regula*, which laid out the rules for monastic life. In his

Regula Benedict listed these requirements: First, each monastery would be administered by an abbot. Second, each monk would take vows of poverty, chastity, and obedience (to the abbot). Third, each monk was required to follow strictly the daily schedule of worship, prayer, work, and study. Fourth, the monks were to live as simply as possible.

The monks represented an important resource for the Roman Catholic Church. They were taught to read and write, rare abilities in the Middle Ages. The monks had no families to impede their deployment; they were free to depart on short notice. Also, their discipline and vows of obedience made them a ready force of trained preachers and evangelists. Certainly, the

---

SIDEBAR 8.2
ACCOMMODATION

Accommodation refers to the . . . missionary practice of accommodating the rituals, practices, and styles of the missionary's sending church to those of the recipient culture. It indicates what are generally conscious processes of adaptation, done with willingness to adopt some of the forms of the receiving culture and at times to leave aside some of the prior Christian church's customs considered to be an impediment to embracing Christian faith in the receiving culture. (Hunsberger 2000, 31)

Accommodation is the approach that Pope Gregory the Great recommended to Augustine and his band of monks. As they worked to Christianize Great Britain, they encountered many pagan people. Pope Gregory sent them this advice in a letter:

The heathen temples of these people need not be destroyed, only the idols which are to be found in them. . . . If the temples are well built, it is a good idea to detach them for the worship of the true God. . . . And since the people are accustomed, when they assemble for sacrifice, to kill many oxen in sacrifice to the devils, it seems reasonable to appoint a festival for the people by way of exchange. (Neill 1986, 59)

Augustine and his monks employed this strategy successfully in Britain, and many other missionary monks of the Middle Ages did so as well.

There are some inherent issues involved with accommodation. First, in accommodation the missionary decides which rituals or practices should be accepted or rejected. Second, accommodation tends to focus on external practices rather than on worldview change. And third, accommodation fails to acknowledge the missionary's cultural background, which affects what is communicated to the recipient culture and the way in which the message is communicated. (Hunsberger 2000, 32)

REFLECTION AND DISCUSSION

- How can missionaries help local believers make sound decisions about traditional cultural practices?

bishops and abbots called on them to lead the church's missionary advance throughout Europe.

The monks' approach usually followed this pattern. A church official would choose an area for evangelization. Then that official would request a letter of introduction from a Catholic ruler. The abbot of the "mother" monastery would then send a band of monks into the new area. They would present the letter of introduction from the ruler in their previous location. Usually the ruler of the target area granted permission for them to begin their work. The monks then built temporary housing and began to go about their normal activities. As they labored to construct a permanent monastery, the monks visited the towns and villages nearby. Gradually, the monks established new churches around their monastery. The monks provided pastoral care for the churches until priests were appointed to tend the churches. Once the new monastery was well established, the abbot of the monastery would send another band of monks to begin work in another area. In this manner much of Western Europe was Christianized (Rudnick 1984, 43).

Columba (521–597) provides a good example of monastic missions. He lived for some years as a monk in Ireland and founded several monasteries there. In 563 Columba gathered a band of twelve monks and founded a monastery on Iona, an island off the west coast of Scotland. He made the Iona monastery his base from which he evangelized the Pict tribe in northern Scotland. After Columba died, monks from Iona continued to deploy missionaries. One of these, Aidan, went to Northumbria in northern England, where he baptized the people and founded a monastery like the one in Iona (Starkes 1984, 65–66).

MONARCHS

Many people groups in Europe came into the Roman Catholic Church through forced conversion. As mentioned above, Pope Gregory and the popes who followed him encouraged rulers to impose baptism on their subjects. It was not difficult to persuade rulers to do this. Medieval rulers believed that they had the right to choose the religion for their people. In other words, they believed that the religion of the king should also be the religion of his subjects. Charlemagne certainly manifested this attitude. Charlemagne (Charles the Great) was king of the Franks. By the end of his life he ruled over much of what is now France and Germany. He sponsored and sent missionaries to Christianize his kingdom. In 800 Pope Leo III proclaimed him to be the emperor of the Holy Roman Empire.

Charlemagne organized a military campaign to conquer the Saxon people. When he entered their land, Charlemagne brought missionary monks with him. He hoped the monks could both convert and pacify the fierce Saxons. The Saxons resisted conquest and conversion, but eventually they surrendered to Charlemagne. He forced the Saxons to accept baptism or be killed. Most accepted baptism. These actions by Charlemagne manifested mixed motives. Charlemagne sincerely wanted to please the pope and expand Christendom; however, he also believed that imposing Christianity on the conquered people would make them peaceful and pliable subjects (Rudnick 1984, 59–60).

Eastern Orthodox Christianity entered Bulgaria in a similar way. Cyril and Methodius were two missionary brothers who went to Bulgaria in 864. Methodius was a gifted artist, and King Bogoris asked him to paint a picture on a wall in his palace. Methodius's painting depicted the joys of heaven and the torments of hell. It affected King Bogoris so profoundly that he and many of his courtiers accepted baptism. The king ordered all his subjects to be baptized or be executed (Carver 1932, 69). The actions of King Bogoris and Emperor Charlemagne exemplify the actions of many European rulers and explain, in part, how Europe was Christianized.

THE CRUSADES

In 1095 Pope Urban II challenged the participants at the Council of Clermont to organize a crusade to liberate the Holy Land (Palestine) from Muslim control. For several hundred years Arab Muslims had controlled Palestine, but they permitted Christian pilgrims to visit holy sites without interference. However, Turkish Muslims had gained control of Palestine, and they had persecuted several Christian pilgrims. This provocation, as well as a desire to see the holy sites controlled by Christians, motivated the pope to speak. Beyond those concerns the emperor of Byzantium had appealed to the Christian rulers of Europe to relieve the pressure exerted on his empire by the Turks.

The princes of Europe responded to the pope's challenge and mounted the first Crusade in 1096. The first Crusade accomplished its main goal when Jerusalem was seized from the Turks in 1099. The crusaders established the Christian Kingdom of Jerusalem, which lasted for about one hundred years. Eventually, the Turks recaptured all the cities and territories lost to the crusaders. The last Crusade set out in 1248, but it failed, as did all but the first.

The Crusades were certainly not a mission strategy. The crusaders did not hope to convert the Muslims of the Middle East to Christianity: in fact, they hoped to kill or enslave them. Still, the Crusades affected European culture and Christian missions in many ways. In terms of their effects on the Roman Catholic Church, the Crusades brought much wealth to the church because many crusaders died and left their estates to the church. Negatively, the papacy suffered a loss of influence because the popes continued to promote crusades long after enthusiasm for them had waned. Also, the crusaders' capture and sacking of Byzantium (Constantinople/Istanbul) in 1204 ended any possibility of reuniting the Eastern Orthodox Church and the Roman Catholic Church.

The Crusades affected Europe by hastening the decline of the feudal system. The crusaders were quite impressed with the Muslim universities they encountered in the Middle East. This prompted the European rulers to begin founding universities in Europe. When the crusaders brought back silk and spices to Europe, they created a demand for those items. This economic demand brought about commercial and cultural interchange between Europe and the Middle East. Ultimately, the Crusades hurt European security. The Byzantine Empire had functioned as a buffer between the Muslim Middle East and Christian Europe. Rather than relieve the Muslim pressure on the Byzantine Empire, however, the Crusades weakened the empire. Eventually the Muslim Turks captured Byzantium and invaded southern Europe.

The Crusades affected missions in two ways: they awakened many Christians in Europe to the need for missionary work among Muslims, and they embittered Muslims in the Middle East against Christians (Neill 1986, 97–98).

Ramon Lull (1235–1315) was one European who sought to evangelize the Muslims rather than exterminate them. He was a native of the Spanish island Majorca, and he lived the comfortable life of a courtier until he experienced the call of God at age thirty. Lull then renounced his frivolous lifestyle and joined the Franciscan order. He felt a strong call to evangelize the Muslims of North Africa and dedicated the rest of his life to that cause.

Lull developed a strategy for reaching the Muslims that involved four key components. First, he insisted that missionaries who work with Muslims must have thorough training. They need to know the language and culture of the people and also know the Qur'an. He founded Miramar College to train missionary monks for missions to Muslims, and he pleaded with the Roman Catholic Church to establish others.

Second, he believed missionaries to the Muslims must possess a good book on apologetics in order to answer Muslim challenges and arguments. So he wrote several apologetics books to meet this need.

Third, he believed that missionaries must be able to preach to the Muslims. To that end he made four trips to North Africa to preach to the Muslims.

Fourth, and finally, he said that missionaries to the Muslims must be prepared to die as martyrs if necessary: "Missionaries will convert the world by preaching, but also through the shedding of tears and blood and with great labor, and through a bitter death" (Neill 1986, 117). True to his beliefs, Ramon Lull was martyred on his fourth trip to North Africa.

CHRISTIANIZATION THROUGH COLONIZATION

In the sixteenth and seventeenth centuries, Spain and Portugal aggressively explored and conquered much of southern Africa and America. These colonizing expeditions were sponsored by the Catholic monarchs of Spain and Portugal, and they sent Catholic missionaries along with the expeditions. They did this in obedience to the pope. In 1493 Pope Alexander VI divided the world into two spheres, east and west. He granted Portugal the rights to new lands discovered to the east of the line demarcation. He gave Spain rights to lands discovered to the west of the line. In this way Portugal acquired colonies in Africa (e.g., Angola and Mozambique) and in South America (Brazil). Spain acquired rights to most of South America, the islands of the Caribbean Sea, Central America, Mexico, North America, and the Philippines. In exchange for these rights the Catholic rulers promised to make Catholics of the peoples they would conquer. The rulers did not take their responsibility lightly. They sincerely wanted the conquered peoples to become good Catholics. However, they also viewed the Catholic Church as a means of pacification.

For their part, the Catholic missionaries made some converts by coercion and some by persuasion. The conquistadors forced some of the indigenes to accept baptism; however, that was not very common. Many of the native peoples willingly accepted baptism because they believed the God of the Europeans to be more powerful than their own. This belief stemmed from two sources: First, the Europeans brought with them diseases against which the native people had no immunity. Millions of Native Americans died due to smallpox, measles, and sexually transmitted diseases. They died in massive epidemics, which their priests were helpless to stop. Seeing that the Europeans did not die from these diseases, the locals assumed that the Europeans' God must be stronger than theirs. Second, the indigenous people were amazed that the small force of Europeans could defeat their far more numerous armies. Of course, the European armies possessed military technology that the local forces had never encountered.

Many of the Spanish and Portuguese missionaries accepted the notion of tabula rasa (literally "clean slate"), and this belief influenced their approach to converting native peoples. They believed that the cultures in the New World and elsewhere were saturated with paganism and there was nothing in them worth saving. They sought to replace the local cultures with Hispanic culture, which was saturated with Christianity. Other missionaries, like the Jesuit Matteo Ricci, practiced accommodation. Ricci (1552–1610) served in China. He mastered the Chinese language and learned the culture. He adopted the apparel of a Confucian scholar. After serving some years in southern China,

Ricci finally gained permission to live in Beijing, the capital city. Because he knew how to make clocks, he made a very special one and presented it to the emperor. The emperor liked the clock, and he named Ricci the imperial clock maker. This gave Ricci much prestige and access to the imperial court.

Ricci was able to bring other Jesuits to Beijing; before he died, he and his fellow Jesuits had baptized two thousand converts. Ricci understood the Chinese prejudice against anything foreign, so he and his companions used Confucian terms to translate biblical and theological words. He also allowed his converts to continue participating in rituals venerating their ancestors. Ricci saw these rituals as cultural rather than religious ceremonies. The Franciscan monks in Macao disagreed with the Jesuits and made a formal complaint to the Vatican. This dispute became known as the Chinese Rites Controversy. The controversy demonstrates the challenge of accommodation. What one missionary sees as an acceptable accommodation another views as a dangerous compromise that will lead to syncretism (combination of two religions).

CASE STUDY: JACK AND JENNIFER

Jack and Jennifer went to work with a Muslim people group. After completing language study they began evangelizing the people of their village. After two years of patient witnessing and discipling, they had a group of believers. When it came time to begin worshiping together, the people asked if they could worship on Friday. Jack and Jennifer asked why they wished to do so. The believers replied, "Friday is our day off from work. That day is the most convenient for us." Jack and Jennifer were surprised and uncertain about how to answer. They had always worshiped on Sunday, "the Lord's Day."

REFLECTION AND DISCUSSION

- How would you respond to the new believers?

9

Pioneer Protestant Strategies

I n this chapter you will learn about the strategies developed and employed by several of the great pioneers in Protestant missions. The strategies they developed still affect missions work today. There is insufficient space to tell their amazing stories of commitment and sacrifice, but missionaries today stand on their shoulders.

JOHN ELIOT'S STRATEGY

John Eliot (1604–1690) was a Puritan pastor who served in Massachusetts. He became concerned about the spiritual condition of the Algonquin tribe that lived near his home. Despite discouragement from the colonial government and his own church's leaders, he began working with the Algonquins. He undertook to learn their difficult language in 1644, and in 1646 he began evangelizing. His ministry developed slowly, but by 1674 he had gathered 1,100 Algonquin converts into fourteen "Praying Towns," villages for Christian Indians that Eliot established.

Eliot labored diligently at Bible translation, and he completed translation of the entire Bible into Algonquin in 1663. His reports inspired the organization of the Society for the Propagation of the Gospel (SPG) in England. The SPG had as its purpose the evangelization of the Native Americans in the American

---

SIDEBAR 9.1
EXTRACTION

John Eliot "extracted" the Christian Algonquins from their homes and villages. That is, he relocated them to "Praying Towns," populated solely by believers. His action is one of the earliest examples of extraction in Christian missions. Eliot believed that left in their villages his converts would deny their newfound faith and return to their old religion. He believed that associating primarily with Christians would reduce the possibility of recantation.

The missionaries in China in the nineteenth and early twentieth centuries also practiced extraction. Like Eliot they worried that their Chinese converts would bow to family and community pressure and renounce Christ. So they often brought them to live at the mission stations, where they were given jobs and encouragement in their faith.

Missionaries to North Africa and the Middle East have practiced extraction for a different reason. They have feared for the physical safety of their converts.

Many Muslims who have converted to Christianity have experienced arrest, beatings, and even death. Knowing this, Christian missionaries have sent Muslim converts to live in other countries to ensure their well-being.

Thus, missionaries have practiced extraction to protect their converts' spiritual condition and physical safety. The disadvantage of extraction is obvious. Removing converts from their homes, workplaces, and schools diminishes the number of believers witnessing to their families, friends, neighbors, and coworkers. It is difficult for the gospel to spread in a people group if few are bearing witness for Christ.

REFLECTION AND DISCUSSION

- How can a missionary who works in a society where converts to Christ are likely to be persecuted balance concern for the new believer's safety with concern for the spread of the gospel?

---

colonies of Great Britain. Eliot trained Algonquins to serve as evangelists, and he and his coworkers eventually won about four thousand to Christ. Sadly, during King Philip's War (1675) most of Eliot's Christian Algonquins died in the fighting or from privation in internment camps (Neill 1986, 192–93).

PIETIST STRATEGY

Pietism began with the ministry of Pastor Philipp Spener, a Lutheran pastor in Germany. In 1675 he published *Pia Desideria* (*Earnest Desires*), in which he called Protestants to make their faith a religion of the heart and not just the head. The Pietists reacted against the cold orthodoxy they saw in the Lutheran Church of that day and embraced experiential Christianity. They did not reject the basic articles of doctrine, but they challenged the Christians of Europe to live their faith. Spener called for believers to engage in personal and group

Bible study. He also challenged laypersons to demonstrate the priesthood of believers by serving in the church, living moral lives, and witnessing for the Lord. In his church Spener initiated cottage prayer meetings where his church members gathered weekly to pray and study the Scriptures together.

Laypersons responded positively to Spener's renewal movement, but many clergy did not. He was forced out of his first church in Frankfurt and later a chaplaincy, but he accepted a call to serve a church in Berlin. While he served in Berlin, he founded the University of Halle, which became the center of Pietism. Spener also won August Hermann Francke to Pietism, and it was Francke who succeeded Spener as the Pietist leader. Francke developed the University of Halle and influenced his students to be mission minded, an unusual thing at that time.

The first Pietist mission work began in 1705, when the king of Denmark called for establishing a mission to evangelize the people in Denmark's new

---

SIDEBAR 9.2
CHARACTERISTICS OF PIETISM

Pietism has exerted a profound influence on evangelical Christianity, including the following elements:

- *The New Birth.* Pietists affirmed Luther's emphasis on justification by faith, but they insisted that the baptism of children did not ensure regeneration. Pietist pastors exhorted their church members to be born again.

- *Joy in Christian Living.* Pietists often spoke and wrote of a joyful relationship with Christ.

- *Sanctification.* Pietists emphasized the doctrine and experience of sanctification. They taught that the Holy Spirit would work in the lives of Christians to make them more like Christ.

- *Biblicism.* Pietists encouraged their people to study the Bible. They judged every doctrine and practice by God's Word. They believed that laypersons could interpret the Bible for themselves with the guidance of the Holy Spirit.

- *Theological Education.* Pietists stressed the importance of educated ministers. They wanted pastors who had educated minds and warm hearts.

- *Missions and Evangelism.* Pietists encouraged their people to witness and engage in missions. Count Nikolaus von Zinzendorf wrote, "My joy until I die . . . [is] to win souls for the Lamb."

- *Social Concern.* Critics have often asserted that Pietists were only interested in spiritual matters; however, the Pietists of Halle established a school for poor children, a free medical clinic, and a home for the poor. (J. M. Terry 1994, 89–90)

REFLECTION AND DISCUSSION

- How has Pietism influenced contemporary Christianity?

trading concession in India. The royal chaplain traveled to the University of Halle to recruit missionaries, and two students, Bartholomew Ziegenbalg and Heinrich Plutschau, responded. They went to India and founded the Danish-Halle Mission. Even though they had no experience and nothing but the New Testament to draw on, the two young missionaries developed a remarkable strategy to guide their work. They said that missionaries to India should study Hinduism carefully in order to understand the barriers to conversion. They also held that missionaries should translate the Bible into the local language. They insisted that missionaries must give themselves to personal evangelism. Finally, they believed that Christian education should be established as quickly as possible, and national pastors must be trained as soon as possible.

In 1715 Ziegenbalg returned to Europe, and he spoke at the University of Halle. There Nikolaus von Zinzendorf, a student, heard him. Zinzendorf was a member of the German nobility. His pietistic grandmother sent him to Halle to study. Later Zinzendorf became the leader of the Moravian Church. The Moravians were the spiritual descendants of John Hus, who had fled to Germany to escape persecution. Zinzendorf gave them land on his family's estate on which to build their village, Herrnhut. Zinzendorf encouraged the Moravians to engage in missions, and after a time of prayer they agreed. Between 1732 and 1760 this church of 600 members dispatched 226 missionaries, a ratio of missionaries to church members of one missionary for every twelve members. The Moravians sent missionaries to many lands, including the Caribbean islands, Greenland, Ghana, South Africa, and the American colonies (where they evangelized Native Americans). The Moravians conducted their missions work according to these principles:

- Missionaries are laypersons.
- Missionaries are self-supporting (tentmakers).
- Missionaries must learn the local language and culture.
- Missionaries must translate the Bible into the local language.
- Missionaries must establish schools and teach the people to read the Bible.
- Missionaries engage in personal evangelism rather than mass evangelism.
- Missionaries emphasize presenting Jesus as the slain Lamb of God.
- Missionaries seek to establish local churches as soon as possible.
- The local church must be self-governing.
- Missionaries should seek to go to the most difficult places.

WILLIAM CAREY'S STRATEGY

Historians call William Carey the father of the Modern Missions Movement (Anderson 1998, 201), and that accolade is appropriate. William Carey was not the first Protestant foreign missionary, but he popularized missions. His example and correspondence inspired the Christians of Europe and North America to embrace missions. His ministry marks the beginning of what Latourette has called "The Great Century of Protestant Missions" (Latourette 1941, 2).

In 1792 William Carey did two things that started the Modern Missions Movement. First, he published a pamphlet titled "An Enquiry into the Obligation of Christians to Use Means for the Conversion of the Heathen." In the pamphlet Carey presented the biblical and theological basis for missions, explained the progress of Christianity around the world, and described how a missionary-sending society could be founded. This pamphlet was widely distributed and stirred up interest in missions.

Second, Carey preached a sermon on missions at the annual meeting of the Northampton Baptist Association in England. In his sermon on Isaiah 54:2–3 he exhorted his audience to "expect great things from God; attempt great things for God" (Anderson 1998, 201). This sermon so inspired his listeners that they soon founded the Baptist Missionary Society. Naturally, Carey volunteered to go as a missionary to India.

In 1793 Carey and his family sailed to India. They endured much suffering during their first years in India, including the death of a young son, Peter. Carey's situation improved significantly when William Ward and Joshua and Hannah Marshman joined him in 1799. Together they established a mission station in Serampore, a Danish colony just north of Calcutta. The Serampore Trio, as they were called, set up a printing press, founded Serampore College, and planted many churches. William Carey and his colleagues adopted this strategy:

- Missionaries should study carefully the language and culture of the people.
- Missionaries should seek to understand the religious beliefs of the people.
- Missionaries should preach the gospel as widely as possible.
- Missionaries should give priority to translating the Bible into the language of the people.
- Missionaries should establish local churches.
- Missionaries should train national pastors and turn over to them the care of the churches as soon as possible. (Neill 1986, 224–25)

SIDEBAR 9.3
MISSIONARY TEAMS

Paul Hartford defines a missionary team in this way: "A ministry strategy and organizational structure that uses a small group format and emphasizes interdependent relationships in order to accomplish a given task" (2000, 22). As shown in this chapter, missionary teams are nothing new, and William Carey would surely remind us that the apostle Paul normally worked with a team. Missionary teams demonstrate several advantages:

- Companionship—missionaries do not suffer so much from loneliness.
- Synergy—the combined efforts of a team are more effective than missionaries working individually.
- Continuity—the ministry can continue if one member has an illness or home leave.
- Varied spiritual gifts—the members of the team can utilize their differing spiritual gifts.

- Greater objectivity—making decisions as a group helps prevent "tunnel vision."
- Encouragement—the members can encourage one another.
- Affinity—the members have a common vision and objectives.
- Biblical model—the apostle Paul employed a team approach.

Of course, teams can and do have problems. Developing and maintaining a successful team takes time and energy, but experience shows this approach can be effective when properly implemented. (Hartford 2000, 934)

REFLECTION AND DISCUSSION

- If missionary teams afford so many advantages, why don't all missions agencies use them?
- How might a multicultural team be more difficult to lead?

In many ways William Carey set the pattern that Protestant missionaries have followed for two centuries. First, he gave priority to Bible translation and distribution. Second, he emphasized planting churches. And third, he founded Serampore College in order to train Indian pastors. His accomplishments are quite remarkable for a man with only an elementary education.

ADONIRAM JUDSON

Adoniram Judson (1788–1850) was the pioneer missionary to Burma. He and his wife, Ann, initially tried to settle in India, but the British East India Company forced them to leave. They entered Burma in 1813. The Judsons both worked hard at learning the Burmese language, and they both learned well. Adoniram often preached to the Burmese people, but he did not make a convert for six years. During those years he labored at translating the entire Bible into Burmese, a project he finished in 1834. His beloved Ann died in 1826, and after a period of severe depression, he married Sarah Boardman, the widow of a fellow missionary. She died in 1845, and he remarried again. In spite of burying wives and children and recurring bouts of depression, Judson persevered with his ministry.

Adoniram Judson developed and demonstrated these principles in his missions strategy:

- He believed in the necessity of mission organizations, and he led in the founding of the American Board of Commissioners for Foreign Missions and the American Baptist Missions Society.
- He devoted himself to learning the Burmese language and culture.
- He was convinced that the Burmese people needed a Bible in their language that would not need to be revised in a few years, so he translated

---

SIDEBAR 9.4
CONTEXTUALIZATION

Contextualization is defined in many ways by different writers. Here is a helpful definition of the term by David Hesselgrave:

> Contextualization is both verbal and nonverbal and has to do with theologizing, Bible translation, interpretation and application, incarnational lifestyle, evangelism, Christian instruction, church planting and growth, church organization, worship style—indeed with all of those activities involved in carrying out the Great Commission. (1995, 115)

For evangelical missionaries contextualization is mainly concerned with communicating biblical truth in such a way that the recipients can understand and make an appropriate response. Adoniram Judson employed contextualized communication when he built a *zayat* (open-air pavilion) in Rangoon, Burma. After he learned to speak Burmese, he often preached to the people, but he made no converts for several years.

Finally, he studied the teaching method of the Buddhist monks. They would sit in a *zayat* and answer questions put to them by passers-by. Judson decided to imitate them. He built a *zayat* in front of his house and began to sit there several hours each day. People began to stop and chat with him, and soon he won his first convert. This is a good example of contextualization.

Judson knew the message to present, and he learned the local language. However, his evangelistic efforts were unsuccessful until he discovered the appropriate form of communication. Contextualization involves communicating biblical truth in the right language and in the right way.

REFLECTION AND DISCUSSION

- How can missionaries decide which language to learn and use?
- What advantages do modern missionaries have over the pioneer missionaries like Adoniram Judson?

his Burmese Bible from the Greek and Hebrew, not from English. His translation, often called the "Judson Bible," is still used in Myanmar.

- He insisted that converts undergo a period of intense discipleship training.
- He challenged missionaries to commit to a lifetime of service.

ROBERT MOFFATT

Robert Moffatt (1795–1883) was a native of Scotland. He had trained to be a gardener, so he had little formal education. Nevertheless, the London Missionary Society appointed him and his wife to South Africa. They arrived in Cape Town in 1816 and eventually they moved to Kuruman in what is now Botswana. They served at Kuruman for forty-eight years. Moffatt completed translating the Bible into Tswana in 1857. This translation prompted a spiritual awakening among the Bechuana people. The Moffatts planted churches in the villages around Kuruman, but they are best known for establishing a prototypical "mission station" there. A mission station was meant to be a self-sufficient center for missionary work. Their station contained housing for missionaries and local staff, storage buildings, a school, a medical clinic, a printing press, an orphanage, irrigation, and a thriving farm. Most of what they needed they raised or produced at the station. Mission stations (or compounds) became standard practice in Protestant missionary work, especially in Africa, China, and India. The Moffatts had several children, and their daughter, Mary, married David Livingstone, who came to Kuruman to serve in their medical clinic.

SUMMARY

The pioneer missionaries of the nineteenth century set the pattern for Protestant missionary work for more than one hundred years. They all labored to translate the Bible into the language of the people they served. Their success in this is remarkable because they had no linguistic training. They also gave priority to evangelism and church planting. Training local pastors was also important. William Carey declared that there would never be enough Western missionaries to evangelize India. If India were to be evangelized, Indians would have to do it. What we witness in India today demonstrates the truth of Carey's statement. These strategies were certainly positive developments. A negative development was the mission station or missionary compound. In Africa mission stations were necessary to sustain the long-term ministries of missionaries. However, in China and India mission stations eventually became Christian havens. As you will see in the later chapter on indigenous missions,

John Nevius called on the missionaries to China to leave their stations and get out among the people.

CASE STUDY:
ARE YOU COMMUNICATING CLEARLY?

Will Martin graduated from a well-respected evangelical seminary in the United States. His seminary emphasized expository preaching, and Will learned that approach to preaching in his homiletics courses. He learned to analyze a biblical text and discover the natural outline. When he preached expository sermons to congregations in the United States, they responded positively.

When he went to serve in a culture different from his own, he was assigned to work with a mountain people. After learning their language, he translated several of his expository sermons and preached them to the people.

The mountain people found his sermons confusing. They had trouble following his sermon from point to point to conclusion. Will was confused himself and quite frustrated. After all, he was preaching just the way he had been taught in seminary.

REFLECTION
AND DISCUSSION

- What do you think is the source of Will's confusion? On the basis of your first answer, what do you think Will should do?

10

Faith Missions Strategy

F aith missions agencies have been the backbone of evangelical missions
for 150 years. In this chapter we explain how the movement began. We
focus on Hudson Taylor because the organization he founded, China
Inland Mission, was the prototype for other faith missions that followed.

JAMES HUDSON TAYLOR

James Hudson Taylor (1832–1905) grew up in England. His parents were dedicated Christians, and his father was a lay preacher in the Methodist Church.
Taylor professed faith in Christ at age seventeen, and soon afterward he declared that God had called him to serve in China. Believing that a medical
mission would open doors for the gospel in China, he studied medicine in
Hull. Before he completed his medical studies, in 1853 the China Evangelization Society appointed him to serve in China.

Taylor arrived in China in 1854. At that time most of the missionaries
confined their ministry to the five treaty ports along the coast of China. Two
early experiences in China shaped his convictions about how missionary work
should be done there. First, he became very frustrated with the administration
of the China Evangelization Society. His financial support arrived irregularly,
if at all. Beyond that, the society had its administrative office in London. This

meant that any question he had about his ministry had to be sent by sailing ship to London, where it had to wait for a meeting of the board of directors, and then the reply would be sent to China via sailing ship. This process took about one year, and often the question was irrelevant by the time the answer arrived. Second, trips into the interior of China convinced him that all of China should be evangelized, not just the east coast. He became so disgusted with the poor administration of the China Evangelization Society that he resigned and became an independent missionary. In 1858 he married Maria Dyer, and they worked together in China. In 1860 Taylor's bad health forced them to return to England, and he spent several months recovering.

While the Taylors were in England, Hudson completed his medical studies in London. He also prayed and planned about establishing a new missions society. In 1865 Taylor founded the China Inland Mission, the first "faith" mission, and began recruiting missionaries. In 1866 the Taylors sailed for China with seventeen new missionaries.

THE CHINA INLAND MISSION

The China Inland Mission's (CIM) name reflected Taylor's reaction to his early experiences in China. The use of *Inland* in the name demonstrated his commitment to bringing the gospel to all of China's provinces and his reaction against the coastal focus of the earlier work in China. By *China* Taylor indicated an exclusive focus; CIM had no other field than China until the Communist government of China expelled all missionaries in the early 1950s.

Taylor adopted innovative policies for the CIM that set it apart from other mission boards. First, he insisted that his missionaries make no direct appeals for financial donations; rather, they were to pray to God to supply their needs. Taylor believed that if his missionaries presented China's spiritual needs, then God would move Christians to give the needed funds. In other words, he challenged his missionaries to live by "faith," which is how the term *faith mission* originated.

Second, Taylor and CIM had no educational requirements for appointment aside from being able to read and write. He did not require a university degree or theological training, in contrast to most agencies of his day, which required prospective missionaries to have theological or medical training.

Third, Taylor invited single women to apply for appointment. This was a true innovation. Great Britain in the Victorian era did not encourage this type of activity on the part of young women. Moreover, many missions leaders criticized Taylor for sending single women into the dangerous interior of China without the benefit of "male protection." Taylor insisted that single

SIDEBAR 10.1
FAITH MISSIONS

"Faith missions is a term generally applied to non-denominational and inter-denominational foreign missionary agencies whose governing concept is to look to God alone for financial support" (Lindsell 1971, 206). Most of the early agencies were denominational. Examples include the Baptist Missions Society, inspired by William Carey, and the Church Missions Society, which was the missionary organization of the Anglican Church in Great Britain. In 1925, 75 percent of the Protestant missionaries served with denominational mission boards (Covell 2000, 353).

Faith missions agencies developed for several reasons. One was a concern that the denominational agencies were not doing enough, especially in reaching the interior regions of Asia and Africa. Additionally, many conservative Christians became concerned about the growing theological liberalism in some Protestant denominations and wanted to support missionaries who reflected their belief in the "fundamentals" of Christianity. A third reason for the proliferation of faith missions was financial. The denominational agencies did not have enough money to send the missionaries needed in the field. So faith missions agencies filled the gap.

Faith missions agencies exhibited several common characteristics. They asked their missionaries to raise their own support. This involved "deputation," visiting churches and individual Christians to present the needs of their prospective places of service and to solicit financial gifts and pledges of monthly support. For many years the missionaries were not allowed to make direct appeals for money,

though most agencies have since relaxed that policy. Further, missionary candidates were required to sign a confession of faith that stated conservative Christian beliefs. Finally, most of the missionaries had graduated from Bible colleges such as Moody Bible Institute and Nyack Missionary College.

For many years the faith missions agencies were general boards, that is, each mission agency engaged in a number of different ministries—evangelism, medical work, education, and so on. However, after World War II a number of specialized mission agencies were founded, including agencies such as Missionary Aviation Fellowship and the Far Eastern Broadcasting Company.

Eventually, several faith mission boards joined together to form the Interdenominational Foreign Mission Association of North America (IFMA) in 1917. Later the IFMA changed its name to CrossGlobal Link, which had seventy-six member agencies in 2010 as well as a number of associate members (churches). They merged into one organization with the Mission Exchange (formerly EFMA) in 2011, finalizing the process by naming the joint organization Missio Nexus in 2012.

REFLECTION AND DISCUSSION

- Perhaps the biggest challenge faith missions face is raising financial support. Given recent financial crises and a gloomy financial outlook in many parts of the world today, what are ways that faith missions agencies can respond to the financial challenges they will face in the coming decade?

women could serve effectively, and, of course, they proved him right. This action by Taylor was a significant step in the development of the Women's Missionary Movement.

Fourth, Taylor made CIM an interdenominational mission by accepting applicants from any Protestant church or denomination. Applicants had only to affirm a basic evangelical statement of faith. Of course, this led to complications such as the mode of baptism used with new converts. The missionaries with a Baptist background practiced immersion, while missionaries with an Anglican background favored sprinkling. Taylor solved this problem by assigning CIM Baptists to one region of China and CIM Anglicans to another.

Fifth, Taylor insisted that the administrative offices of the organization be located in China. The CIM established an office in London and eventually in other major Western cities, but the administration of the mission was done in China. He did not want his missionaries to experience the communications and supervisory frustrations that he had in his early years in China.

Sixth, the CIM challenged all its missionaries to identify as closely as possible with the Chinese people. Taylor exhorted them to learn to speak the Chinese language/dialect of their location and to learn the culture. He wanted them to dress like Chinese, speak like Chinese, eat like Chinese, and live in Chinese houses. Taylor practiced this principle himself. He wore the silk robe of a Chinese teacher and wore his hair in the Chinese style. His position on identification prompted many Western missionaries to ridicule him and his policies. However, as time passed, his policies proved their worth, and CIM missionaries functioned more effectively than did the missionaries who wore Western clothing.

Seventh, China Inland Mission emphasized rapid evangelization. Taylor encouraged his missionaries to engage in widespread evangelism rather than church planting. He wanted his missionaries to do itinerant preaching, going from town to town and village to village. This type of strategy is called a "diffusion strategy," as mentioned in chapter 6. This approach also brought criticism from other missions agencies, and Taylor eventually conceded that church planting was necessary (Neill 1986, 283).

Eighth, and finally, Taylor directed his personnel to occupy the provincial capitals first. Once they had established a ministry there, they could itinerate in the surrounding towns and villages. This reflected the apostle Paul's strategy, which focused on urban centers in the Roman Empire.

Taylor's faithful ministry bore fruit. By 1882 the CIM had achieved his primary goal and had placed a missionary in every province in China. By 1895 the CIM counted 641 missionaries in China, half the total number of Protestant missionaries. By 1929 the CIM had 1,300 missionaries serving in China, making it by far the largest Protestant mission organization in the

---

SIDEBAR 10.2
IDENTIFICATION

Missionary identification is the effort missionaries make to become one with their adopted people groups. One aspect of identification is to become a "bicultural" person, a person who is comfortable and functional in two cultures. Missionaries must navigate between two extremes. One extreme is to reject the local culture completely. Missionaries who do this seek to duplicate the lifestyle they enjoyed in their home settings. They may live in a new country, but they do not live *with* the local people. The other extreme is to "go native." Missionaries who do this reject their own cultures and completely embrace their host cultures, sometimes to the point of rejecting Christianity and converting to the local religion. A bicultural missionary retains a love for home culture, but also becomes an insider in the local culture.

The missionary's model in identification is Jesus Christ, who identified with humankind by becoming a man. Of course, a missionary cannot choose to be reborn as Japanese or Nigerian, but a missionary can make the effort to identify as much as possible.

One important aspect involves missionary lifestyle. This includes learning the language and adopting the dress, food, lodging, and a host of cultural traits. As mentioned in this chapter, Hudson Taylor identified by wearing the silk gown of a Chinese teacher and wearing his hair in a long queue, after the Chinese fashion of that time.

Ultimately, no missionary can identify completely. A Caucasian missionary from Canada would never be mistaken for a local person in southern Africa, but the missionary can become an accepted person in the local society. The missionary can learn the language, culture, and communication forms well enough to communicate the gospel clearly. (King 2000, 349–50)

REFLECTION AND DISCUSSION

- Jesus became God incarnate—God in the flesh. In what ways might missionaries work to "become" the gospel incarnate?
- How long should it take a missionary to become bicultural?

---

world. Perhaps the greatest accomplishment of Taylor and CIM is that they demonstrated that missionaries could survive and evangelize in every part of China. Inspired by the example of CIM missionaries, other agencies began extending their work inland (Neill 1986, 284).

Taylor himself suffered much for the sake of the gospel. He buried two wives and four children in China. In 1900 the Boxer Rebellion, a nationalistic uprising in northern China, sought to purge China of foreign influence and institutions. The Boxers destroyed Western factories and railroads, and they especially targeted foreign missionaries and Chinese Christians. Thousands of Chinese Christians died as martyrs. The Roman Catholic Church and the CIM suffered higher losses because their missionaries served in the interior and could not escape to the coast. The CIM lost 135 missionaries and 53 missionary children. This horrible loss of life depressed Taylor so much that he resigned his position as director of the CIM. After he recovered from his depression, Taylor returned to China and served as a missionary until his death in 1905.

FAITH MISSION ORGANIZATIONS

China Inland Mission provided a model for other missions agencies. It continued to minister in China until the CIM missionaries were expelled by the Communist government, beginning about 1950. Today, the CIM is known as the Overseas Missionary Fellowship, and its missionaries work in Taiwan and with diaspora Chinese throughout Asia, as well as doing tribal ministry.

The agencies that were founded according to the pattern of the CIM include:

- Christian and Missionary Alliance (1887)
- The Evangelical Alliance Mission (1890)
- Central American Mission (1890)
- Sudan Interior Mission (1895)
- African Inland Mission (1895)

CASE STUDY:
CONCENTRATION OR DIFFUSION?

Rick and his team were assigned to work with a mountain tribe in the southern Philippines. The people lived in small villages scattered over a wide area. Many of the villages could be reached only by hiking over rugged trails that snaked through the mountains. Rick and his team gained the *datu's* (chief's) permission to live in the central village, Kabukiran. They studied for two years to learn the language and culture of the people. They also spent several months developing the Bible stories they would use to evangelize the people group.

When they finished their preparatory work, the team met to discuss the next phase of their work. Some of the team members wanted to hike from village to village, telling the people the Bible stories they had translated. Rick urged the team to focus their efforts on Kabukiran. He said, "Let's plant a strong church here in our village. Then, we can train the believers to tell the Bible stories and reach out to the other villages."

REFLECTION
AND DISCUSSION

- If you had been a member of the team, how would you respond to Rick?

11

Mission Strategies on the American Frontier

I n 1800 the young nation, the United States of America, looked westward. Following the Revolutionary War and the organization of their government, Americans began a movement to the West that lasted for two generations. This population shift posed a problem for American church leaders: how could they establish churches on the western frontier? In this chapter we describe the strategies employed in the "churching" of the United States.

SPIRITUAL INFLUENCES

Two spiritual awakenings shaped American Christianity. The First Great Awakening began in New Jersey through the ministry of Theodore J. Frelinghuysen. He was a Pietist pastor in the Dutch Reformed Church. When he arrived in New Jersey in 1719, he was appalled at the unbelief and poor morals he observed among his church members. He began evangelizing his church members and exhorted them to live committed lives. At first his congregation and many of the local pastors opposed his approach, but eventually a spiritual awakening broke out. It soon spread into the local Presbyterian churches. Gilbert Tennent, a Presbyterian pastor, met Frelinghuysen and realized that they both shared a commitment to spiritual renewal. Tennent challenged the "presumptuous security" of his church members. They assumed that their baptism and church membership guaranteed them an eternal home in heaven. Tennent called on them to be born again and live faithful lives (Hatch, Noll, and Woodbridge 1979, 139).

The revival in New England was led by Jonathan Edwards, a Congregational Church pastor. In 1727 he went to serve the Congregational Church in Northampton, Massachusetts. Like Tennent and Frelinghuysen, he was disappointed by the level of morality he observed. Through personal visits and challenging sermons, he called the people to repentance and commitment to Christ. When the revival broke out, the congregation and the town were transformed. During the revival his church added three hundred new members. News of the revival spread through the area, and eventually forty towns experienced a spiritual awakening. Edwards described the awakening in his famous book *A Faithful Narrative of the Surprising Work of God*. Indeed, the title expresses Edwards's view of revival, which he considered a sovereign action by God, a miracle of God's grace (Hatch, Noll, and Woodbridge 1979, 139–40).

Surely, the leading light of the First Great Awakening was George Whitefield. While Tennent and Frelinghuysen ministered only in the Middle Colonies and Jonathan Edwards in New England, George Whitefield preached up and down the east coast of the American colonies. His ministry unified the awakening in America and connected it to the Evangelical Revival in Great Britain. George Whitefield was a large man with a booming voice, fully able to preach to the crowds of thousands in the open-air meetings he conducted. In 1740 Whitefield made a successful preaching tour of New England in which he preached 130 sermons in seventy-three days. When Whitefield left Boston, twenty thousand people came to hear his farewell sermon (Hatch, Noll, and Woodbridge 1979, 139–40).

The revival sparked controversy, and those opposed (the Old Lights) condemned it as emotional extremism. The New Lights supported the revival and pointed to its positive results. Baptists and Methodists supported the revival and reaped many of its benefits. For example, in Massachusetts the number of Baptist churches increased from six to thirty, and in Rhode Island from eleven to thirty-six. Between 1740 and 1760, 150 new Congregational churches were organized in New England. Perhaps forty thousand new members were added to New England churches during the awakening.

The First Great Awakening produced nontangible results as well. It affected the nature of American religion, making it individualistic. The revival's emphasis on personal conversion suited a culture of rugged individualists. The awakening also enshrined revival meetings as the most common method of evangelism. Last, the awakening popularized extemporaneous preaching. George Whitefield practiced this method, and many preachers imitated his style (J. M. Terry 1994, 123–24).

The Second Great Awakening began in the eastern United States in 1786 with a campus revival at Hampden-Sidney College in Virginia. Yale College in Connecticut experienced revival in 1802, when Timothy Dwight, the president, preached a series of stirring chapel messages. When the revival broke out on campus, one-third of the students professed faith in Christ. From Yale the revival spread to other New England colleges and churches.

The awakening began in the West in about 1800. The Presbyterian Church, like all the churches, struggled to provide pastoral care for its scattered members on the western frontier. James McGreedy, a Presbyterian pastor, announced a worship and Communion service at his church near the Red River close to the Kentucky and Tennessee border. Many people attended, and a number were saved or revived. A month later a bigger meeting was held at Gasper River. This meeting was the first true "camp meeting," so called because the people camped at the site and built a platform and crude benches from felled trees. The preachers held the services in the open air, and they usually had morning, afternoon, and evening services. The order of worship was simple: hymn singing, fiery preaching, and a public invitation. The pastors led early morning prayer meetings also. The settlers enjoyed both the worship services and the opportunity to socialize.

In about 1805 the Presbyterians ended their involvement in camp meetings, concerned that they had become too emotional. The Baptists and the Methodists continued to sponsor them until about 1840. The Methodists called the camp meetings their "harvest time," and Bishop Francis Asbury guessed that as many as five hundred were held in 1811. Bishop Asbury attended a camp meeting in Ohio in 1808 and reported that twenty-three preachers were present and two thousand worshipers (Sweet 1944, 136).

Like the First Great Awakening, the Second Awakening influenced American religion, especially religion in the West. The camp meetings saw thousands of people converted, and the churches grew rapidly. For example, between 1800 and 1805 Methodist members in Kentucky increased from 3,030 to 10,158. The camp-meeting preachers emphasized human free will to choose salvation. This shifted the theology of the frontier from Calvinism to Arminianism. The Second Great Awakening made Methodists and Baptists the dominant churches in the South. By 1850 in the twelve states of the South there were 6,061 Methodist churches and 5,298 Baptist churches, in contrast to 1,647 Presbyterian churches and 408 Episcopal churches, of which 315 were located along the

Atlantic coast (J. M. Terry 1994, 137). Certainly, the awakening changed the moral climate of the frontier, as piety replaced drunkenness.

METHODIST CHURCH PLANTING

The Methodists succeeded remarkably well in their efforts to plant churches along the western frontier. Four factors contributed to their success. First, they had good leadership. The outstanding bishop of the Methodist Episcopal Church in America was Francis Asbury (1745–1816). Ordained by John Wesley, he remained a bachelor so that he could devote more time to his ministry. He traveled unceasingly, visiting the Methodist circuits and churches throughout the United States. He ordained three thousand circuit riders, and by the time of his death Methodists in the United States numbered 250,000 (Starkes 1984, 149). Asbury's vision and activity contributed greatly to this growth.

Second, the Methodists also succeeded because of their strategy for evangelism and church planting. They employed "circuit riders" to evangelize the people, plant churches, and disciple new believers. Almost all the early Methodist preachers were itinerants, that is, they traveled along a regular "circuit" or route. They preached in the Methodist societies and classes, and they also evangelized in individual homes and new villages. The size of the circuits varied according to the number of Methodist classes in the area. If no classes existed, the circuit riders established them. Usually there were twenty to thirty classes in each circuit. The goal was for the class to develop into a church, and most did so.

The circuit riders could not be everywhere at once, so they encouraged and authorized lay preachers to conduct ministry in their localities while the circuit rider preached elsewhere. These lay preachers proved a great asset in the evangelization of the frontier. When a young man showed evidence of faith and ability to speak publicly, the circuit rider would encourage him to preach some trial sermons. If his efforts pleased the congregation, the circuit rider granted the novice preacher an "exhorter's license." Some of the exhorters became circuit riders, but many remained exhorters throughout their lives. These lay preachers, or exhorters, typically had little education, but they made up for that with their passion for Christ.

Third, the Methodists had a polity (pattern of church government) that proved itself conducive to growth. John Wesley had established groups of believers who met weekly to pray and study the Bible. He modeled his groups after the Pietists' cottage prayer meetings. A "society" was composed of the Methodists who lived in a particular area. The society was divided into "classes." The class members were taught to gather weekly and to encourage one another. Laypersons led the classes, and circuit riders visited the classes on a regular schedule. In the beginning John Wesley established "chapels" or meetinghouses for the Methodist society in each area. When the Methodists broke away from the Anglican Church in Great Britain and Episcopal Church in the United States, the chapels became Methodist churches, though many continued to be called "chapels." Wesley appointed bishops to supervise the circuit riders. Eventually, as the Methodist Church grew, the bishops appointed district superintendents to assist with denominational administration.

Fourth, John Wesley's theology could be summarized in four points: universal salvation, free salvation, sure salvation, and full salvation. These correspond to justification by faith alone, true freedom of the human will, assurance of salvation through the witness of the Holy Spirit, and sanctification. Wesley espoused Arminian theology, and he explained his beliefs in the Twenty-Five Articles, which served as a guide for the Methodist societies and the circuit riders. The Methodist preachers preached free grace for sinners and the free will of people to choose Christ. These themes appealed to the frontier settlers, who valued democracy and equality. The preachers also sought to follow the instructions on preaching laid down in the Methodist Book of Discipline, which directed them (1) to convince, (2) to offer Christ, (3) to invite, and (4) to build up. They were supposed to do all four in every sermon. Their faithfulness in following these instructions is evident in the growth of the Methodist Church on the frontier.

BAPTIST FARMER-PREACHERS

The Baptists on the frontier certainly were not as organized as the Methodists, but they did plant many churches in the West. Much of their success was due to their simple gospel message, emotional preaching, and flexible polity. All these elements suited the frontier quite well. The Baptist advance on the frontier was led by bivocational pastors. Some of these pastors taught school or tended stores in order to feed their families, but most worked as farmers. The farmer-preachers possessed little education, but they believed that God had called them to preach and they preached the gospel of salvation through Jesus Christ with boldness and conviction.

The farmer-preachers lived among and worked like their people. Most lived in log houses with dirt floors. They worked with their neighbors to pull tree stumps, plant crops, and build barns. They struggled to feed their families just like the other men in the community. These preachers understood the needs of their people because they shared those needs.

John Taylor serves as a good example of the farmer-preachers. In 1783 Taylor and his family made the arduous trip across the mountains from Virginia to Kentucky. They settled in Woodward County and cleared the land for their farm. He and several other believers organized the Clear Creek Baptist Church. He served that church as pastor for nine years. As his farm prospered, he was able to make preaching tours each summer. On these trips he took part in establishing seven churches in Virginia, North Carolina, and Tennessee. He never received any formal training, nor did he receive financial support from churches or a mission agency (Sweet 1950, 216).

SIDEBAR 11.1
JOHN MASON PECK

John Mason Peck (1789–1858) was a pioneer missionary on the western frontier. Peck grew up in New York and became a Baptist in 1811. Soon afterward, he announced that God had called him to preach, and his church encouraged him to do so. He served two churches in New York as pastor, teaching school to augment his meager pastor's salary. In 1815 Peck heard Luther Rice speak on missions, and he received a call to missions. Peck believed his calling was to domestic missions, not foreign missions, and Rice encouraged him to apply to the Baptist Convention for appointment as a missionary.

In 1817 the Baptist Convention appointed Peck and James Welch to serve as missionaries in the Missouri Territory. When Peck and Welch arrived in St. Louis, they began to preach, organize Sunday schools, and plant churches. They also organized women's "mite societies" (missions societies) in the St. Louis area. In 1820 the convention discontinued mission work in Missouri due to a lack of funds. The convention instructed Peck to transfer to Indiana to work with Native Americans. He refused to leave St. Louis and worked independently until 1822, when the Massachusetts Baptist Missionary Society employed him as a missionary for five dollars per week.

In 1822 he moved to Rock Spring, Illinois, and began to devote himself to organizing Sunday schools and societies for the distribution of Bibles. He realized his societies and Sunday schools would die without encouragement, so he appointed circuit riders like the Methodists had. In 1832 he and Jonathan Going led in the founding of the American Baptist Home Mission Society. He established a theological seminary on his farm in Rock Spring. Eventually, the seminary moved to Alton, Illinois, and became Shurtleff College. During the 1830s and 1840s he continued to itinerate in Illinois and Missouri and Iowa. He became concerned about the lack of Christian literature for the Sunday schools and churches on the frontier, and that prompted him to accept the leadership of the American Baptist Publication Society. In 1852 Harvard University conferred on him a doctor of divinity degree. The editor of Peck's memoirs states, "Little less than two thousand Baptist churches were in flourishing existence in his field ere he left it, where there were not a score on his entrance." (Southern Baptist Historical Library and Archives, http://www.sbhla.org/bio_peck.htm)

REFLECTION AND DISCUSSION

- How do the church planter's convictions about ecclesiology affect church planting?
- How does formal theological education affect church planting?

101

DEVELOPING A STRATEGY FOR MISSIONS

Most of the frontier Baptist churches began like the Clear Creek Baptist Church. When a farmer-preacher settled in a new area, he would canvass his neighbors to discover their spiritual condition and whether there were Baptists among them. Then he would hold Sunday meetings at a convenient location—in a cabin, barn, or clearing. When the church began to grow, the members would erect a building, usually a log church. Many of these early churches took their names from the creeks nearby. For that reason many of the older churches in Kentucky and Tennessee have names like Turkey Creek Baptist Church or Rocky Creek Baptist Church.

The preaching style of the farmer-preachers suited the settlers quite well. The preachers preached hell hot and heaven sweet. They had no patience with ambiguity or spiritual neutrality. A person either followed Jesus or served the devil. This type of preaching appealed to the people on the frontier. They had little education and less interest in doctrinal distinctions, and they liked to hear simple sermons, forcefully preached.

Baptist polity also proved conducive to church growth on the frontier. The Baptists believe in the autonomy of the local church—that each church should be self-governing. This meant the churches could multiply without restraint. A group of Christians who wished to organize a Baptist church could do so without authorization. Baptists also practiced democracy in congregational decision making. This emphasis on democracy appealed to people on the frontier.

The Episcopal and the Presbyterian denominations required that their pastors have theological education, but the Baptists did not. A candidate for ordination in the Baptist church only had to demonstrate a call from God to preach, a gift for preaching, and a rudimentary knowledge of the Bible in order to be ordained. These simple requirements meant that more men could be ordained, and the number of pastors could increase along with the needs of the frontier for more pastors and churches. The Presbyterians and the Episcopalians tended to grow at slower rates due to their higher educational standards for ministers. Their high standards meant they deployed fewer ministers (Baker 1974, 87).

CASE STUDY: TRAINING LOCAL LEADERS

Sandy Martin evangelized the Idata people of West Africa for several years. Gradually, the Idata began to come to Christ and receive baptism. Sandy saw the need for churches, but she had no pastors to lead them. Her seminary professor had told her class, "The workers will come from the harvest." Sandy had not forgotten that statement, but she remained uncertain about what to do. There were believers in her group who showed spiritual maturity and gifts for ministry, but they had no training. How could they be trained to lead the churches? Sandy knew there was a Bible college in the capital city, but she was not sure her people would fit in there.

She considered developing a training program especially for her people, but she was not sure what should be included.

REFLECTION AND DISCUSSION

- What advice would you give to Sandy?

12

The Indigenous Mission Strategy

The word *indigenous* is often used in biology to refer to a plant or animal native to an area. For example, pine trees are indigenous to North America just as durian trees are indigenous to Malaysia. In the nineteenth century missiologists applied the word to churches that were able to reproduce themselves and reflect the cultural characteristics of their ethnolinguistic group. Missionaries employing the indigenous strategy seek to plant reproducing churches that are "at home" in their culture, not churches that are essentially western (J. M. Terry 2000, 483–85).

THE APOSTLE PAUL'S STRATEGY

All proponents of indigenous missions refer to Paul's missionary strategy. They seek to understand the apostle Paul's strategy and implement it in modern times. In chapter 6 we described Paul's missionary strategy. In sum, we noted that Paul planted churches in the cities of Asia Minor and Greece, expecting those churches to plant daughter churches. He did not ask for financial support for those churches but instead asked the new churches to support themselves. Paul provided general supervision for the new churches, but he delegated daily oversight to the church elders. He worked with a team of missionaries, and he maintained contact with the churches in Antioch and Jerusalem.

EARLY INDIGENOUS MISSIONS ADVOCATES

Henry Venn

Henry Venn (1796–1873) of the (Anglican) Church Missionary Society and Rufus Anderson (1796–1880) of the American Board of Commissioners for Foreign Missions coined the term *indigenous church* in the mid-nineteenth century. They developed their strategies separately, but they later unified the strategy through correspondence. Neither had served as a missionary, but they studied Paul's strategy through the biblical narrative. They advocated planting "three-self" churches—churches that would be self-supporting, self-governing, and self-propagating (Venn at first used the term "self-extending"). They challenged missionaries to establish churches that could support themselves financially, make their own decisions, and evangelize their localities. They forbade missionaries from becoming bogged down in pastoring and maintaining churches. They believed that missionaries should be pioneer workers, planting "self-reliant" and "purely native" churches. They instructed missionaries to train local pastors and entrust the leadership of the churches to them as soon as possible. Venn also advocated "euthanasia" in missions, by which he meant that missionaries should do the pioneering work and then move on to another place. He viewed missionaries as temporary workers in a locale, not permanent personnel.[1]

John L. Nevius

John L. Nevius (1829–1893), a Presbyterian missionary to China, further developed the indigenous principles of Venn and Anderson in his classic book *Planting and Development of Missionary Churches* (1899). Nevius's principles came to be called the "Nevius Plan," summarized here:

1. Christians should continue to live in their neighborhoods and pursue their occupations, being self-supporting and witnessing to their coworkers and neighbors.
2. Missions should develop only programs and institutions that the national church desires and can support.
3. The national churches should call out and support their own pastors.
4. Church buildings should be built in the native style with money and materials given by the church members.
5. Intensive biblical and doctrinal instruction should be provided for church leaders every year.

1. To learn more about Henry Venn, see M. Warren 1971. To learn more about Rufus Anderson, see Beaver 1967.

Nevius reacted against the heavily subsidized work that he had observed in China. He personally implemented his principles in China, with good results. However, the Nevius Plan had little impact in China because most of the missionaries rejected the strategy. They preferred the status quo: maintaining their mission stations; controlling the Chinese church; and financially subsidizing churches, pastors, and institutions. However, when the American Presbyterians and Methodists began work in Korea in the 1880s, the new missionaries invited Nevius to advise them. He and his wife traveled to Korea in 1890 and spent several weeks coaching the novice missionaries. They followed the Nevius Plan, and historians today note that the strength of contemporary Korean Christianity is in part due to the plan's effectiveness (Nevius 2003; Reapsome 2000).

Roland Allen

Roland Allen (1868–1947) served as an Anglican missionary in China from 1892 until 1904. Like Nevius he faulted the methods employed by most missionaries in China. He expressed his indigenous strategy most fully in two books: *Missionary Methods: St. Paul's or Ours?* (1912) and *The Spontaneous Expansion of the Church* (1927).

Like other proponents of the indigenous approach, Allen exhorted missionaries to follow the pattern set by Paul. Allen also emphasized the role of the Holy Spirit in missions and encouraged missionaries to practice itinerant church planting, entrusting the care of the churches to the Holy Spirit. He affirmed the three "selfs," but he stressed "self-propagating" above the others. He believed an indigenous church would certainly be a reproducing church. The key points in Allen's strategy are these:

1. All permanent teaching must be intelligible and so easily understood that those who receive it can retain it, use it, and pass it on. The teaching provided by missionaries must be easily understood so that the new believers can teach it to others.

2. All organizations should be set up so that national Christians can maintain them. By Allen's time the work in China had become highly institutionalized. There were missionary stations (compounds), schools, Christian colleges and universities, orphanages, seminaries, publication centers, agricultural centers, hospitals, dispensaries, and vocational training centers. Allen questioned the need for all these institutions and the Chinese church's ability to support them financially.

3. Church finances should be provided and controlled by the local church members; the local churches should be supported financially through the church members' tithes and offerings.

4. Christians should provide pastoral care for one another. The people of China often suffered famine, brought on by drought, floods, and locusts. During the periodic famines the missionaries provided rice for church members. Naturally, the missionaries could not bear to see the believers starve. During the famines many Chinese would join the local church in order to obtain rice. This is where the phrase "rice Christian" originated. While we should not reject feeding the hungry, the local Christians should learn to care for one another, rather than relying on the missionaries.

5. Missionaries should give local believers the authority to exercise spiritual gifts freely and at once. The Holy Spirit has given the national Christians all the spiritual gifts necessary for church leadership. Missionaries who refuse to relinquish control to local leaders are a hindrance to the growth of the churches.

Allen's writings influenced many twentieth-century missiologists, including Donald McGavran, the founder of the Church Growth Movement.

Melvin Hodges

Melvin Hodges (1909–1986), a missionary to Latin America and mission administrator with the Assemblies of God, wrote *The Indigenous Church* ([1953] 1976). Widely used in Bible college and seminary missions courses, this book expresses the ideas of Venn, Anderson, Nevius, and Allen in an updated, popular format. Hodges explains how difficult it is to change from a subsidized approach to an indigenous approach. He also emphasizes training national workers and empowering them to care for the churches, thus freeing the missionaries to start new churches.

Alan Tippett

In 1955 Donald McGavran began what came to be called the Church Growth Movement. When McGavran founded the School of World Mission at Fuller Theological Seminary in 1965, one of the first professors he hired was Alan Tippett, an Australian and former missionary in the South Pacific. In his book *Verdict Theology in Missionary Theory*, Tippett (1911–1988) updated and expanded the three-self formula of Anderson and Venn.

In *Verdict Theology* Tippett proposes a sixfold description of an indigenous church:

1. *Self-image.* The church sees itself as being independent from the mission, that is, the church has self-identity. It is serving as Christ's church in its locality.

2. *Self-functioning.* The church is capable of carrying on all the normal functions of a church—evangelism and missions, worship, discipling, fellowship, and ministry—without the assistance of expatriate missionaries.

3. *Self-determining.* The church can and does make its own decisions (described as "self-governing" in earlier writings). The local churches do not depend on the missionary to make their decisions for them; rather, they rely on the guidance of the Holy Spirit and the Holy Bible. Tippett echoes Venn in saying that the mission must die for the church to be born.

4. *Self-supporting.* The church bears its own financial burdens and finances its own service projects. The national church supports itself with the tithes and offerings given by its own members rather than with financial assistance from abroad.

5. *Self-propagation.* The national church sees itself as responsible for carrying out the Great Commission. The church gives itself wholeheartedly to evangelism and missions—locally, nationally, and internationally.

6. *Self-giving.* An indigenous church knows the social needs of its community and endeavors to minister to those needs.

Tippett explains his understanding of the indigenous church:

When the indigenous people of a community think of the Lord as their own, not a foreign Christ; when they do things as unto the Lord, meeting the cultural needs around them, worshipping in patterns they understand; when their congregations function in participation in a body which is structurally indigenous; then you have an indigenous church. (1969, 136)

In recent years Paul Hiebert and others have added yet another mark to the list: self-theologizing. They believe a truly indigenous church will develop its own theology, one that is true to the Bible but expressed in culturally appropriate ways. These theologies would affirm the central doctrines of the Christian faith, but they would express them using metaphors and concepts that reflect their own unique cultures. Historically, young churches have struggled to self-theologize, and typically it is the last mark to develop.

CONTEMPORARY APPLICATION

Today missiologists talk and write more about "contextualization" than about indigenous missions. Students are confused about the difference between the two terms. Early evangelical writers on contextualization emphasized the accurate and intelligible communication of the biblical message of salvation—in other words, they focused on effective cross-cultural communication. In recent decades evangelicals have come to view contextualization more broadly. It includes all aspects of the Christian faith, and not simply communication or theology (see Moreau 2012). Indigenization focuses on the churches that result from good missionary work; contextualization goes further in focusing on the scope of the things addressed by local bodies of believers in addition to the composition of those local bodies.

Missionaries who seek to establish indigenous churches should remember these principles as they do their work: First, missionaries should plant churches with their desired goal in mind (as noted in chap. 5; Steffen 1993). Sometimes missionary trainers call this the "End Vision." This means that the desired outcome—indigenous churches—should influence the methods employed. The Bible teaches us that we shall reap what we sow (2 Cor. 9:6). That is certainly true in church planting. If you employ a highly subsidized approach to church planting, then it will prove quite difficult to transition to self-supporting local churches.

Second, there will always be a dynamic tension between supracultural doctrines and variable cultural traits. Basic Christian doctrines, like the bodily resurrection of Jesus Christ and the second coming of Christ, are true in every culture and in every age. However, the church must adjust to the cultures it enters. For example, many churches in Indonesia worship on Fridays because that is the day off for their members. Sunday is certainly the normal day for worship, but in light of the situation in Indonesia, worshiping on Friday could be permitted. As another example, Christians in North America typically sit on pews or chairs during the worship services; however, worshipers in Indonesia often sit on mats on the floor. Many similar examples could be mentioned.

Third, church planters should expect the churches to support themselves from the beginning. Paul did not solicit money from the church in Antioch of Syria or in Jerusalem to help the new churches in Asia Minor. Rather, he requested donations from the new churches in Greece and Asia Minor to relieve the saints in Jerusalem, who were suffering due to a famine (1 Cor. 16:1–3). Some have called indigenous church planting "tough love." That means the missionary must resist the temptation to help financially. An indigenous approach to church planting requires the new congregations to be self-supporting from the beginning. Sometimes this results in slower growth in the early stages, but it produces greater growth later. If the church planter uses lots of money in church planting, then the availability of funds will determine the number of churches that can be planted. However, if the church planter employs an indigenous approach, there is no limit on the number of churches that can be planted.

Fourth, Bible study groups (or storying groups) should be encouraged to make their own decisions even before they organize as churches. Often the church planter will invite people to gather for Bible study on a regular basis. These Bible study groups develop naturally into house churches. The church planter can help the group become a self-governing church by encouraging the members to make their own decisions—such as when and where to meet—long before the Bible study group becomes an organized church.

Fifth, missionaries should encourage new congregations to evangelize their communities and seek opportunities to plant new churches. The church planter should infuse evangelism, church planting, and missions into the DNA of the new congregations. The church planter should encourage new believers to share their testimonies with their families, friends, neighbors, classmates, and coworkers. The church planter should also assist the new congregations in identifying opportunities for church planting. Church planters should teach the missionary mandate of the Bible. In this way even new Christians and congregations will understand their missions responsibility.

Sixth, missionaries should always use reproducible methods of evangelism, teaching, preaching, and leadership. This means that the church planter should evangelize, pray, lead worship, preach, and minister in ways the local believers can imitate. In other words, the church planter should intentionally model methods for new believers and novice pastors. For example, in the 1950s a missionary church planter worked hard at planting churches in the southern Philippines. He purchased a truck, tent, lights, benches, electrical generator, movie projector, and films. He would go to a village or town and set up his tent, lights, projector, and so on. Then he would publicize free movies. This was quite an attraction in the rural Philippines of that era. He would show half of a movie, preach a gospel message, and then show the second half of the movie. He would remain in the town or village until he had won some people to Christ, baptized them, discipled them, and organized them into a church. Then he would go to the next village. Using this method the faithful missionary planted more than forty churches. Sadly, few of these churches ever reproduced. The church planting method he modeled required a truck, tent, generator, projector, and films. The local Christians could not afford that equipment, so they did not plant daughter churches.

Seventh, missionaries should give priority to training local believers to serve as church leaders. There will never be enough international missionaries to evangelize the world. Effective world evangelization requires multiplying pastors, evangelists, church planters, and missionaries. Jesus spent much time training his twelve disciples so that they could continue his mission (John 20:21). Paul trained a number of workers to assist him in his missionary work. From the very beginning missionary church planters should pray for God to raise up workers from the new disciples (Matt. 9:35–38). Missionaries should be sensitive to the leading of the Holy Spirit in this regard and then mentor those who demonstrate spiritual gifts.

Eighth, missionaries should view themselves as temporary church planters rather than permanent pastors. Venn and Anderson stressed the temporary nature of missionary work. They taught that church planters should seek to work themselves out of a job. If they do their work well, the time will come when they are no longer needed in that place or among that people group. This

---

SIDEBAR 12.1
STRATEGIZING WITH LOCAL LEADERS

In chapter 15, we emphasize that proper contextualization can be done only in conversation and consultation with the local believers. The same should be said of indigenization. In a pioneer situation the missionary or team of missionaries have no local believers to consult in the beginning. Those believers are yet to be won to Christ, and there are certainly no local leaders. Later, though, the missionaries should involve the local church leaders in their strategy planning. This involvement brings two benefits. First, the local leaders will add deep cultural insights to the discussion. Second, the local leaders will learn about planning and missions strategy.

After I (Mark) had served in the Philippines for fourteen years, the Filipino leaders invited me to a meeting. They said, "You know that all these years the American missionaries have planned the strategy, and we have cooperated with them."

I replied, "Yes, that's true. You have cooperated, and we've planted lots of churches."

The leaders answered, "Yes, we've started many churches. Now, though, we

want to plan the strategy, and we want the missionaries to cooperate with us."

I responded by saying, "I agree. You all know very well what should be done. It is time for you to take the lead in planning strategy."

The leaders replied, "We're glad you agree. Now, go tell the other missionaries what we want."

I consented, and I carried their message to the other American missionaries. I advised them to consent, also, and they did. True indigenous missions passes leadership responsibility to local leaders as soon as possible.

Finally, some view the indigenous approach as missionary-centric because it is the missionary who decides what is good for newly established churches, leaving the missionary in control. This criticism misses the point of the church becoming self-governing. A missionary who properly implements the strategy empowers new believers to discover the Lord's will concerning their worship style, ethics, cultural practices, and so on, enabling them to make decisions according to the Scriptures and the guidance of the Holy Spirit.

is a difficult thing for some missionaries to accept. When they have planted a church, they have a natural desire to stay and develop that congregation. This approach could be called *entrepreneurial church planting*. That is a good thing in some contexts, but in international missions, church planters usually are expected to be *apostolic church planters*. This means they are expected to plant a cluster of reproducing churches and then move on to another area—just as the apostle Paul did. Another difficulty for missionary church planters is psychological bonding. It is difficult to commit oneself to a group of people and then leave them. Acts 20 shows how Paul had bonded with the believers in Ephesus. The Ephesians found separation difficult, and we can assume Paul did also. As noted previously, Steffen's excellent book *Passing the Baton* explains how church planters can develop and implement an effective exit strategy (1993).

Ninth, missionaries should resist the temptation to establish institutions and wait for the national church to take the initiative. It is tempting for missionaries to insist that the new national churches need all the institutions and programs the missionaries knew "back home." The list might include Christian camps, hospitals, retreat centers, Christian bookstores, Bible colleges, and such. These are good things, but their development should arise from "felt needs" expressed by local Christians.

Tenth, missionaries must allow the national churches to develop theologies and practices that are biblical yet appropriate in their cultural settings. Critics of Christianity around the world declare that it is a foreign religion. Truly indigenous churches should manifest worship and church practices that are biblical but also reflect the local culture. In this way the national church will not seem imported.

CRITIQUE OF THE INDIGENOUS STRATEGY

Venn and Anderson developed the indigenous strategy almost 150 years ago. Given the place the strategy has enjoyed in evangelical circles, it is not surprising that it has received its share of criticism over the years. German missiologist Peter Beyerhaus agrees that churches should support themselves and propagate, but he writes that the church should be "Christonomous" (Christ-governed), not self-governed (Beyerhaus 1964, 393–407). However, to date no viable alternative term for *self-governed* has gained acceptance.

A second criticism is that missionaries have striven to plant churches according to the three selves, but they have ignored other aspects of indigenization. For example, the pioneer Presbyterian missionaries in Korea embraced the three selves, but they did not promote indigenous worship. Worship in Korea was and is quite Western in its music and style. This was one of the concerns Tippett addressed by adding three additional selfs to the model (1969).

Some critics agree that the indigenous strategy does follow Paul, but they do not believe that Paul's strategy is a necessary determiner for contemporary strategy.

CASE STUDY:
WHO WILL BRING A LAMP?

Christi began work in a mountain village in Central America. She invited the residents to meet with her for a weekly Bible study. Their free time was at night, so they agreed to meet on Thursday nights. The village had no electricity, so a light source was needed. One of the villagers asked, "What shall we use for a light?" Christi owned a kerosene pressure lantern, but she did not offer it. She waited, and an older woman spoke.

"I have an oil lamp that I can bring," she said. The others agreed that would be fine.

REFLECTION AND DISCUSSION

- The urge to help a new church is naturally strong. What are some other urges the church planter must resist?

13

The Church Growth Movement

he Church Growth Movement greatly affected evangelical missions between 1955 and the end of the twentieth century. Peter Wagner defines
the movement this way:

> Church growth is that discipline which seeks to understand through biblical,
> sociological, historical, and behavioral study, why churches grow or decline. True
> church growth takes place when "Great Commission" disciples are added and
> are evidenced by responsible church membership. The discipline began with the
> functional work of Donald McGavran. The Church Growth Movement includes
> all the resources of people, institutions, and publications dedicated to expound-
> ing the concepts and practicing the principles of church growth. (2000, 199)

The Church Growth Movement changed the way missionaries and mission
administrators thought about missions and measured their progress. This
movement reflected a new philosophy of missions, one that emphasized evangelism and church planting.

The Church Growth Movement began in 1955 with the publication of Donald
McGavran's book *The Bridges of God*. Before 1955 many mission agencies had
become content to establish and maintain permanent mission stations. These
mission stations involved considerable property and buildings, and they required
a lot of maintenance and attention from their missionary residents. Missionaries

often spent their entire careers at one station. In many settings missionaries served mostly in and through institutions like hospitals, schools, orphanages, seminaries, agricultural stations, and leprosariums. All these institutions required significant missionary personnel and funds. Agencies were reluctant to abandon these costly institutions because so much money and time had been spent to build them. As a result missionary evangelists and church planters were routinely called in from their fieldwork to supervise these institutions. Many "field" missionaries also continued to serve unproductively for years on end. Though others in similar circumstances baptized many and established multiple churches, people involved in these institutions rationalized their lack of success by offering platitudes such as, "I may not be fruitful, but I am being faithful."

Theologically, shifts occurred in the World Council of Churches that eroded the motivation to do missions on the part of the member churches. The World Council gradually came to describe missions as social ministry and economic and political activism rather than as evangelism and church planting. Donald McGavran addressed these problems and called the church back to its missional purpose.

DONALD ANDERSON MCGAVRAN: THE FOUNDER

Donald McGavran was born in India in 1897, the son and grandson of missionaries. He grew up in India and then went to the United States for his higher education. He earned his bachelor of arts degree at Butler University, his bachelor of divinity at Yale Divinity School, and a master's degree at the College of Missions in Indianapolis. Later he earned a doctorate in education from Columbia University. As a student he participated in the Student Volunteer Movement and volunteered to return to India as a missionary.

In 1923 McGavran returned to India, serving under the United Christian Missionary Society (Disciples of Christ). During his missionary career, which lasted thirty-four years, he served in many different capacities: school superintendent, hospital administrator, rural evangelist, and Bible translator. Through these varied positions he saw missionary service from every possible angle.

After several years of service, McGavran became aware of the efforts by J. Waskom Pickett and others to survey the progress of Christian missions in India. Bishop Pickett had a special interest in what he called "mass movements." By mass movements Pickett meant occasions when large numbers of people became Christians within a short period of time. Pickett's survey, *Christian Mass Movements in India*, was published in 1933.

Pickett asked McGavran to continue the survey by studying the status of Christianity in central India. McGavran agreed to do so, and his life was changed. McGavran recounted that he became fascinated by church growth. Why was the church growing in one district, while in an adjacent district it was not growing at all? He dedicated the rest of his life to answering the question, Why do churches grow? McGavran published his research and conclusions in his first book, *Christian Mission in Mid-India* (1936). The book was republished later as *Church Growth and Group Conversion* (1956).

In 1953 McGavran rented an isolated cabin in the jungle and devoted himself to writing his philosophy of missions, resulting in the publication of *The Bridges of God* (1955). In it McGavran challenged the mission station approach to missions and laid out his ideas for a better alternative. Reaction—both positive and negative—was swift. Kenneth Scott Latourette writes in the foreword, "To the thoughtful reader this book will come like a breath of fresh air, stimulating him to challenge inherited programmes and to venture forth courageously on untried paths. It is one of the most important books on missionary methods that has appeared in many years."

McGavran's ideas were truly revolutionary at the time. He challenged almost every form of conventional missionary wisdom and practice. Theologically, he insisted that the missionary's primary task is helping lost people become Christians, but he also emphasized making disciples, and not just converts. Missiologically, he exhorted administrators to hold missionaries accountable for their work by demanding and analyzing statistics from every field. McGavran also called for fierce pragmatism in evaluating missionary methods. He rejected winning people one by one and called on missionaries to use the new converts' networks of social relationships as bridges that would lead to "people movements." McGavran desired to see people come to Christ in masses, and his research convinced him that this was possible.

After the publication of *The Bridges of God*, McGavran's life changed considerably. He was invited to lecture at a number of seminaries, and his own mission agency began to send him on research and consultation trips around the world. In 1957 he and his wife retired from active missionary service and returned to the United States. During the next four years McGavran traveled widely, doing field research and writing *How Churches Grow* (1959), in which he explained his philosophy of missions more fully and answered his many critics.

In 1961 he established the Institute of Church Growth in Eugene, Oregon, on the campus of Northwest Christian College. He meant for this to be a "think tank" for church growth research and seminars. During this period McGavran also started *Church Growth Bulletin*, a simple newsletter on church growth that attracted thousands of subscribers.

In 1965 Fuller Theological Seminary named McGavran the founding dean of its new School of World Missions. The move to Fuller provided McGavran with a platform to promote his strategy. He recruited an outstanding faculty that included Arthur Glasser, Ralph Winter, Alan Tippett, Peter Wagner, and Charles Kraft. Students flocked to Fuller to enroll. During his years as dean, McGavran found time to write *Understanding Church Growth* (1970), which summed up his strategy for international missions.

McGavran served as dean of the School of World Missions from 1965 until 1971 and taught as an emeritus professor for years after his retirement. He continued to write and lecture until his death in 1990.

DEVELOPMENT OF THE MOVEMENT

As noted previously, the Church Growth Movement began with the publication of *The Bridges of God* in 1955. McGavran did not intend to start a movement, and he did not consciously name it the Church Growth Movement. His main concern was fostering "people movements." In his later years McGavran said he should have used the term *effective evangelism*. In writing about church growth McGavran sought to use a term without the negative baggage that liberal churchmen had piled on the traditional terms *missions* and *evangelism*. They had redefined missions as social ministry and evangelism as "dialogue" with adherents of other religions. McGavran fought to return missions to making disciples and planting churches.

From 1955 until 1972 McGavran and his colleagues concentrated their research, teaching, and writing on international missions. After 1972 the Church Growth Movement exhibited a clear North American emphasis. This came about through the courses that McGavran taught at Fuller Seminary. Many students took the missions courses even though they did not intend to serve as missionaries. As they graduated and began to work in churches, they discovered McGavran's principles could be applied in North America as well. When Fuller Seminary began to offer a doctor of ministry in church growth in 1975, hundreds of North American pastors responded and received a graduate-level education in church growth.

In 1972 McGavran and Peter Wagner team-taught a course on North American church growth at Fuller Seminary. Among the students in that class were Win Arn and John Wimber. Soon afterward Arn founded the Institute of American Church Growth, and Wimber was named the first director of the Department of Church Growth at the Fuller Evangelistic Association, later known as the Charles E. Fuller Institute. Both organizations provided seminars, materials, and church growth consultation. The 1970s proved to be a period of great popularity for the movement.

In the 1980s the Church Growth Movement divided into several streams. The first stream was the Megachurch Movement. This movement focused on the development of megachurches, that is, churches with more than two thousand in weekly attendance.

A second stream from the Church Growth Movement was the Cell Church Movement. Led by Paul Yonggi Cho and Ralph Neighbour Jr., this movement highlighted the virtues of cell churches. The primary example was Yonggi Cho's Yoido Full Gospel Church in Seoul, Korea, which grew to over eight hundred thousand in weekly attendance during the 1980s.

A third stream developed—what could be called the Signs and Wonders Movement. As McGavran aged, Peter Wagner seemed to be his anointed successor as leader of the movement. However, in 1988 Wagner published *How to Have a Healing Ministry without Making Your Church Sick*. This book revealed Wagner's fascination and identification with the Signs and Wonders Movement (sometimes called the third wave of Pentecostalism). Wagner's identification with the Signs and Wonders Movement negatively affected his standing in the eyes of many proponents of church growth.

A fourth stream was strategic spiritual warfare. Peter Wagner and others began to teach the importance of spiritual warfare and what they called "strategic spiritual warfare mapping" as a means of engaging territorial spirits. Wagner came to believe that a host of demonic spirits oppose the expansion of God's kingdom. Proponents of this approach believe that we must map out an area by research, including historical information as well as the contemporary setting. They argued that part of that research could include interrogation of evil spirits in those afflicted by the spirits. The information gained through interrogation can then be used to attack the demonic hierarchy by means of prayer. Wagner articulated his views on this subject through his books *Confronting the Powers* (1996) and *Warfare Prayer* (1992).

A fifth stream is Church Health. Two names stand out in connection with this stream: Rick Warren and Christian Schwarz. In 1980 Rick Warren founded the Saddleback Community Church in southern California, which now reports a weekly attendance of more than sixteen thousand. He also wrote *The Purpose Driven Church* (1995), which became a best seller. Warren teaches that the main thing is not church growth but church health. He believes healthy churches will naturally grow. Christian Schwarz has promoted a similar concept through his book and seminar *Natural Church Development* (1996).

The sixth stream stemming from the Church Growth Movement is the Unreached Peoples Movement. McGavran taught that missionaries should not view nations as cultural monoliths but rather as cultural mosaics. Most missiologists agreed with McGavran's point, but little had been done about it.

In 1974, speaking at the International Congress on World Evangelization held in Lausanne, Switzerland, Ralph Winter called on the participants to identify and evangelize every ethno-linguistic group (people group) in the world. Winter's address inspired the creation of several different organizations devoted to researching these people groups and facilitating their adoption by missions agencies. These organizations included AD 2000 and Beyond, the Caleb Project, and the Peoples Information Network. These organizations and the leaders of evangelical missions agencies developed the concept of "unreached people groups" (UPGs), which drives missions strategy today.

The last stream is the Church Planting Movement strategy. David Garrison and others have taught that missionaries should be planting churches that multiply rapidly and exponentially. They call these multiplication movements Church Planting Movements (CPMs). This idea seems to be an extrapolation of McGavran's concept of people movements.

Listing all these streams raises two pertinent questions: Where is the Church Growth Movement today? Does it still exist? Surely it has gone to places that Donald McGavran never imagined or intended. Church growth as he meant it to be is still practiced overseas, often by missionaries who would not recognize the name Donald McGavran or understand the contribution he made to the missions strategy they are implementing. The continuing emphases on identifying and reaching all the people groups of a nation and multiplying churches trace back to McGavran's early writings.

PRINCIPLES OF CHURCH GROWTH

The following principles are a summary of McGavran's writings.

Emphasize Evangelism

McGavran emphasized evangelization. He said and wrote over and over again: God wants his lost sheep found. McGavran believed that evangelism and church planting should always be missionary priorities. His emphasis on the priority of evangelism should be understood in light of his long debate with the World Council of Churches. McGavran believed that the World Council of Churches had abandoned spiritual salvation for social ministry and political liberation. He did not reject social ministries completely. His writing on "gospel lift" shows his concern for human needs, but he believed evangelism should be primary. McGavran believed that when people were redeemed, they would forsake destructive habits and lifestyles that harmed their families and communities. The resulting improvements represented "gospel lift."

119

Disciple All People Groups

McGavran's greatest ongoing legacy is seeing nation-states as cultural mosaics of people groups. Today's "adopt a people group" thinking and practice comes directly from McGavran's insights. We take them for granted today, but they were startling when first explained in 1955. McGavran, and later Ralph Winter, urged missionary strategists to identify all the people groups and systematically evangelize them, using contextualized methods. Together they laid the foundation for people-group thinking that is used throughout evangelical missions today.

Sociology and Anthropology Can Be Helpful

McGavran's graduate studies in education helped him to understand how the social sciences could help missionaries. When McGavran and his colleagues founded Fuller's School of World Mission, they emphasized cultural anthropology. Anthropology is now accepted as a standard element in missionary training, but it was not always so.

Emphasize Discipling (Evangelism) Rather Than Perfecting

McGavran observed many missionaries in India who would win a few converts to Christ and then halt their evangelistic efforts in order to "perfect" (teach) the new converts. McGavran believed this practice stifled any possibility of a people movement. He believed that the Holy Spirit ripens people groups at different times. Therefore, when a people group is ripe for the gospel, the missionary must not stop harvesting (evangelizing) until all the ripened souls have been gathered. This concept has prompted some to say that McGavran rejected nurturing new believers. That does not reflect McGavran's view. He insisted that those won to Christ as part of a people movement need instruction; he just rejected the idea of stopping evangelistic efforts in order to do the teaching/nurturing.

Missionaries Should Identify and Avoid Hindrances to Church Growth

In *Understanding Church Growth* McGavran discusses many hindrances to avoid. These include:

1. *Statistical hindrances.* McGavran laments that few agencies kept careful records of the number of churches, newly baptized members, new churches, newly established preaching points, and so on. He insists that

these records are like a medical patient's vital statistics—an indication of health or illness, progress or regress.

2. *Administrative hindrances.* McGavran notes that missions administrators often fostered mediocrity by not rewarding productivity. Generally, all the missionaries were treated alike, regardless of their success or failure. He believes strongly that administrators should pour money and personnel into situations where the church is growing.

3. *Cultural hindrances.* In many cases missionaries have assumed what worked back home in North America would work just as well overseas. Sometimes those programs prove effective, but often they do not due to cultural differences.

4. *Semantic hindrances.* McGavran expresses much frustration with the fuzzy language used by missionaries. For example, a missionary might report that he opened a "work" in Santa Cruz. What does that mean? It might mean that he planted a church or preached a sermon or distributed gospel tracts or visited a family there. "Witness" is another ambiguous term. A report might say, "We have a witness in seven villages in Padagor province." Of course, this leaves the reader wondering if the "witness" is seven churches planted or seven preaching points opened or simply seven villages visited by the missionary.

5. *Psychological hindrances.* Typically, missionaries or missions administrators with few results to report seek to rationalize their failures. Often reports and promotional literature abound with high-sounding phrases but little hard data. McGavran argues that every statistic represents another person added to the kingdom of God. He makes no apology for seeking to win as many to Christ as possible.

6. *Promotional hindrances.* Missionaries and administrators must raise the money necessary for missionary work. So promotional materials tend to be general and optimistic. They seek to touch the emotions of the givers by dwelling on stories of human interest. The recounting of one extraordinary response to the gospel may give the listeners or readers the impression that this response is typical. The impulse to use this approach is natural, but McGavran observes that it obscures the reality of church growth and makes it difficult for supporters to understand exactly what they are funding.

7. *Theological hindrances.* McGavran notes that several theological issues might hinder church growth. One such issue is a nonconversionist theology. For example, many today contend that ultimately all persons will be saved. Such universalism necessarily discourages evangelism and missions. A second theological issue is pluralism. In the worst case pluralists believe that all the world's religions are equally valid or efficacious; therefore, missionaries should refrain from proselytizing their

adherents. A final theological hindrance is a more exclusive focus on humanitarianism. Those who advocate "presence evangelism" believe that missionaries should give their attention to ministering to the physical needs of the world's people, letting their presence and Christlike attitudes influence people. McGavran understands these positions, but he rejects them.

Resources Should Be Concentrated in Responsive Areas

This is sometimes called the "harvest principle." McGavran and his disciples taught that spiritual harvests, like grain harvests, have a limited life. Missionaries must reap the harvest of souls while a people group is ripe for the gospel. One common example is the response of the Japanese after World War II. From 1945 to 1955 the Japanese were responsive to the gospel, but after 1955 the response slowed dramatically. McGavran contended that agencies need to consider this phenomenon and pour money and resources into situations where there is a good response to the gospel.

Missionaries Should Make Cultural Adaptations

Proponents of the Church Growth Movement taught that missionaries should make every effort to achieve fluency in the appropriate language and learn to function in their host culture. McGavran believed that people need to hear the gospel in their heart language. He also taught that missionaries should adjust their lifestyles in order to win more to Christ.

Missionaries Should Use Reproducible Methods

Church growth proponents hold that missionaries should do everything in ways that can be duplicated by local Christians. McGavran taught his students to be careful to use methods of church planting the local people could duplicate.

The Church Multiplies Fastest by Planting New Churches

The Church Growth Movement has always contended that church planting is the key to fulfilling the Great Commission (Matt. 28:18–20). The first-century Christians obeyed Jesus's command by planting churches throughout the Roman Empire. Church growth research has demonstrated that new churches are more evangelistic than older churches and more active in church planting. In other words, new units multiply more rapidly than older units. It is easy to see why the Church Growth Movement advocated aggressive church planting.

Homogeneous Units Grow Faster

Undoubtedly, this has been the most controversial principle advanced by Donald McGavran. Some speakers and writers have even accused him and the Church Growth Movement of racism. Actually, McGavran was simply making a sociological observation. He noted that people like to worship with people like themselves, and they are more likely to come to Christ if they can do so without crossing language, racial, or cultural barriers. He meant that missionaries would see more church growth if they planted churches that focus on one caste or language.

McGavran was not a racist; he lived most of his life in India. When he returned to the United States to live, he wrote several articles suggesting how the United States might resolve its racial problems. In church growth the homogeneous factor could be almost anything—language, job, caste, age group, or worship style—that people have in common. McGavran's point is simply that people cannot demonstrate a kingdom ethic until they come into God's kingdom. He believed that homogeneous churches would bring more people into God's kingdom.

Evaluate Methods Regularly and Honestly

McGavran and Wagner both took pride in being fiercely pragmatic. They insisted that missionaries assess their results on a regular basis in order to evaluate their methods. They believed the task of world evangelization was so important that missionaries could not waste time or money on ineffective methods. McGavran taught his followers the value of statistical research in making these evaluations. In response to the critics who sneered at their pragmatism, the church growth proponents asked if their critics advocated using impractical methods. The point of this is simple: missionaries should regularly analyze their approach to see where improvement can be made.

THE IMPACT OF THE CHURCH GROWTH MOVEMENT

A retrospective look at the Church Growth Movement reveals several significant accomplishments. First, the movement helped the Protestant missions movement, or at least the evangelical wing, to rediscover its traditional emphasis on evangelism and church planting.

Second, the Church Growth Movement's emphasis on homogeneous units prompted missions leaders in North America to plant ethnic churches. Today many denominations report that their most dynamic growth is in their ethnic congregations.

123

Third, the movement challenged the theology of the World Council of Churches. As the World Council's theology became increasingly liberal, Mc-Gavran and his associates challenged all Christians not to abandon the unreached billions in Africa, Asia, and Latin America.

Fourth, the Church Growth Movement affected North American seminaries and Bible colleges. Today, most evangelical seminaries and Bible colleges offer courses on church growth. If church growth is not mentioned in the course title, it is certain to be found in the syllabus.

Fifth, the Church Growth Movement has impacted the local church. Every year dozens of church growth seminars and conferences are offered for the benefit of local church practitioners. Church growth consultants across North America assist churches in evaluating their programs and facilities. Several periodicals have been published, including *Growing Churches* and the *Church Growth Bulletin*.

Finally, the Church Growth Movement helped missionaries in several ways. The research emphasis of church growth helped missionaries and field administrators to learn how to assess the potential for church growth in unreached areas and evaluate progress in existing fields. The movement also promoted the study of anthropology, and this equipped new generations of missionaries to acculturate more quickly and minister more effectively. The innovations that the Church Growth Movement introduced in leadership training, like Theological Education by Extension (TEE), made possible the rapid multiplication of churches. Last, the movement taught missionaries *how* to plant churches. Missionaries knew that they should plant churches, but many did not know how. Indeed, the title for many missionaries changed from "field evangelist" to "church planter."

NEEDED IMPROVEMENTS IN CHURCH GROWTH

Ebbie Smith, longtime missions professor and disciple of McGavran, has listed the following corrections that the Church Growth Movement needs to make today (1994):

- The Church Growth Movement needs to return to its roots. Most church growth literature today pertains to the growth of individual North American congregations, not the multiplication of churches in the 10/40 Window.
- Most of the church growth literature today focuses on the growth of middle-class churches that appeal to baby boomers and baby busters. McGavran would call the movement back to consider the needs of the poor and oppressed.

- The Church Growth Movement should avoid overemphasizing the role and importance of megachurches. Certainly, they are an interesting phenomenon, but most churches are small. That fact will not change. Smaller churches need affirmation and attention from the movement.

- The Church Growth Movement needs to reaffirm its emphasis on reproducibility. Western fascination with technology and media is understandable, but the methods employed in premodern societies should be technologically appropriate for those environments.

- The Church Growth Movement has accomplished much in evaluating quantitative growth. The movement should now turn to research into qualitative growth. How can churches grow better, as well as bigger?

- The Church Growth Movement should resist the temptation to teach that a set of missionary methods will work in every circumstance. All aspects of the missionary task must be contextualized, including the methods.

- The Church Growth Movement never developed a thorough theological foundation. McGavran was a missionary practitioner, not a theologian. The definitive book on the theology of church growth remains to be written.

- The Church Growth Movement's antagonism toward institutions in the mission field is understandable but overly broad. The movement needs to revisit this issue. One student of church growth has noted that McGavran never met an institution that he liked. His successors need to develop a more nuanced approach to institutions overseas.

CONCLUSION

In 1973 Peter Wagner wrote an article on church growth for *Christianity Today*. He concluded the article with these words:

Three moods characterize all church-growth advocates, I have found, and these can therefore be said to be moods of the movement in general:

Obedience. Full obedience to the Word of God and the will of God is essential. No apologies at all are made for whatever unswerving obedience might involve.

Pragmatism. Church-growth people do not hesitate to use whatever means God provides to do the best possible job in reaching the goals. They are not very much interested in what *should* bring unbelievers to Christ, but they are acutely interested in what does, in fact, bring unbelievers to Christ.

Optimism. Christ said, "I will build my church and the gates of hell shall not prevail against it." There is no warrant to be gloomy in Christian work. We are ultimately on the winning side. If God be for us, who can be against us? (1973, 14)

CASE STUDY:
RESPONSIVE AREA
GETS MORE RESOURCES

Richard Gordon studied church growth in seminary and became convinced that it was a good strategy. He served for years as a missionary, and later his agency named him director for Asia. In his new role he had to decide where to assign new missionaries. After comparing the statistics of Thailand and the Philippines, he realized that the Philippines was more responsive. So he sent the new missionaries to the Philippines, and he canceled all personnel requests for Thailand.

REFLECTION AND DISCUSSION

- What is your initial response to Richard's actions?
- In light of church growth strategy, how might you defend his decisions?
- In light of church growth strategy, how might you critique his decisions?
- What would you have done in his place?

14

Frontier Strategies

Throughout most of the history of missions, missions administrators and missionaries have focused on nations. They have reported on their progress toward world evangelization in terms of the number of nations "reached." However, toward the end of the twentieth century evangelicals turned their attention to the unreached *peoples* of the world. Many different terms were used to describe this emphasis: unreached people groups, hidden peoples, frontier missions, World A, the last frontier, and the 10/40 Window. This chapter will explain three strategies that reflect the frontier emphasis.

THE UNREACHED PEOPLE GROUPS STRATEGY

As mentioned previously, in *The Bridges of God* McGavran urges missionaries to view nations as cultural *mosaics* rather than cultural *monoliths*. He writes that missionaries should identify all the people groups in a nation and devise strategies to reach all of them. The missions community heard McGavran, but little was done to follow his recommendation. In 1974 Ralph Winter gave a plenary address at the Lausanne Congress on World Evangelization in which he challenged the participants to strategize to bring the gospel to the thousands of unreached people groups (UPGs) in the world. Winter declared, "I'm afraid that all our exultation about the fact that every *country* has been penetrated has allowed many to suppose that every *culture* has been penetrated." He reminded the congress that the Greek word translated "nations" in Matthew 28:19 actually means "ethnic groups" (Winter 1981, 302). Eventually evangelicals responded enthusiastically to Winter's challenge and founded organizations and wrote books to research people groups and facilitate their evangelization, including the Joshua Project, the

---

SIDEBAR 14.1
HOW MANY UNREACHED PEOPLE GROUPS ARE THERE?

The precise number of UPGs is difficult to determine. A review of the various websites reveals some variation in the numbers. For example, the Joshua Project listed 16,350 for the total number of people groups in the world in 2010, while the World Christian Database listed 13,674. The research department of the International Mission Board listed 11,642. Why the differences?

One simple reality is that it is challenging to determine how to count some people groups. For example, a particular people might include seven subgroups. This raises a question for researchers. Should they be counted as one group or seven? Because different researchers and different organizations answer that question differently, the final counts of the numbers of peoples will also vary (Mandryk 2010, 1).

Researchers do agree—at least approximately—that there are roughly 6,600 unreached people groups when they use a common definition of a UPG as a group in which evangelicals comprise less than 2 percent of the population. Of the 6,600 unreached, 3,800 people groups are currently unengaged, meaning that no organization or agency is actively evangelizing them. These are sometimes referred to as Unreached, Unengaged People Groups (UUPGs). Of the

3,800 UUPGs, 565 have a population of more than 100,000 (Mandryk 2010, 1; groups with a population of greater than 100,000 are referred to as "megapeoples").

When we consider this question in terms of languages, we still find that different organizations provide different answers. In 2013 *Ethnologue* stated the number of languages as 7,105. The *World Christian Encyclopedia* lists 13,511 languages, and the Global Recordings Network estimates the number at 10,000 (Mandryk 2010, 1).

Clearly the broad framework of what constitutes a people group has been identified. However, just as clearly, the boundaries are not always distinct enough such that different researchers arrive at the same counts. There are several cooperative ventures through which agencies and researchers continue to refine their definitions and offer ever more definitive counts (see, e.g., the World Mission Atlas project at http://www.worldmap.org).

REFLECTION AND DISCUSSION

- Given some of the issues identified in this sidebar, if you were to try to develop the definitive definition of a people group, what characteristics would you include?

Caleb Project, AD 2000 Movement, and Patrick Johnstone's highly successful Operation World.

In 1982 the Lausanne Committee wrote the standard definition of an unreached people group: "An unreached people is a people group among which there is no indigenous community of believing Christians with adequate numbers and resources to evangelize this people group without outside (cross-cultural) assistance" (Winter 1984, 37). Thus, a UPG is a group of people with their own language and culture without a viable Christian community, that is, local churches with the capability of evangelizing their own people.

The Modern Missions Movement began more than two hundred years ago with the ministry of William Carey. Why are there still so many UPGs in the world? Many factors affect the access that these people groups have to the gospel.

- Political gatekeepers: Governments in most of the countries where the UPGs are located strive to keep Christian missionaries out. They believe that Christianity will disrupt their societies, both religiously and socially.

- Geographical factors: Many of the UPGs are located in isolated areas, like deserts, mountains, and jungles.

- Religious opposition: Most of the UPGs are found in societies dominated by a major world religion. Religious leaders in those cultures seek to maintain their religion's position of dominance. They fiercely resist incursion by Christian missionaries. Persecution of new converts is usually swift and severe.

- Communication and transportation issues: Many of the UPGs have limited access to gospel media, and what access they do have may be censored. Moreover, because of their isolation, it is often quite difficult to travel to many of the smaller UPGs.

- Poverty: Many of the UPGs are among the poorest populations in the world. This means that they have less access to education and information in general.

- Oral learners: Most of the UPGs are composed of people who acquire information orally, rather than by reading. Most contemporary/modern missionary methods have been literacy based. These methods have included tract distribution, Bible distribution, evangelistic home Bible studies, expository preaching, and the like. The percentage of people in the world who are oral learners has been estimated at 60 percent, and some suggest 70 percent (Steffen 1996).

- Lack of attention: Between the beginning of the Modern Missions Movement in 1792 and 1982 few missionaries went to these people groups.

Travel to them was difficult, and the governments restricted admittance. Also, missions administrators assumed that these people groups would be unresponsive to the gospel, which meant that allocating missionaries and money to reach those people groups would be poor stewardship of scarce resources.

- Few Christians and churches: In these people groups there are few evangelical Christians who can witness to their neighbors and friends. There are few churches, and those that do exist tend to be ancient churches that focus on survival in a hostile environment rather than evangelistic outreach.

In 1989 at Lausanne II in Manila, Luis Bush challenged the participants to reach the "10/40 Window." He referred to the region from 10 degrees north latitude to 40 degrees north latitude, from the west coast of Africa to the east coast of Asia. Bush informed the conference that 90 percent of the UPGs in the world live within the 10/40 Window. It includes sixty countries and more than two billion people. It contains the major unreached population blocs: Muslims, Hindus, Buddhists, and Chinese of various religions. At the time he spoke only about 3 percent of the evangelical missionary force was working in the 10/40 Window. In response to his challenge the number rose to 8 percent in 1999 and 15 percent in 2008.

FIGURE 14.1: THE 10/40 WINDOW

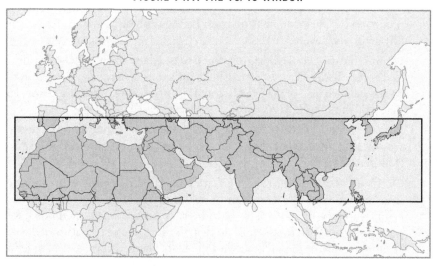

The proponents of frontier missions proposed a strategy with two key elements: prayer and focus. In regard to prayer they encouraged churches and individual Christians to "adopt a people group" and pray for their salvation.

Databases and organizations provided the information and matching of believers with UPGs (see, for example, http://www.worldmap.org). The proponents also called for focus; that is, they called on missions agencies to commit to focusing on a particular UPG. Numerous meetings were held to identify UPGs and solicit the commitment of agencies to reach them. In other words, the proponents enlisted churches and Christians to pray for UPGs and missions agencies to engage UPGs.

Missions agencies developed a strategy for reaching UPGs. The strategy involves these steps:

- Identify a UPG
- Commit to engaging that UPG
- Appoint a strategy coordinator (a missionary to strategize and focus resources on the UPG)
- Enlist prayer support
- Recruit a team of missionaries to reach the UPG, under the leadership of the strategy coordinator
- Learn the language and culture
- Develop a people-group profile (see chap. 17)
- Evangelize the people, using their heart language
- Plant churches that can reproduce
- Train local leaders
- Implement an exit strategy

While it was necessary to list these tasks sequentially, in practice some steps can be done at the same time. For example, developing a people-group profile is a great way to learn something about the culture. Missionaries also can combine language learning and evangelism.

CHURCH PLANTING MOVEMENTS

In the 1990s the administrators of the International Mission Board (IMB) became frustrated with the meager results from many areas in the 10/40 Window. Though the IMB had deployed missionaries to more than one hundred countries, 90 percent of the baptisms and new church starts came from just five countries: Brazil, Kenya, Nigeria, the Philippines, and Korea. During the same period they learned of instances where missionaries had experienced extraordinary increases in the number of churches. So in 1998 the administrators convened a meeting in Richmond, Virginia, and later another in Singapore to discover why and how these multiplication phenomena had occurred. David Garrison, then the chief strategist for the IMB, published their findings in a booklet titled *Church Planting Movements* (1999). Later he wrote a book with the same title (2004). The Church Planting Movement (CPM) strategy became *the* strategy for the IMB, and many other mission agencies have since embraced it (Garrison 2004).

A Church Planting Movement is defined as "*a rapid multiplication of indigenous churches planting churches that sweeps through a people group or population segment*" (Garrison 2004, 21, emphasis in original). Embedded in the definition are components of the underlying strategy, seen especially in several of the terms used. The first is *rapid*: CPM proponents believe that it is important for new churches—including new daughter churches—to reproduce themselves rapidly. The second is *multiplication*: the essential aim of a CPM is many new churches multiplying themselves until the whole people group is evangelized. A CPM has multiplication inculcated into the DNA of the new churches. The third is *indigenous*: though a foreign missionary may start the CPM, the goal is for the movement to quickly become locally led, financially self-supporting, and rapidly reproducing. The fourth, and final, is the idea of *churches planting churches*. Obviously, a church planter must start the first church, but afterward the CPM envisions churches planting daughter churches. That is why Garrison describes a CPM as a "church multiplying movement" (2004, 23).

In the strategy development meeting the participants listed ten universal elements found in all the CPMs:

- Extraordinary prayer
- Abundant evangelism
- Intentional planting of reproducing churches
- The authority of the Bible
- Local leadership
- House churches
- Churches planting churches
- Rapid reproduction
- Leadership by laypersons
- Healthy churches (carrying out the basic functions of a church: worship, evangelism/missions, discipleship, fellowship, and ministry) (Garrison 2004, 172)

The participants also listed ten common elements that were observed in most, but not all, of the church planting movements studied:

- A climate of uncertainty in the society
- Insulation from outsiders (Christians from outside the people group)
- High cost of following Christ
- Bold, fearless faith
- Family-based conversion patterns
- Rapid incorporation of new believers (into the churches and into leadership)
- Worship in the heart language
- Divine signs and wonders
- On-the-job leadership training
- Missionary church planters and their families suffer (Garrison 2004, 221).

The CPM advocates reject anything that might slow or hinder the rapid reproduction of churches. For example, they caution against church buildings, residential theological education, and ordination. They view these as extrabiblical and a hindrance to multiplying churches.

In evaluating the CPM strategy, even critics agree that the CPM has much to commend it. Employing this strategy has led to amazing CPMs among Hindus and Muslims in South Asia. These are populations in which missionaries have experienced little success in the past, demonstrating the significance of these recent successes. The CPM strategy stresses fervent prayer, widespread evangelism, and planting indigenous churches. It also emphasizes local leadership, reproducibility, and limited foreign involvement. These are all good things.

The CPM strategy has been criticized as well. In *Reaching and Teaching*, David Sills cogently argues that the CPM neglects thorough training for disciples and especially church leaders. Other critics contend that the CPM has a weak ecclesiology. For example, CPM advocates use new converts as pastors. Critics argue that this practice ignores Paul's instruction not to allow a novice to serve as a church leader (1 Tim. 3:6). Further, CPM literature says little about the nature of the church, and its practitioners seem to take a minimalistic approach to ecclesiology. For example, Garrison mentions Matthew 18:20 ("wherever two or three are gathered" KJV) in his description of "church" (2004, 259). Also, many of the featured CPMs seem to have a short life span. That is, after a few years researchers cannot find the churches. Several of the CPMs highlighted in the CPM booklet have vanished. In John 15:16 Jesus told his disciples: "I chose you and appointed you so that you might go and bear fruit—fruit that will last." It seems the rapidity emphasized by the CPM strategy does not always produce fruit that lasts.

Many missions leaders and church planters have embraced CPM, but many missions professors, like Hesselgrave, have expressed caution (Hesselgrave 2005, 235–36). Why is there disagreement between professors and practitioners? Perhaps the professors are more sensitive to theological concerns, while the church planters are more concerned with results. The shortcomings of the CPM strategy could be overcome by more attention to disciple training, leadership training, and a more biblical ecclesiology.

THE CHURCH MULTIPLICATION STRATEGY

The church multiplication strategy was developed by George Patterson, a long-time missionary church planter and church planting coach. Patterson served for many years in Honduras. For several years he taught in a residential Bible institute, but he did not see many churches planted by the institute's students or graduates. He decided there must be a better way to train effective church planters. Through wise counsel and trial and error, he developed a program of leadership training that he called Theological Education and Evangelism by Extension (TEEE).

Theological education by extension (TEE) had existed since 1961, but Patterson's innovation was to combine TEE with training for church planting. By emphasizing church planting in his TEEE program, he saw his students plant one hundred churches in northern Honduras. Later he became a church planting coach, and in that role he met Richard Scoggins in New England. Patterson trained Scoggins and his companions in church planting, and a network of house churches resulted. Scoggins collaborated with Patterson to write a book, *The Church Multiplication Guide* (Patterson and Scoggins 1993, 6). The authors endeavor to convince their readers that churches can multiply around the world—including in North America.

The church multiplication strategy emphasizes planting churches that will reproduce. Of course, this is the natural, healthy pattern. A foreign missionary is always alien and almost always temporary. The churches will remain long after the missionary is gone. Patterson and Scoggins insist that "church multiplication" is essential "because church growth by multiplication is more strategic and biblical than growth by addition *only*" (1993, 6). If the missionary can assist the churches in developing a pattern of church planting, then the church planting will continue in the missionary's absence. In other words, churches planting churches is natural and reproducible.

In his TEEE courses Patterson emphasized "obedience-based" study. That is, he insisted that the students learn and obey the biblical lessons presented. He taught his students the biblical pattern of church planting, and he required them to follow that example. He also taught his students to evangelize their own social networks. These "web-movements," as McGavran called them, led to a rapid increase in the number of believers.

The church multiplication strategy has been proven effective in North America and around the world. Its emphasis on training church leaders first differentiates it from other strategies. Most strategies emphasize evangelism and discipling primarily and leadership training secondarily. Church multiplication recognizes that authentic discipleship and equipped leaders are the key elements in a sustainable movement of reproducing churches. Church growth research has shown that an adequate number of church leaders is essential for church planting to continue. Church leaders come from the pool of disciples. Therefore, discipling and leadership training are the fuel that propels a surge of church planting.

CASE STUDY:
WHOM SHOULD WE FUND?

Imagine that you have just been elected to your church's missions committee. When you attend the first meeting, two missionaries make appeals for funding. Jack Martin serves in Brazil, and he has been an evangelist and church planter there for fifteen years. He has planted twelve churches and conducted many effective evangelistic meetings. Jacob Morton and his wife plan to serve in Uzbekistan in the 10/40 Window. Both missionaries make good presentations, but the church can afford to support only one. As the committee discusses its decision, some committee members argue for supporting the harvest field missionary, while others insist it is more strategic to send missionaries to the 10/40 Window.

REFLECTION AND DISCUSSION

- What would you say?
- How would you vote?

15

Contextualization Strategies

I n recent years evangelical missiologists have written many articles and
books on the subject of contextualization. Contextualization has become
a key element in mission strategies. This chapter briefly surveys four strategies that employ contextualization theory.

DEFINING CONTEXTUALIZATION

In 1972 two scholars connected with the Theological Education Fund of the
World Council of Churches coined a new word, *contextualization*. They
stated that "contextualization implies all that is involved in the familiar term
indigenization, but seeks to press beyond it to take into account the process of
secularity, technology and the struggle for human justice which characterized
the historical moment of nations in the Third World" (Nicholls 1979, 21). By
context the writers meant the cultural situation in which the gospel takes root.
The proponents of this approach in the World Council of Churches (WCC)
insist that there is no absolute or eternal theology. Rather, they believe that the
continuing dialectic between text (Christianity) and context (culture) will produce a theology that is correct for that particular situation. Basically, the WCC
placed context in the dominant position and text in a subordinate position.

SIDEBAR 15.1
CRITICAL CONTEXTUALIZATION

The late Paul Hiebert served for many years as a professor of missionary anthropology at Trinity Evangelical Divinity School. He advocated an approach to contextualization that he called "Critical Contextualization." This approach involves four steps that lead to an appropriately contextualized expression of Christians (1994, 88–91).

First Step—Hiebert maintained that missionaries and the leaders of the local churches should study the customs and traditions of the culture. This should be an uncritical gathering of cultural data.

Second Step—The local pastor or missionary then leads the believers to study the Scriptures that pertain to the cultural practices. That is, the missionary assists the believers by exposing them to the biblical texts that address their cultural practices.

Third Step—Local Christians meet to evaluate their traditional customs in light of scriptural teaching. It is necessary for the local believers to do this for themselves. They understand their customs, and especially the religious overtones, better than the missionary ever can. It is also important for them to go through the process,

owning it, so to speak. This will provide them with a pattern of biblically informed decision making that they can apply in other situations. Their decisions will be guided by their cultural understanding, the Bible's teachings, and the guidance of the Holy Spirit, as they pray for wisdom.

Fourth Step—The last step involves implementing the decisions made by the body of believers. Many customs will be retained, while others will be modified or rejected.

Hiebert believed that his approach would enable the missionary and national churches to avoid syncretism. His belief was based on four reasons: (1) Critical contextualization acknowledges the Bible as the "rule for faith and life." (2) This approach recognizes the role of the Holy Spirit in guiding the new churches. (3) In this approach the church functions as a "hermeneutical community," interpreting the Scriptures as the body of Christ. And (4) the conclusions drawn by these new churches can inform believers and theologians in other cultural contexts.

Evangelical writers took *contextualization* and redefined it for evangelical missions. They realized that evangelical missionaries, though devoted to the Bible and theological orthodoxy, had not always dealt sensitively with host cultures. Sometimes missionaries and theologians have hurt the majority world churches by failing to distinguish between Western theology and biblical theology. Bruce Nicholls writes, "The failure of missionary communicators to recognize the degree of cultural conditioning of their own theology has been devastating to many Third World churches" (1979, 25).

At this point a definition of *contextualization* from the evangelical perspective is necessary. Darrell Whiteman of Asbury Seminary defines contextualization

---

SIDEBAR 15.2
WHY IS EVANGELIZING MUSLIMS SO DIFFICULT?

Mission strategists recognize the importance of evangelizing Muslims. With over 1.4 billion adherents to Islam, Muslims represent the largest bloc of unevangelized people. Many missionaries and agencies have dedicated themselves to bringing Muslims to Christ. Nevertheless, successes have been few and frustrations many. Why have Muslims been so resistant to the gospel? Over thirty years ago, J. Herbert Kane compiled a list of six reasons why the evangelization of the Muslim world has been so difficult (1982, 114–17):

1. **ISLAM IS YOUNGER THAN CHRISTIANITY.** Islam borrowed stories and concepts from both Judaism and Christianity. Islam "has just enough Christianity in it to inoculate it against the real thing" (Kane 1982, 114). Muslims claim that God's revelation to Muhammad corrects and replaces the Bible.

2. **ISLAM DENIES THE DEITY AND THE DEATH OF CHRIST.** Islam rejects categorically

the belief that Jesus Christ is the Son of God. Kane writes, "If a missionary but mentions the deity of Christ the fanatical Muslim is likely to spit on his shadow to show his utter contempt for such a blasphemous suggestion" (1982, 115). Muslims also reject the physical death of Jesus on the cross and his bodily resurrection.

The Christian missionary can find many points of similarity between Christianity and Islam, and certainly he will want to make full use of these, but sooner or later he must come to the central theme of the gospel—the cross. At that point he runs into a stone wall. He can remove many offending things, but he can never do away with the offense of the cross. That and the deity of Christ are hurdles that can never be removed (Kane 1982, 115).

3. **ISLAM TREATS DEFECTORS VERY HARSHLY.** "All religions, including the broadest

---

this way: "Contextualization attempts to communicate the Gospel in word and deed and to establish the church in ways that make sense to people within their local context, presenting Christianity in such a way that it meets people's deepest needs and penetrates their worldview, thus allowing them to follow Christ and remain within their own culture" (1997, 2).

This definition is helpful because it clarifies two important points. First, as Whiteman writes, the gospel must be communicated clearly. Contextualized communication involves the right person communicating the right message in the right language in the right form in the right place to the right people. Second, contextualization is more than just the gospel message—it includes the forms, structures, and life of the church in its setting (Moreau 2012). In this sense a contextualized church will fit its own society or culture. It should feel local to local people rather than foreign to them. The church that of them—Hinduism—look with disfavor on the devotee who changes his religion," Kane writes. "But it remained for Islam to devise the Law of Apostasy, which permits the community to kill the adherent who defects from the faith" (1982, 115). Not all Muslim societies apply the death penalty to apostates, but Muslims everywhere know that converting to another religion will bring ostracism and persecution, at the least.

4. **MUSLIM SOCIETY HAS VERY STRONG SOLIDARITY.** Muslim societies reject the separation of religion and state. They seek to integrate religion, politics, economics, education, and culture. They also seek a community that is unified, bound together by Islam. Christian missionaries are viewed as home wreckers and disrupters of public order. The Muslim community views converts to Christ as countercultural traitors.

5. **THE PUBLIC PRACTICE OF RELIGION IS A CHARACTERISTIC OF ISLAM.** Christians practice much of their faith privately; however, faithful Muslims demonstrate their devotion by public prayers and worship. A Muslim who accepts Christ and stops worshiping at the mosque comes under suspicion quite quickly. This expectation of public prayer and worship reinforces Islam and represents a deterrent to conversion.

6. **THE MEMORY OF THE CRUSADES HAS BEEN KEPT ALIVE IN THE MUSLIM WORLD.** For Christians in the West the Crusades of the Middle Ages are ancient history; however, for Muslims the Crusades happened yesterday. They view Western soldiers and Christian missionaries as modern crusaders, bent on destroying Muslims and Islamic societies.

REFLECTION AND DISCUSSION

- Much has transpired since Kane wrote these words in 1982. In light of today's world, how would you update Kane's list?

results from contextualized missionary practice should proclaim biblical truth without dislocating the believers from their own culture. So if missionaries contextualize correctly, a new church in Nepal would be obediently biblical and fully Nepalese.

While cultural considerations are essential, the church's belief and practice must be defined by the Holy Scriptures and guided by the Holy Spirit. Thus pioneer missionaries must carefully teach both Scripture and contextualized hermeneutics. When the new believers learn the Bible and how to interpret it correctly, they can develop a church organization and a system of ethics that are true to the Bible and attuned to their cultural setting.

Evangelical missionaries always walk a tightrope, trying to maintain a balance between biblical fidelity and cultural sensitivity. An uncontextualized church would be foreign and "imported." Incorrect contextualization can also result in problems. Rick Brown has warned that the "main threat" in contextualization is syncretism. *Syncretism* is the combination of two or more religions or cultures. In many places the pioneer missionaries did not give sufficient attention to culture and worldview. This resulted in syncretized Christianity in which Christianity became a veneer over the traditional religion of the people. This is often called "folk Christianity." In these situations the Christians identify themselves as Christians, but their worldview remains unchanged (Brown 2006, 128). In modern times missionaries understand worldview change, and they can avoid the problem of folk Christianity. However, in seeking to reduce cultural and religious barriers to conversion, missionaries can go too far and compromise biblical truth. Thus, contextualization is like salting your scrambled eggs. You need just the right amount. Missionaries and missiologists do not always agree on the right amount.

PHIL PARSHALL'S STRATEGY

Phil Parshall initiated one of the first evangelical attempts to contextualize strategy. Parshall served for many years as a missionary to Muslims, first in Bangladesh and then in the Philippines. During his years in Bangladesh he developed a contextualized approach to evangelizing Muslims and planting churches. He described his strategy in *New Paths in Muslim Evangelism* (1980). Parshall sought to remove as many cultural barriers as possible in his ministry. He wanted his churches to feel "comfortable" for the worshipers, without compromising biblical teaching.

In the churches that Parshall's team planted, the believers worshiped on Fridays, left their shoes at the door, and washed their hands before entering. The Bible teacher and the worshipers sat on mats on the floor. The worshipers raised their hands in the Muslim way as they prayed. The Bible was shown great reverence and placed on a special folding stand, as is the Qur'an in Muslim settings. The worshipers used local tunes for their hymns and praise songs. The word *Christian* was avoided, and the believers described themselves as "followers of Isa" ("Isa" is Arabic for Jesus).

The missionaries on Parshall's team made lifestyle changes in order to effectively evangelize the people. The male missionaries wore local clothing and grew beards. The female missionaries wore dresses like the women in their people group, and sometimes they wore veils. The missionaries lived as simply as possible, and they refused to eat pork. They did not make photographs of the new believers, nor did they invite foreign visitors to meet the new believers. Using these methods the missionaries planted a cluster of churches in Bangladesh and demonstrated that a contextualized approach could be effective in evangelizing Muslims (Parshall 1980).

JOHN TRAVIS'S C1–C6 SCALE AND RESULTING STRATEGY

John Travis (a pseudonym) has served for years as an evangelist and church planter among Muslims in Asia. He developed a helpful spectrum for categorizing mission work among Muslims according to the degree of contextualization. His descriptive spectrum (Travis 1998b), known as the C1–C6 Scale, is not a strategy per se. However, he and others have written articles advocating the use of a C5 approach to reach Muslims for Christ (see, e.g., Brown 2007; Higgins 2006, 2007; Lewis 2007, 2009).

C5 Strategic Approaches

Travis and other missionaries to Muslims have advocated using the C5 approach to evangelizing Muslims. Travis contends that Muslims can accept Jesus as Savior and still attend the weekly services at the mosque. C5 advocates make much of the meaning of the word *Muslim*, reminding us that it means "submitted one." Thus, in their opinion, a Muslim-background believer is a "Muslim." He is submitted now to Jesus Christ. Because Muslims view converts to Christ as betrayers of their family, community, and faith, Travis believes converts should be encouraged to maintain their position in the Muslim community. In this way they can witness to worshipers at the mosque and avoid persecution and expulsion from their community (1998a).

Travis acknowledges the danger of syncretism in using the C5 approach. However, he believes the benefits are worth the risk. To minimize the possibility of syncretism he suggests these guidelines:

1. Jesus is Lord and Savior; there is no salvation apart from Christ.
2. New believers are baptized, meet regularly for worship, and take the Lord's Supper.
3. The new believers study the Injil (the four Gospels).
4. New believers reject harmful animistic practices often attached to Islam, such as shamanism, occult practices, charms, and prayers to Islamic saints.
5. Normal Muslim practices like circumcision, fasting, almsgiving, attending the mosque, wearing a head covering, and abstaining from pork and alcohol are continued; they allow new believers to express their love for God and respect for their neighbors.
6. New believers are taught to examine and evaluate Muslim beliefs and practices in light of biblical teaching. Biblically acceptable Islamic beliefs and practices are retained. Other beliefs and practices are modified or rejected.

141

SIDEBAR 15.3
THE C1–C6 SPECTRUM (ADAPTED FROM TRAVIS 1998A)

C1 refers to traditional churches in Muslim cultures. Many of these churches are quite ancient and have managed to survive the Muslim conquest and domination of their nation. These churches use a minority language in worship. For example, the Coptic Church in Egypt uses the ancient Coptic language in its worship services, not Arabic, the national language. C1 churches use traditional Christian terms, forms, and rituals. They worship on Sundays and call themselves Christians. Generally, they do not attempt to evangelize the Muslim majority; rather, they exist as a Christian enclave in a Muslim culture.

C2 describes traditional churches that use the national or majority language. Many of these churches were planted by Protestant missionaries a century ago. These churches use Christian vocabulary, and the members call themselves Christians. They worship on Sundays, and their worship forms reflect Western Protestant worship in the early twentieth century.

C3 refers to contextualized communities of evangelical Christians. These churches use the majority language and cultural forms that do not carry religious baggage. Most of their members are Muslim-background believers. The churches use local folk music, art, and dress. The believers call themselves Christians, and they may worship in a church building or at a neutral site. Many of these churches have been planted by evangelical missionaries in the last thirty years.

C4 indicates contextualized Christian congregations, like those planted by Phil Parshall. The members are all Muslim-background believers. They use the majority language and biblically permissible cultural and Islamic forms. They worship on Fridays. The believers call themselves "followers of Isa." They reject eating pork and drinking alcoholic beverages. They leave their shoes at the door of the place of worship, wash their hands before entering, sit on mats on the floor, and pray with raised hands.

C5 speaks of Christ-centered communities of messianic Muslims. All the believers are former Muslims. The believers seek to remain in the Islamic community. They call themselves Muslims (submitted ones) who follow Isa as the Messiah. Some believers continue to worship at the mosque. They share their faith in Isa with Muslims. Sometimes the believers are expelled from their mosques because their views are judged deviant.

C6 refers to small Christ-centered groups of secret, underground believers. Typically, these believers live in places where they would be killed if their conversion to Christ became known. They worship individually or in small groups. Many have come to Christ through dreams and visions, while others have come via radio or television broadcasts, Christian literature, or travel abroad. These believers continue to attend the mosque, and they try to keep their faith secret.

REFLECTION AND DISCUSSION

- Which positions on the spectrum make you uncomfortable? Why?

7. New believers are expected to show growth in their spiritual lives, as evidenced by the fruit of the Spirit, loving relationships, and witnessing for Christ (Travis 1998b).

Travis notes that many C5 believers have been expelled from their mosques, and he believes that for many Muslim-background believers C5 may be a transitional phase. Still, he contends that the C5 approach provides enhanced opportunities for evangelism in the Muslim community.

The C5 strategy has generated much controversy and criticism. The International Mission Board, one of the largest evangelical missions agencies, has forbidden its missionaries to employ the C5 strategy. Parshall also reacted with great alarm (1998), arguing that C5 likely will lead to syncretism. He believes that encouraging new believers to attend the mosque is questionable because Islam teaches that Muhammad is the greatest prophet of God and denies the divinity, death, and resurrection of Jesus. Parshall recommends these guidelines to avoid syncretism:

1. Missionaries must be acquainted with the Bible's teaching on syncretism, and they must emphasize the uniqueness of Jesus Christ.
2. Missionaries must study Islam and Islamic culture carefully.
3. Experimentation is desirable, as long as safeguards against syncretism are in place.
4. Proper contextualization requires constant monitoring and evaluation.
5. Missionaries must be careful not to preach a gospel that has been syncretized with Western culture (1998, 404–10).

THE INSIDER MOVEMENT STRATEGY

The insider movement strategy, like the other strategies in this chapter, reflects the passion of evangelical missionaries to bring Muslims to Christ. This strategy differs somewhat in that it has been employed among Hindus (anonymous 2004) and Buddhists (DeNeui 2002). Still, it is an extrapolation of Travis's C5 strategy, utilizing that strategy while adding insights from missionary experience in India. Rebecca Lewis has defined an insider movement as follows: it is any movement to faith in Christ where "(a) the gospel flows through pre-existing communities and social networks, and where (b) believing families, as valid expressions of the Body of Christ, remain inside their socio-religious communities, retaining their identity as members of that community while living under the Lordship of Jesus Christ and the authority of the Bible" (2007, 75).

143

Practitioners of the insider movement strategy seek to achieve four goals. First, they want to see more Muslims, Hindus, and Buddhists come to Christ. All three groups have been resistant to conversion. Second, the missionaries who use this strategy hope that their converts can retain their religious identity and thus remain accepted persons in their societies. This relieves them of persecution and enhances their ability to witness to family, friends, and neighbors. As Lewis writes, "Today we should . . . free people groups from the counter-productive burden of socio-religious conversion and the constraints of affiliation with the term 'Christianity' and with various religious institutions and traditions of Christendom" (2007, 76). Third, missionaries want to eliminate the problem of double conversion, "by which they refer to the two-fold decision to believe in Christ and to identify oneself as a 'Christian'" (2007, 76). In some cultures the term *Christian* carries significant historical and cultural baggage. In those settings to declare oneself a *Christian* is like changing one's religion *and* rejecting one's culture. Fourth, and finally, proponents end "extractionism," the practice of extracting new believers from their communities.

For theological support some proponents of insider movements point to fulfillment theology, contending that Jesus Christ can "fulfill" or complete Hinduism. Fulfillment theology holds that world religions represent general revelation that can be fulfilled or completed by Jesus Christ. Most insider

---

SIDEBAR 15.4
FIELD RESEARCH ON A C5 CHURCH PLANTING EFFORT

Dean Gilliland, former professor in the School of World Mission at Fuller Theological Seminary, led a team of researchers that surveyed a group of Muslim-background believers in South Asia who were converted through the efforts of a church planting team that used the C5 strategy. Here are the results of the survey (Travis 1998a):

- 76 percent meet weekly for Christian worship
- 55 percent believe in the Trinity
- 97 percent say Jesus is the only Savior
- 100 percent pray to Jesus for forgiveness

- 50 percent continue to attend the mosque
- 96 percent say that the Qur'an was given by God
- 66 percent say the Qur'an is more important than the Bible
- 45 percent say they feel at peace hearing the Qur'an

REFLECTION AND DISCUSSION

- Phil Parshall believes this survey confirms his concerns that the C5 strategy has a tendency to lead to syncretism (1998, 409). Do you agree or disagree? Explain why.

movement advocates point to the practice of the first-century Jewish believers (see, e.g., Higgins 2007) and remind opponents that New Testament believers continued to worship in synagogues after they had professed faith in Christ.

Critics of insider movements point out that worshiping in a synagogue where the Old Testament was read and Yahweh was worshiped is much different from worshiping in a Hindu temple or a Muslim mosque. They also note that the Christians did not continue in the synagogues for very long. The critics concede the issue of "double conversion" but insist that properly contextualized churches can minimize this problem. The critics are rightly concerned with the likelihood of syncretism should the converts continue to worship in their temples or mosques (see, e.g., the October 2005 issue of *Mission Frontiers*; Tennent 2006; Corwin 2007; and *St. Francis Magazine* at http://www.stfrancis magazine.info/ja/). Insider advocates concede the danger of syncretism, but they plead for time to see how the movements develop (Lewis 2011).

THE CAMEL METHOD

The Camel Method was developed by Muslim-background believers in South Asia, and a book describing the method was written by Kevin Greeson, a longtime missionary to Muslims in that region (2004). In the Camel Method an evangelist uses verses from the Qur'an that mention Jesus as a bridge to sharing from the Bible. Specifically, the Qur'an contains ninety-nine names for Allah. Muhammad declared that there are actually one hundred names for Allah, but only the camel knows the one hundredth.

Greeson teaches people to ask Muslims questions about the Qur'an's teachings about the one hundredth name and about Isa (Jesus). Although the Qur'an does contain several passages that speak of Jesus, most Muslims are not familiar with them. If a Muslim shows interest, then the witness directs the inquirer's attention to the Bible. Greeson uses this acronym as an aid to remembering the witnessing sequence (2007, 58–60):

- Mary was Chosen to give birth to Isa.
- Angels announced the good news to her—
- that Isa would do Miracles;
- that Isa knew and was the way to Eternal
- Life.

Many veteran missionaries to Muslims report success in using the Camel Method. The method has several advantages. First, it is a good point of contact. It is always good to begin by asking questions and adopting the attitude

145

of a learner. Second, it is good to start where people are and then take them to where they need to be. Third, this method has proven effective in many different parts of the Muslim world.

While the response to the Camel Method has been generally favorable, some critics have raised objections. One criticism is that the Camel Method exalts and affirms the Qur'an as a holy book. By beginning with the Qur'an, the missionary might unintentionally communicate that the Qur'an and the Bible have equal authority. A second criticism is that the method is deceptive because the missionary initiates the conversation by posing as an inquirer who is asking sincere questions about Islam. However, the missionary is not truly inquiring about Islam (see, e.g., Walker 2010).

CASE STUDY:
WHAT TO WEAR?

Kelli and Jacob Wilson served as missionaries in North Africa. When they arrived, they discovered that the people group among whom they served was very traditional in its cultural values. The women all wore the burka (a black gown covering the body from head to toe). Kelli refused to wear a burka or change her style of dressing in any way. She told her supervisor, "We have come to liberate these women from spiritual and cultural oppression. How can I adopt a practice I believe to be wrong?"

REFLECTION AND DISCUSSION

- What are arguments *for* and *against* Kelli's position?
- In what ways (both positive and negative) do you anticipate that her lifestyle will affect her witness to the women?

16

Understanding Cultural Research

A significant part of developing healthy mission strategies is having a proper understanding of the people who will be served by the team and the national believers with whom your team may be entering into partnership. For centuries missionaries traveled to other lands with very little advance knowledge of the people they were going to serve. More recently, however, the church has been blessed with many resources to assist in conducting good cultural research to help shape strategy.

It is important to have zeal for doing the Lord's work. However, zeal without knowledge can result in serious problems (Prov. 19:2). Consider the following unfortunate situation:

Our friend Raju made the mistake of not doing research before he established his street youth project. He saw a need, and met that need based upon a series of assumptions. This is common among children-at-risk workers. Many feel the need to respond urgently, and do so without taking the time to understand the issues or context. Raju forgot to find out why the youth were on the streets, why they were not at school, or who else was working with them. The local schools in which he enrolled the children were basically nonfunctional. He employed youth who could not go to the local school to assist him with outreach . . . and broke child labor laws in the process. The youth were already enrolled in a skills training program with another project; however, because they started to go to school and were not attending training, they could not graduate and missed a whole year. Unfortunately, Raju caused more harm than good. (Burch, Sexton, and Murray 2009, 478)

Our purpose in this chapter is not to advocate that social science is the key in reaching the world with the gospel. Rather, we want to offer guidelines to assist missionaries in understanding the value of cultural research and to provide helpful tools for strategy development. In the following chapters we will address the specifics of such things as developing a people-group profile, discerning a people's receptivity to the gospel, and developing a communication strategy.

CONTEXTUALIZATION

Contextualization includes understanding the people well enough to communicate effectively with them the good news about Jesus and assist them in living according to his commands within their cultural environment and throughout the world. David Hesselgrave and Edward Rommen note that "Christian contextualization can be thought of as the attempt to communicate the message of the person, works, Word, and will of God in a way that is faithful to God's revelation, especially as it is put forth in the teachings of Holy Scripture, and that is meaningful to the respondents in their respective cultural and existential contexts" (1989, 200).

Although entire books have been written on the topic of contextualization (e.g., Kraft 1979; Hesselgrave and Rommen 1989; Moreau 2012), we are able to provide only a glimpse into this important area as related to cultural research. Such research is designed to provide the strategist with an understanding of the people that includes what they believe, how they think and communicate, and how they live life. Knowing these things is basic to the development of contextualized strategies. Such understanding is so important to mission strategy that Dayton and Fraser write: "Understanding a people is at the heart of planning strategies for evangelism. It serves as the basis for all the steps that must later be considered and planned. An awareness of the various facets of a people enables us to see how best to communicate the gospel" (1980, 147).

HOW TO UNDERSTAND THEM

While there are numerous ways to do cultural research, we believe developing a good understanding of the people in each of the following areas will greatly assist in developing healthy strategies. Although sociological and anthropological wisdom is of tremendous value to the strategist, it is not our purpose to train social scientists. We anticipate that these categories will help missionaries and their teams better understand the people and societies among whom they serve and how best to communicate the gospel and carry out the Great Commission among them. (For a great starting point for numerous online resources related to cultural research, see http://www.mislinks.org/understanding/.)

Geographically

Geography has a great bearing on how people live. Groups residing near the shanties or slums on the perimeter of a city will have a different way of thought and life than those living in a high-rise apartment in the downtown area. While living in Indianapolis I (J. D.) noticed this reality when I crossed over a set of railroad tracks on my side of the city. A couple of blocks to the north of the tracks, the city was well groomed and contained many nice stores and restaurants. To the south of the tracks, the homes and businesses were run-down. Bars were placed on the windows to keep out thieves.

Strategists should obtain a map of the area in which they are serving. Natural (e.g., forests, rivers, mountain ranges) and man-made (e.g., roadways, railroads, industrial parks) landmarks should be noted. While looking over their maps, strategists should be asking questions such as:

- How do these landmarks affect people's normal traffic patterns?
- How does the geography of the area influence where the people work, play, and live?
- How does the geography affect how people will gather together?
- Are there geographic barriers that would require different meeting places for different groups? (For some resources related to geographical study, see http://www.mislinks.org/understanding/maps/.)

Demographically

Demographics are facts about the people, largely consisting of statistics. Many national, regional, and local governments collect and use demographic information, though obtaining this type of information is more difficult in some parts of the world than in others. Fortunately, in addition to governmental data there is a wealth of information that has been obtained over the years by social scientists (see, for example, http://www.mislinks.org/understanding /statistics/ and http://www.worldmap.org/ for links to such resources online). By obtaining demographics strategists seek to answer questions such as:

149

SIDEBAR 16.1
REACHING NATIVE AMERICANS

In the following excerpt, Bruce Terry discusses the cultural barriers that exist between certain Native American groups and the Anglo majority population in the United States, hindering missionary activity. His observations offer an excellent reminder of the value of cultural research in developing missionary strategy.

One of the barriers to evangelism which exists is the antagonism between the Indians and white men. This is more pronounced among some tribes than among others. The Hopis of Arizona, for example, have a sign posted outside the old Oraibi pueblo which reads, "Warning. Warning. No outside white visitors allowed. Because of your failure to obey the laws of our tribe as well as the laws of your own, this village is hereby closed." The trust which is needed to overcome this kind of antagonism cannot be built overnight.

In some tribes there is tremendous social pressure to remain true to the old traditions and loyal to the group. One who becomes a Christian is a social outcast. This is especially true in those tribes which are group-oriented—for example, the Pueblo tribes. And even if a tribe does present a solid front to outsiders which exerts social pressure against the acceptance of the gospel, the same tribe may have internal factions within the society which can also prove to be a hindrance. The Southern Baptists of Zuni, for example, discovered that several small groups for teaching children were much more effective than trying to have a few larger groups. The reason for this is that when the children in one faction discovered that children from

- What types of people live here?
- What are their ages?
- What are their marital statuses?
- What are their income levels?
- What are their educational levels?
- What is their literacy rate?
- What are their occupations?
- Is the community growing or declining? What is the rate of change?
- What ethnic groups (if more than one) are present?
- How large are the groups?
- What is the crime rate?
- What types of crime are the most prevalent?
- What religions (if more than one) do people follow?

Such information provides a team with the general standard of living found in the area. If much diversity exists, demographic information will assist in another faction were to be in the Bible class, they would stay at home.

But the lack of response experienced by most missions cannot simply be attributed to the culture of the Indians. Rather, it has to a great extent been due to a failure of the missionaries to understand and appreciate Indian culture. In reporting on a recent interdenominational conference on Indian evangelism, the MARC Newsletter says, "However, it was obvious from the papers presented that the major failure of missions to the Indians, particularly in the United States, has been a failure to realize that tremendous cultural differences exist between white missionaries and Indian people." It goes on to state that we have been assuming all along that they required the type of evangelism we usually use in the US, when in reality they need the type of evangelism used in foreign countries. All too often, missionaries have assumed that since most of the Indians could speak English as a second language, there was no reason for them to learn the native language. But somehow English often fails to communicate like one's own mother tongue does. And the missionary deprives himself of really being able to participate fully in the Indian culture because of his failure to learn the language. In fact, he cannot even correctly understand the culture. (1975)

REFLECTION AND DISCUSSION

- If you were working to reach the Hopi, what are some cultural and historical matters that you would need to know before starting your work?
- Why do you think some missionaries did not learn the Indian culture? How did this affect their strategies in the short term and in the long term?

providing such insights. Demographic information aids in the development of methods to engage people. If a team's research reveals that many of the people are oral-based learners (e.g., low literacy rates), then communication methods will need to reflect this reality.

Culturally

The information gleaned from cultural research is helpful in understanding the heart of the people. Cultural research can provide a window into the soul of the community. While a people may profess to be Buddhist, at home, work, and play they may be found to be less Buddhist and more animistic because of their values. Questions asked by researchers at this level include:

- What is the general lifestyle of the people?
- What is the general mind-set?
- What are the interests of the people?
- What do the people value? Why?

- What are the hurts of the people? Why?
- What causes them the most fear? Why?
- What causes them the most joy? Why?
- What are their dreams for the future?
- What are their most important material possessions? Why?
- What value do they place on family and children?
- What value do they place on education?
- What value do they place on work?

Spiritually

Obviously, the religiosity of a people is important to the work of the mission-ary strategist. Instead of just understanding a group's religion, we encourage strategists to get to know the spirituality of the people. In many places of the world a person may be officially, ethnically, or familially a member of a major world religion, but in practice that person's life may not closely reflect the of-ficial tenets of the religion. Researchers studying a people group's spirituality ask questions such as:

- What is the spiritual climate of the people?
- How open to spiritual matters are they in their daily lives?
- Are they more hostile, highly open, apathetic, or agnostic?
- What are the religious traditions and rituals of the people?
- What do the sizes and architecture of the religious buildings in the com-munity reveal about the people?
- What are the population counts of the different religious groups in the community?
- Where are the merchants and/or shamans in the community who sell religious/spiritual resources?
- Are there any ministries and/or teams serving among the people?
- What percentage of the population is evangelical?
- What is the ratio of evangelical churches to the entire population?

While we should not overlook the possibility of significant online resources that can help answer these questions (e.g., http://www.mislinks.org/understanding /folk-religions/), neither should we anticipate they will answer in specific details the types of questions that should be asked.

Historically

The past always influences the present, even when people are not aware of its influence. Researchers need to study the history of the people and the community. Also, if the people have been highly transient or, as in some urban contexts, have a high annual migration rate, then a study into the history of the migrants is also necessary. Why did they move? What "pushed" them from their communities, and what "pulled" them to this new one? A study of the history of a people may provide numerous clues about what to embrace and use as a point of contact with the people, as well as what to avoid in conversations.

Politically

The politics of a people affect the way they think and live. What political parties or philosophies, if any, do the people subscribe to? If the people you are attempting to reach have migrated from another location, then you also need to know the political views they held when in their previous locations. I (J. D.) remember being driven through the streets of New York by a Haitian taxi driver. As we conversed, I quickly discovered that even though he had been living in the United States for many years, he was part of the larger Haitian community in the city, which stayed in close connection with friends and family members living in Haiti, and he was very much interested in political matters in his home country.

Linguistically

Language provides a window into the heart and worldview of a people. Missionaries should learn the language, including the colloquialisms, of the people. While the trade language is important for survival, knowledge of the people's heart language is where you will begin to develop a more accurate understanding of their worldview. (For some links to resources on intercultural communication, see http://www.mislinks.org/communicating/intercultural-communication/.)

Economically

The wealth of an individual or people can provide a great amount of insight into their worldview and lifestyles. Status, security, power, and education are among some of the matters that wealth influences. It should be noted that wealth should not simply be attributed to the money of a people. While many societies of the world are cash based, others are not. Agriculture and livestock and a certain barter system may be in place. Families with little money but

SIDEBAR 16.2
NOT ALL EVANGELISM IS THE SAME

The gospel that is preached never changes. The message remains the same. Of course, different contexts will challenge the way the message is shared. When missiologists speak of evangelism, they do so recognizing the need to consider how the gospel is contextualized.

The following four types of evangelism (see Winter and Koch 2009) should be kept in mind by mission strategists to assist in understanding societies and strategy development. Different types of evangelism will require different methods of communicating the gospel.

It should be noted that the differing factor among these four is that of culture and not language. While language may play a part in cultural differences, it is not always the determining factor. Also, geography is not a determining factor in what defines the following categories. Evangelism can be occurring among a particular people within the same city as that of the evangelist, but both groups may be culturally different.

E-0. This type of evangelism is that which is found among individuals who would be classified as nominal Christians, or those who may be gathered with churches for times of fellowship and worship. For example, this type of evangelism would come in the form of an evangelistic sermon on Sunday morning.

E-1. This approach to sharing the gospel is done among individuals who are of the same culture as that of the one sharing the message. The cultural gap between the communicator and the receiver is not very great. In addition to many cultural similarities, both parties have the language in common as well. E-1 can be applied to church planting. Teams working among those of a similar cultural background will find themselves categorized according to this type.

E-2. This category of evangelism and church planting includes serving among a people who are of a slightly different culture as that of the evangelists. While language may or may not be different, there is a similar worldview. Americans engaged in evangelizing Western Europeans could be an example of E-2 evangelism.

E-3. This final category of evangelism and church planting is characterized by great differences between the evangelists and the people hearing the gospel. There are typically many cultural differences and challenges to the communication of the gospel and planting healthy churches. Again, while language and geography are not the determining factors for what constitutes E-3 evangelism, an example of this work would be Americans working among Chinese. Here there are often stark worldview and communication differences that affect the birth and growth of churches.

REFLECTION AND DISCUSSION

- In light of these four categories, in what ways does cultural research help us to better understand each point of the scale?
- Which of these four categories best describes the sense of calling you or others you know have experienced?

who possess many animals may be some of the wealthiest in the community. Questions worth considering include:

- What is considered the normal standard of living for this people?
- What constitutes a "wealthy" person?
- What is considered poverty?
- Is this society a cash-based society?
- What are the typical desires among the people for economic advancement?

SIDEBAR 16.3
DANCING: BLESSING OR BANE?

The following story was shared by Charlie Davis, based on his service with the Evangelical Alliance Mission in Caracas, Venezuela. While the excerpt does not reveal the details of how he and his family wrestled with contextualization (see the full article for those), it does draw attention to the challenges that arise when cultures collide. Even without knowing their full story in Venezuela, you should allow the "Reflection and Discussion" to guide your thoughts related to the value of cultural research.

I grew up with the understanding that dancing was sin. In sixth grade my parents sent written permission allowing me to sit out while my physical education class learned how to square dance. The closest I came to a real dance while growing up was watching on my grandmother's TV as the old folks vied for the pleasure of dancing with Lawrence Welk.

Fifteen years ago my wife and I began working in Venezuela, eager to see some new churches started in this predominately Catholic country. Dancing was never a question. The established evangelical church had traditions that almost precisely matched those with which I was brought up.

We did, however, get more exposure. Instead of a TV set, which could be easily turned off, we heard and felt dancing in ways never before imagined as neighbors around us celebrated late into the night. Our solution was to buy ear plugs, put pillows over our ears, and turn up the white noise of the fans. Dancing was at best a nuisance, at worst a tool of the devil for promoting licentious behavior. We did not realize how little we really understood the Venezuelan cultural presuppositions that made dancing such a central part of their culture. (1997, 50)

REFLECTION AND DISCUSSION

- How might the Davises' attitude toward dancing hinder evangelism in Venezuela?
- What do you think may have happened that caused the Davises to recognize that they had misunderstood the Venezuelans?
- How might cultural research have assisted the Davises early in their work?
- Every missionary should anticipate the likelihood of encountering similar misunderstanding. What attitudes do you need to cultivate and what actions do you need to take to help avoid this?

What Do They Know about the Gospel?

In the process of a team's cultural research, one of the most important questions that needs to be answered is related to the people's knowledge of the gospel. Of course, the answer obtained is purely a generalization projected on the people, but it should be based on the majority position. Some peoples of the world will have little to no understanding of the gospel. Others will have a great amount of understanding, yet often mixed with grave distortions of what is found in the Scriptures. There are numerous online resources available to help you understand this, including the World Mission Atlas Project (http://www.worldmap.org/). We will address this topic in more detail in chapter 19.

What Is Their Attitude toward the Gospel?

Another important question to answer concerns the general affection of the people for the gospel message. Knowledge of the truth is one matter, but their attitudes are quite another. The people can have a very accurate understanding of the gospel and be hostile to it. Of course, they can also have little knowledge of the message and be very receptive to it. We will address attitudinal matters in more detail in chapter 19.

Strategists should plan to help the people come to a more accurate understanding of the gospel *and* develop a more favorable attitude toward it. In most cases the latter will be accomplished as methods are established to permit the people to observe the godly ways of the team members and how they love their neighbors. In some highly resistant areas, progress should be evaluated based on how the methods move people in a more favorable direction toward the gospel.

I (J. D.) once asked a missionary who had served in a predominately Islamic country to share with my class about his work. On this particular day he told the story of how a team of sports trainers led a clinic at a local school for teenagers. The presentation was related to physical health. During the presentation one of the trainers spoke of the need to stay in good health and avoid drugs and sexually immoral activity. The missionary was surprised when the Muslim leader of the event stood before the crowd and told the people that they needed to "start living like these Americans." This event was a step in the right direction in changing negative attitudes toward the truth.

CONCLUSION

Cultural research assists us in developing strategies. It will not prevent all problems, misunderstandings, embarrassments, or faux pas from occurring.

However, refraining from taking the necessary time to develop a better understanding of the people is a sure guarantee for mistakes that could have been easily avoided. People are social beings and live and function within societies. It is very important that the strategist have a good understanding of the people geographically, demographically, culturally, spiritually, historically, politically, linguistically, and economically. Knowing a people's knowledge of and attitude toward the gospel message is essential for proper communication. With this information in mind, it is now time to consider how to develop a profile of a people group.

17

Developing a People-Group Profile

A missionary strategist functions somewhat like a medical doctor. A medical doctor gathers data such as blood pressure, pulse rate, temperature, and symptoms in order to make a correct diagnosis and prescribe the correct medicine for the patient. A missionary strategist must also gather information in order to develop an effective strategy. Penicillin might work well for a patient with a sore throat, but it would not help one with a broken leg. In the same way a strategy well suited for reaching the Central Thai in Bangkok, Thailand, will almost certainly not work well among the Masai of Kenya. Each people group requires a unique strategy, and in order to develop a unique strategy missionaries need to understand their people group thoroughly.

WHAT IS A PEOPLE-GROUP PROFILE?

James Slack, a mission researcher with the International Mission Board, defines a people-group profile as "a profile of the way the people within a specific culture live, act, think, work, and relate. It is a 'map' of the culture's social, religious, economic, and political views and relationships" (personal communication). In other words, a people-group profile is like a CAT scan

SIDEBAR 17.1
UNDERSTANDING WORLDVIEW

A key concept in developing a people-group profile is *worldview*. Everyone has a worldview, but most people are not conscious that they do. If you asked people, "What is your worldview?" most would answer, "The world is round." So, what does *worldview* mean in regard to missions? James Sire has defined *worldview* as "a set of presuppositions (assumptions which may be true, partially true or entirely false) which we hold consciously or subconsciously, consistently or inconsistently about the basic constitution of reality, and that provides the foundation on which we live and move and have our being" (2004, 17). David Burnett defines *worldview* this way: it is "the shared framework of ideas held by a particular society concerning how they perceive the world. Everyday experiences are fitted into this framework in order to give a totality of meaning and comprehension for the individual" (2002, 13).

Sire writes that worldview answers seven basic questions about reality:

1. What is prime reality—the really real?
2. What is the nature of external reality, that is, the world around us?
3. What is a human being?
4. What happens to a person after death?

5. Why is it possible to know anything at all?
6. How do we know what is right and wrong?
7. What is the meaning of human history? (2004, 20)

Sire believes that when one has answered these seven questions, the worldview becomes much clearer.

The quest to discover a people group's worldview is not simple or easy, but it is quite important. In the past, missionaries failed to determine worldview, and as a result their biblical teaching did not penetrate to the core of the culture. This led to syncretism. The people believed in Jesus for eternal salvation, but they went to the local witch doctor or shaman to solve their daily problems because their worldview had not changed. The missionary's aim is not to persuade people to adopt a Western worldview but rather to persuade them to adopt the biblical worldview.

REFLECTION AND DISCUSSION

- How does a society's approach to decision making affect evangelism?
- How is folk religion different from classic or textbook religion?

of the people group. It helps the missionary to understand the people group from all angles.

Figure 17.1 helps explain how a culture appears to a missionary researcher. It is easy to observe what the people do and wear, but the researcher must probe deeper. By conducting interviews and asking questions, the researcher can understand the people group's morality, how they judge right from wrong. Further questioning can uncover their beliefs about what is true and their worldview (what is real). Only through this effort can the missionary understand the culture on a deep level.

FIGURE 17.1
(ADAPTED FROM KWAST 1981, 363)

WHY IS A PEOPLE-GROUP PROFILE NECESSARY?

Missionaries are naturally eager to present the gospel to the people group among whom they serve as quickly as possible. As a result they may resist the idea of spending time developing a profile (ethnography) of their people group if they consider the effort required a waste of time. While we may empathize with that attitude, cross-cultural workers must resist the temptation to skip this step. A well-done profile will enhance evangelism and save time in the long run. For example, a missionary in East Africa secured permission to do Bible storying in a village. He faithfully visited the village each week for a year and told the Bible stories in the shade of a large tree. He began with the story of creation and concluded with the ascension of Jesus. When he finished the last story, one man in the group said, "It is a shame those stories are not true." "What do you mean, not true!" exclaimed the missionary. "All the stories are true." "Oh, no," the African answered. "This is the tree where we tell the stories that are not true. That tree over there is where we tell stories that are true." Some preliminary research would have saved this well-intentioned missionary a lot of time and effort.

There are a number of reasons for preparing a people-group profile:

1. A profile will establish a foundation for understanding the culture and how the people will comprehend the gospel.
2. The profile will highlight contrasts between the people's culture and Christianity.
3. The profile will reveal issues that the missionary will need to address, such as polygamy in Africa or widow burning in southern Asia.
4. The profile will provide the missionary with lists of barriers and bridges to evangelization. "Barriers" are cultural elements and/or religious beliefs that will hinder the people from coming to Christ. "Bridges" are cultural elements that will likely aid the process of evangelization. For example, most animistic cultures believe in a "high god" who created the world. This belief is a bridge to evangelizing those cultures—a starting point for biblical teaching.
5. The profile will help the missionary understand which biblical doctrines to emphasize in the teaching.
6. The profile will aid the missionary in determining the learning objectives for biblical teaching.
7. If the missionary is doing Bible storying, then the profile will help the missionary choose Bible stories that speak to cultural issues.
8. The profile will enlighten the missionary about the implications of the gospel for the people group. In other words, it will identify the issues that the new believers need to confront.
9. The profile will enable the missionary to plot the people group's position on the learning scale and the receptivity scale.
10. The profile will help the missionary avoid syncretism among the new believers.[1]

The last point in the list may be the most important of all. The pioneer missionaries did not know about worldview. As a result their teaching and preaching changed the people's behavior, ethics, and beliefs (especially about eternity), but it did not change their worldview. The result has been folk Christianity or syncretistic Christianity. Folk Christians trust in Jesus for salvation, but they go to the shaman (witch doctor or spiritual practitioner) for help with

---

1. This material comes from a presentation that James Slack provides to new missionaries of the International Mission Board at the International Learning Center (used with his permission).

their daily problems. African church leaders bemoan this situation in their churches, as do American, Brazilian, and Indian church leaders.

One way to avoid syncretism is to ensure that the message of salvation has been fully contextualized. Seminaries insist that their students master hermeneutics so that they will be able to interpret the Bible accurately (2 Tim. 2:15). They also require their students to study homiletics so that the graduates will be able to preach clearly. Missionaries need to know hermeneutics and homiletics, but they also need to understand contextualized communication. That is, they need to learn to discern the worldview of the people group they are serving so that they can be sure that the people truly do understand the gospel message.

Robertson McQuilken, former president of Columbia International University, served as a missionary in Japan. He has stated that he preached eternal life to Japanese Buddhists for ten years and made only a few converts. Then he realized that the Japanese understood his preaching in a way he did not intend. A basic premise of Buddhism is that "life is suffering." Buddhists seek nirvana, which is the state of nonbeing or escape from life/suffering. Thus, when he preached that those who believe in Jesus would receive everlasting life, the Buddhists decoded his message as "believe in Jesus, and you will suffer forever." It is no wonder that few responded to his preaching. He reported that he then began preaching: Believe in Jesus, and you'll experience abundant life (John 10:10). When he emphasized abundant life, the Japanese began to respond to his message. Of course, later he helped them to understand the wonderful truth of eternal life (McQuilken 1995).

Bryan Galloway, a missions researcher in Asia, summarizes the importance of a people-group profile this way: "Applied ethnographic research helps missionaries not only understand the socio-cultural problems within a people, but also assists in solving those problems through the people's existing institutions and cultural forms. In other words, an applied ethnographic approach identifies and works through existing cultural bridges of the host people and culture. . . . [This] aids missionaries in bringing the gospel close to home for the host people and culture" (2006, 7).

HOW CAN I DEVELOP A PEOPLE-GROUP PROFILE?

There are several steps to follow in developing a profile of a people group (see the appendix for a useful guide). The first step is to understand the basics of ethnographic research. A number of guides are available that will help the novice (e.g., Agar 1996; Fetterman 1998; Spradley 1979; Wolcott 2008). The second step is to map the location of the people group. It is important to know where the people live. With a small, isolated people group, this may be simple; however, often the missionary researcher will discover that the people group is scattered. For example, a researcher in Kenya might discover that while most of his people live in their traditional tribal homeland, many have migrated to Nairobi to seek work.

The third step is to study the demographics of the people group. This involves determining the population of the people group. How many persons are there in this group? Of course, the number might vary from one hundred to one hundred million. The researcher will also need to discover the number of people in different age divisions. Some people groups are predominantly composed of young people under the age of twenty-one, while other people groups have an aging population with a significant percentage of elderly persons. The number of people in the different age divisions will affect the strategy and methods chosen by the missionary team. Population and demographic information is usually available on websites maintained by the United Nations (http://unstats.un.org/unsd/databases.htm), GapMinder (http://www.gapminder.org/), Ethnologue (http://www.ethnologue.com/), the World Christian Database (http://www.worldchristiandatabase.org/wcd/), the Mission Atlas Project (http://www.worldmap.org), and the Joshua Project (http://www.joshuaproject.net/).

The fourth step is to conduct the ethnographic study. Reading books and articles about the people and their culture provides a good starting point. The researcher will also need to conduct many interviews and conversations. Finding helpful cultural informants is usually a critical part of the process, for they are the ones who can both validate and correct what the researcher finds. It is important to note that many countries have strict regulations for researchers engaged in formal research. It is critical that missionaries be aware of any regulations regarding human research and follow them closely.

When interviewing, it is important to get a broad variety of samples, which means that the interviews should include persons of different age groups, gender, social status, and so on. A person of twenty might answer quite differently than a person eighty years old. A woman's perspective might be different from a man's. Urban dwellers may respond differently than those who live in rural settings. Soliciting a variety of perspectives will provide the researcher with a well-rounded profile. The researcher will also want to spend time observing the daily life of the people.

The ethnographic researcher will study the life cycle of the people, including their rituals and ceremonies, such as birth celebrations, coming-of-age initiations, weddings, and funerals. The researcher will need to observe the people's daily routine and schedule, including such things as household habits. Understanding the family life of the people is essential. The researcher will want to answer questions such as: What gender roles exist? How does this people group raise their children? How are the children enculturated at home and in school? What are the issues affecting families?

Another significant aspect of the culture is the economic profile of the people. If the group is small, are they rich or poor? Are they farmers or fishermen or miners? How is wealth distributed among the people? Do the farmers own their own land, or do they work land owned by others? Do the people have the potential for economic development? What are their felt needs in regard to economics? The larger the population of the group, the greater the diversity in these areas.

The missionary researcher will want to discover how the people prefer to learn. Are they oral learners, or do they prefer to learn through reading? What percentage of the people can read? Are there schools for the children? What percentage of the children go to school? How extensive and effective are the schools? What are common methods of teaching used in the schools or other educational institutions?

The researcher also will seek to understand how the people group governs itself. What type of national government does it have? What about local groups? How are communities governed? How are decisions made, and who makes them? Who are the influential people in the local community and in the larger society?

The people-group profile will include information about the religious beliefs of the people. What is the dominant religion in their culture? Are other religions represented? If so, what percentages of the population do they represent? What role does religion play in the lives of the people? What are the religious rituals performed by the people? What are their values? What are their core beliefs? What is their worldview? Who are the religious leaders, and what influence do they exert in the culture?

As the answers to these questions and many others are secured, the researcher will be developing the profile based on what is discovered. This type of information comes not only from the interviews and observations; it should also come from books, articles, websites, documentaries, newspaper articles, and so on. The profile may become a rather extensive document, but it is critical that the missionary strategist become as much of an expert as possible on the people group. The information contained in the people-group profile will prove invaluable in making decisions about strategy and methods.

HOW CAN A MISSIONARY USE THE PEOPLE-GROUP PROFILE?

The people-group profile is not an end in itself; rather, it is a means to an end. The end is the evangelization of the people group. The profile will inform the many strategic and methodological decisions that the missionary team must make. For example, distributing gospel tracts has been a popular and traditional method of evangelism in some Western settings; however, there is no point in distributing tracts to a people group composed of oral learners or where antagonism to this type of evangelism process already exists.

The information gained about the economic situation of the people group might point toward human needs ministries. Often ministering to a people's needs opens their hearts to hear the gospel message. I (Mark) made a weekend trip through forty-three villages in West Africa. In every village where our group stopped, the village leader asked for a water well. A church planting team working in that area ought to consider well drilling as a way to win the people's favor.

Determining the people group's worldview will help the missionaries understand how to explain the gospel clearly. Most adherents of the major world religions do not practice these religions "purely." Most adherents practice folk Islam, folk Hinduism, folk Buddhism, and so on. This represents a challenge for missionaries, who usually have studied world religions. They understand the classic forms of those religions from their textbooks, but the reality "on the ground" is quite different. Most people practice a combination of a world religion and animism. Their worldview may be more animistic than Islamic or Buddhist. Thus the missionaries must develop an approach that speaks to their syncretistic or blended religion. For example, one missions researcher in Thailand has speculated that the paucity of converts from Thai Buddhism to Christianity may be due to worldview issues (see, for example, Cohen 1990 and 1991). The missionaries have approached the Thai as Theravada Buddhists, but many of the people's religious practices are animistic, not Buddhist.

The people-group profile will provide valuable information for making strategic decisions. It will also help the missionaries come to love the people group more deeply.

CASE STUDY:
UNINTENDED CONSEQUENCES

A pioneer missionary to Africa discovered that many of the men who became Christians had multiple wives. The missionary believed this practice was sinful, so he insisted that the men send all their wives, other than the first, home to their families. The fathers of the women refused to take them back. Their fathers did not want to repay the bride prices they had received for their daughters. So the women were left with no homes and no means to support themselves and their children. As a result they turned to prostitution in order to support themselves.

REFLECTION AND DISCUSSION

- Did the missionary do the right thing? What are some alternative approaches that the missionary might have tried?
- How could ethnographic research have helped the missionary make the right decision?

18

Developing
a Communication Strategy

As mentioned in a previous chapter, communicating the gospel clearly is a key element in establishing an indigenous, contextualized church. If the people do not understand the gospel clearly, then their faith will be shallow at best. Further, the newly established church will rest on a flawed theological foundation. In this chapter we discuss the essential factors involved in communicating the gospel and biblical truth effectively.

FUNCTIONS OF COMMUNICATION

Communication fulfills many functions in a missionary's work. First, communication makes it possible to have meaningful contact with a people group. Learning the language of the people makes it possible to communicate with them, and communication is truly a dialogue, not just a monologue. Communicating provides a way to learn the culture. It is often said that language is the key that unlocks culture. While one can learn a lot about culture by reading and observing, communicating with the people—asking questions and understanding the answers—takes one much deeper into the culture. Of primary concern to a missionary, communication affords a way to convey a message. Missionaries believe they know the greatest message of all, and they want to convey that message clearly. Communication also provides a way to get feedback from the people group. A missionary can ascertain the clarity of the message he or she presents only by soliciting responses from the people.

NATURE OF COMMUNICATION

Communication can be verbal or nonverbal. A missionary can speak or write words that convey a message. The words, whether spoken or written, are symbols that encode a message. True communication is two-way—a dialogue, in other words. One party encodes information, and a second party decodes the information. This process sounds simple, but it is not. If you have ever asked a computer expert for instructions, you realize that decoding the information he or she provides is problematic at best. The problem comes when the second party, the recipient of the message, decodes the communicated message. The recipient decodes (interprets) those ideas according to her or his own culture, knowledge, and personal experience. Even if people speak the language well, they may not know the vocabulary used. This presents a problem in communicating both spiritual truth and computer instruction. Thus wise communicators anticipate how the recipients will decode the message, and the communicators will solicit a response. The response will reveal whether and to what degree the message was understood.

Missionaries face a daunting task because they are dealing with three cultures: the biblical culture, their own culture, and the recipients' culture. This situation is called the three-culture model. In missionary communication the culture of the Bible is filtered through the brain of the missionary, which is affected by the enculturation that the missionary received as a child. Then the missionary communicates the biblical message to the recipients in the people group. The recipients decode (interpret) the message according to their own culture. Therefore, an effective missionary communicator must understand three cultures: the biblical culture, the missionary's own culture, and the people group's culture (see Hesselgrave 1992).

Missionaries must also learn nonverbal communication. Nonverbal communication includes facial expressions, body posture, hand gestures, personal space (how close one stands), nodding/shaking the head, greetings, and touching. Often we make almost instantaneous decisions about people on the basis of nonverbal cues rather than verbal ones (Gladwell 2005). For example, Americans greet each other by shaking hands, while Koreans and Japanese bow. South Americans tend to stand closer when they converse than do North Americans. Some gestures that are innocent in one culture are obscene in another. This means missionaries must learn how to communicate, both verbally and nonverbally.

WHAT LANGUAGE SHOULD BE USED?

Choosing the language for communicating with a people group can be perplexing. For example, in the southern Philippines a missionary working with the Saragani Manobo people is forced to choose between three languages. Tagalog is the national language of the Philippines. Cebuano is the regional language spoken in the southern Philippines. Saragani Manobo is the local or tribal language. Of course, it would be helpful, even ideal, if the missionary learned all three. However, most on-location supervisors would be delighted if the missionary learned one language well. So what should the missionary do?

Most people respond better to the gospel when they hear it in their heart language, that is, the language learned from one's mother. The national language is not the heart language for many people. That would seem to indicate that the local language, Saragani Manobo, is the best choice here. However, Saragani Manobo is not widely spoken, and the missionary would find it difficult to communicate outside the tribal area. Some missionaries try to learn the national or regional language and then the local language. Thus, they learn two languages. Other missionaries learn the national or regional language at the survival level (enough to travel) but focus their intensive learning on the local language. When a couple or a team of missionaries is involved, they may choose to learn different languages, so that someone can function in every needed language. Veteran missionaries and supervisors connected locally can provide valuable advice about language learning.

Regardless of the choice made, language learning is a key to missionary effectiveness. Language competency goes a long way toward ensuring that the message is understood. Also, language proficiency helps one to understand the culture more fully. For example, in Cebuano one would never say, "Gibuak ko ang plato" (I broke the plate). Rather, a Cebuano would say, "Nakabuak ang plato" (The plate "happened" to break). This difference in expression reveals an important truth about accepting personal responsibility in the Cebuano culture. This, in turn, helps the missionary understand how the people understand sin and shame. So contextualization begins with learning the appropriate language well.

WHO SHOULD COMMUNICATE?

This question might seem frivolous. Should not the missionary communicate the gospel to the people group? The answer is it depends. Of course, missionaries should always seek to tell the good news of Jesus Christ; however, in some cultures various factors may affect who should communicate and to whom. For example, in many Muslim cultures it would not be appropriate for a male missionary to communicate the gospel to a woman or vice versa. So in those cultures, female missionaries witness to the women and male missionaries witness to the men.

In other cultures communication is governed by age. In some East African settings important information must be shared by someone of the same age group or an older person. In one instance a young male missionary witnessed again and again to the elders in a village in Kenya. They listened carefully to his messages, but they did not respond. His father, a retired pastor with white hair, came to visit, and the missionary shared his frustration. The son said, "Would you help me to witness to them?" "Sure," replied his father, and they traveled to the village. The old pastor shared the gospel with the village elders, and the son translated the message. At the conclusion of the message all the elders trusted Christ for salvation. The young missionary asked, "I told you this message many times. Why did you believe the message now?" The elders replied, "You are not old enough to tell us this truth." Similarly, a field leader in northern Africa bemoaned the fact that all his missionaries were young. He said, "If I had older missionaries, they would get more respect and more would believe in Christ. However, life is so hard here that the missionaries do not stay long enough to get gray hair." So gender and age can affect communication, depending on the culture.

In cultures where there is enmity or distrust of Westerners, it may be advantageous for respected indigenes to do most of the witnessing. In this way the gospel and the church will not seem foreign. Of course, the hard part for a pioneer missionary is winning and training respected insiders to do the witnessing.

Another answer to the question of who should communicate is "someone who is trusted." Before people will believe any message, they must trust the person who delivers it. For example, a used-car salesman might say, "This car was owned by a little old lady who only drove it to church on Sundays." Would you believe what he said? Most likely you would not, because used-car salesmen have a reputation in the United States for not being truthful. Of concern for us is that missionaries encourage people to change their lives radically. Why should people believe their message?

In order to become agents of spiritual change, missionaries must build trust among their people group. This is one reason why ministering to human needs can enhance evangelism. Demonstrating love and concern for the people and their needs is embedded in the command to love our neighbors as we love ourselves. This type of love builds trust. Additionally, missionaries should endeavor to build trust among their people by displaying personal virtues such as humility, teachability, availability, generosity, sensitivity, and trustworthiness—but do so in light of how those traits are demonstrated in the local setting. By loving people unconditionally and becoming fluent as a bicultural person, we become believable. One result is that the gospel we live out in front of our neighbors will also become believable.

HOW TO COMMUNICATE?

As the missionary develops the people-group profile, much attention will be given to patterns of communication. How do the people communicate with one another? How do they pass on their cultural heritage to the younger generation? How do schoolteachers present their lessons? How do these people prefer to learn? The answers to these questions will help the missionary choose effective means of communication with the people group.

Most Western missionaries are comfortable with formal communication. Formal communication includes sermons and lectures. In Bible college or seminary the professor lectures, while the students listen attentively (hopefully) and take notes. In church services found in many Western settings, the pastor preaches while the people sit quietly and listen. Missionaries who come from these types of churches are very familiar with this manner of communicating spiritual truth, and their natural tendency is to employ this type of one-way formal communication in their ministries.

Although formal communication makes it possible to convey large amounts of cognitive knowledge, this communication style rarely convinces people to change. Studies show that people remember only 5 to 10 percent of what they hear in a sermon or a lecture. Lack of feedback is a problem with this approach. This approach also may not be familiar or comfortable for the people in a particular culture.

For example, Adoniram Judson preached publicly in Burma for six years with no response. Then he began to observe how the Buddhist monks taught the people. They often sat in open-air pavilions, called *zayats*, where they sat on mats and taught the Burmese conversationally. So Judson built a *zayat* and began sitting in it for several hours each day. The people began to stop by to talk, and within one year he had baptized nineteen converts (Judson 1883). A locally contextualized approach to communication proved much more effective than the method that Judson had learned while growing up.

In recent years researchers have determined that at least 60 percent of the world's population learns orally (see, e.g., http://www.oralbible.com

/oral-learning/statistics-facts). This means that they acquire knowledge by hearing rather than by reading. This not only affects their modes of learning; it also affects their ways of thinking. Research into orality has prompted missionaries to develop oral means of communicating the gospel. This involves communicating the message of the Bible through Bible stories. One approach based on this methodology is chronological Bible storying (https://www.oralitystrategies .org/strategies.cfm?id=1), which is sometimes referred to as Bible storying.

As a whole, the Bible is roughly 75 percent narrative (stories), so the Bible lends itself to this approach. Typically, missionaries who use the chronological Bible storytelling approach begin with the story of creation and teach their way through the Bible until they end with the ascension of Jesus. The number of stories used varies from missionary to missionary, ranging from 30 to 150. One advantage of storying the entire Bible is that the hearers can understand God's whole plan of salvation. Learning about the Passover lamb and the sacrificial system helps them to understand Jesus's identity as the Lamb of God. Storying has proved effective throughout the world. All societies use stories to pass on their cultural traditions to the younger generations, so the story approach is familiar and comfortable (see Steffen 1996 for a helpful introduction to orality and Bible storying).

Missionaries use other culturally accepted methods to convey the gospel. In the Arabic language poetry is important; thus poetry can be used effectively in Arabic cultures. In the southern Sudan the missionaries use dramas to present Bible stories to the Denka tribe. Songs are used all over the world to communicate spiritual truth. In Bali (Indonesia) Christians tell stories by means of stylized dances. One missionary organized a Christian dance troupe that developed a set of Bible story dances. This method proved quite popular throughout Indonesia.

Protestant missionaries have used mass media since the days of William Carey. Carey and his associates translated the Bible and gospel tracts into many Indian languages and distributed the materials as widely as possible. Since the early twentieth century missionaries have used radio, television, films, cassette tapes, CDs, DVDs, MP3s, satellite broadcasts, and the internet to communicate the gospel. Mass media has the advantage of presenting information to many people at a minimal cost per person.

However, those using mass media always struggle with the problem of feedback. It is hard to determine who is receiving the communication and what impact it has had. Another issue in the use of mass media is that it typically employs a Western format with programs done in a Western way. Wise missionary communicators will seek ways in which to contextualize the programs to enhance their appeal. For example, years ago in the Philippines the Southern

Baptist Foreign Mission Board sponsored a radio program that was broadcast throughout the country. The program featured a choir that sang hymns translated into the national language and a sermon in the national language. At the end of the program listeners were encouraged to write to request a Bible correspondence course or to submit their questions and concerns.

This format did elicit some response; however, a revised format proved more effective. The media team observed that Filipinos love to listen to radio soap operas. So it hired writers and actors to develop and present a Christian soap opera. This format became quite popular, and responses increased tenfold. Similarly, broadcasts produced in the Middle East in a variety of local languages and sent via satellite (Sat-7; http://www.sat7.org) have been very effective in communicating Christ and Christian issues to audiences in Muslim settings.

Mass media is a good way to sow gospel seeds and to make initial contact with people; however, mass media alone will seldom bring about spiritual change. Eventually someone will need to deal with the respondent personally. Thankfully, this now can be either in person or via email, social media, Skype, texting, or other internet-based communication programs.

COMMUNICATION CONSIDERATIONS

Communication is essential to the missionary task. Many factors influence effective communication as explained in this chapter. Here are some pointers for better communication:

1. *The message is affected by the communicator's image.* In communication perception is reality; that is, people act according to what they perceive to be true. If people believe Sudso is the best laundry detergent, they will buy Sudso, regardless of its true quality. In the same way, if the people in your people group have a negative perception of Westerners, that will affect your communication negatively, regardless of your love and concern for them.

2. *Communication is affected by the personal characteristics of the communicator.* If the missionary learns the language well, becomes bicultural, and earns the trust of the people, they are more likely to believe the gospel message.

3. *The use of technology in communication may prove to be a help or a hindrance.*

4. *The "who" and "how" of communication are important.* Learning the worldview of the people is essential, but understanding their communication patterns and learning styles is also important (D. K. Smith 1992, 18).

CASE STUDY:
WHAT MESSAGE DID THEY RECEIVE?

A missionary team traveled to a remote village in Africa to show the "Jesus" film. The team members set up their electrical generator and projector, and they strung up a white sheet to serve as a screen. The villagers had never seen a movie before, and they watched the film with keen attention. When the movie ended, the headman of the village said, "We want you to stay here in our village. You are the most powerful sorcerers we have ever met. No other sorcerer can make people walk and talk on a cloth."

REFLECTION AND DISCUSSION

- Where did the missionaries go wrong?
- What might they have done differently?

19

Discerning Receptivity

The world is a very big place. There are seven billion people alive today. Four billion of those people are not followers of Jesus, and two billion of those have never even heard about Jesus. Even in places such as the New England area of the United States, it is common to find entire states where evangelicals represent only 3 percent of the population (see Payne 2010). Need appears to be omnipresent. Also, scattered across this vast world are people who are very receptive to the gospel, some apathetic, and others extremely hostile to this truth.

Part of conducting research and developing a people-group profile involves ascertaining both a people's receptivity level to the gospel and the need for new missionary labors among those people. Both are critical in developing wise strategies. Our ability to discern receptivity is so important that we devote two chapters to exploring the issues involved. In this chapter, we discuss the importance of discerning receptivity.

WHAT IS RECEPTIVITY?

While the Scriptures are clear that everyone is an enemy toward God when they are dead in their sin (Eph. 2:5), not everyone responds to the gospel in the same way. Some unbelievers become angry when confronted with the message of God's love. Others reveal a lackadaisical attitude. But others are very receptive to the message and are open to hearing more. This matter is noted both in the Scriptures and throughout history. McGavran has observed: "The common people, the Gospels tell us, received our Lord's message better than the Pharisees and Sadducees. For the first three decades of the Christian era, the Jews responded far more than the Gentiles. When Judea had been Christian for a hundred years, Philistia on one side and Arabia on the other still remained solidly pagan" (1970, 217).

Receptivity is a description of the responses of individuals, peoples, and societies to the gospel message when they are confronted with this truth through a contextually appropriate method and in a way they can understand. The wise strategist takes receptivity into consideration when planning mission strategy for reaching a region or a people.

Several times a year my family and I (J. D.) travel a few miles from our home to an orchard to pick strawberries, apples, and pumpkins. We are not farmers and therefore have no idea when we need to show up at the orchard to harvest some of the crops. Because of our ignorance, every year we wait for the owners of the orchard to send us a calendar informing us when the strawberries, apples, and pumpkins are ripe and ready.

Drawing from this agricultural (and biblical, see John 4:35) metaphor, missiologists recognize the connection to the principle of receptivity. Like some ripe orchards, some people are ready to repent and place their faith in Jesus. More resistant people are akin to the apples that are still green. Other peoples are more apathetic to the gospel but may be ripening to it.

THE IMPORTANCE OF RECEPTIVITY

There are several reasons why this principle is critical to kingdom work. Unfortunately, many strategists and missionaries do not take it into consideration. The following are five reasons for your consideration.

Biblical Example

Throughout the New Testament both Jesus and the apostolic church allowed the principle of receptivity to influence their approaches to reaching people with the gospel (Matt. 10:1–15; Mark 6:7–13; Luke 9:1–6; 10:1–12; Acts 13:44–52; 14:1–7; 16:38–40; 18:1–8).

Time Is Short

There is both a personal and a cosmic eschatology that strategists must keep in mind. On the personal level, people do not live forever and need to hear the gospel. On the cosmic level, strategy is always to be developed in light of the imminent return of Jesus. The healthy and rapid dissemination of the gospel is to be taken into consideration.

Results in Rapid Growth

Missionaries will see receptive peoples come into the kingdom and churches multiplied among them at a much faster rate than is the case with nonreceptive peoples. While this fact is obvious, it is not always considered by many strategists and teams.

Limited Resources

Teams do not have an unlimited amount of time, money, and people to carry out the task that the Lord has set before them. Therefore, strategists should recognize that generally speaking, the best place to invest their God-given resources is among those peoples and population segments that are the most receptive to the gospel message.

Wisdom Points in This Direction

Wise strategists will develop plans that give priority to the most receptive peoples. God-given wisdom shouts aloud that efforts and energies should go to those asking the Philippian jailer's question (Acts 16:30) rather than to those who stuff their ears to avoid hearing about Jesus. This only makes sense.

ABUSES OF THE PRINCIPLE

The obvious abuse of the principle of receptivity is that it provides an excuse to withhold the gospel from resistant or apathetic groups. For example, George Harper, attempting to summarize the problem, notes that "gauging a group's 'receptivity' is basic to determining how, or even if, it ought to be approached with the gospel. Peoples who are judged to be stubbornly resistant to the gospel must be by-passed" (1982, 205).

While Harper's concern is a legitimate one, any such practice reveals disobedience to the command of Jesus. We are to take the gospel to all peoples, receptive and hostile. The church is to preach the good news to everyone regardless of his or her response to this great hope. No one is to be passed over with the gospel message. The church is to preach the gospel to all nations. So how do we avoid advocating the neglect of unreceptive peoples when applying this principle?

In regard to strategy, utilizing the principle affects prioritization and resource allocation. Proper use does not support avoiding the unreceptive or not sending

177

teams to serve among them. Rather, it guides strategists in discerning how much of their resources should be placed in what areas. For example, McGavran noted his concern with flooding unreceptive peoples with missionaries: "No one should conclude that if receptivity is low, the Church should withdraw mission. Correct policy is to occupy fields of low receptivity lightly. . . . But they should not be heavily occupied lest, fearing that they will be swamped by Christians, they become ever more resistant" (McGavran 1990, 191).

The light occupancy approach is a wise strategic decision. In a time when multitudes are very open to the gospel while others are antagonistic to such truth, strategy should involve concentrating resources among the most receptive and sending fewer resources to the least receptive.

Teams that serve among the least receptive should stay in good communication with those in the more receptive areas for at least two reasons. First, as they share the gospel, they need to discern if the people are becoming more receptive to the truth. And second, as the people become more receptive, the teams need to share this information with those in the more receptive areas, requesting additional teams to be sent to their areas. Another strategic matter in regard to this principle is that by the time resistant fields become ripe, those who have been working in the ripe fields will already have new workers equipped and prepared to be sent to the ripening fields to serve.

TOOLS TO ASSIST

Receptivity is a nonconcrete reality. While the manifestation of receptivity levels can be observed in the ways people respond to the gospel, receptivity itself cannot be studied as if it could be placed inside a test tube. Since the 1970s three scales have been developed to assist in quantifying receptivity. Although the following can be helpful to the strategist, they should not be considered a substitute for prayer and the leading of the Holy Spirit. Rather, they are simply resources to assist in helping understand the reality of an ethereal subject such as receptivity.

Resistance-Receptivity Scale

Missiologists have for years attempted to discern the general receptivity levels of peoples. While such attempts are only broad statements describing the peoples, and therefore it should not be assumed that everyone in the group is at the same point of receptivity, they have been helpful in understanding how to develop mission strategies. One of the first attempts to visually describe resistance and receptivity was developed by McGavran in his book

Understanding Church Growth (1970, 228). A variation of his original scale is shown below (fig. 19.1). Individuals and peoples falling at letter A on the scale would be very receptive to the good news, while those at letter E would be very resistant and maybe even hostile to the message.

FIGURE 19.1: RESISTANCE-RECEPTIVITY SCALE

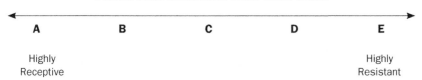

The practical reality of such a scale is that it reminds the strategist of the importance of contextualized methods (see chap. 15). Almost any method will work to reach those at letter A. However, almost any method will not be effective in reaching those at letter E. The wise use of methods is more critical when it comes to reaching peoples found at letters B, C, and D. Although the Lord can work through even the worst of methods, generally a bad method hinders missionary work.

Commenting on the relationship of methods to discerning receptivity, Harper makes a very important observation, one that should cause strategists to take caution. He writes, "Since others' ability to respond is thus unavoidably bound up with our facility of communication . . . our judgment of a group's resistance or receptivity will be as much of a function of how we have expressed the message as of how they have responded to it." In other words, the *means* by which missionaries communicate the gospel and live among the people has a significant effect on how the missionaries understand the people's attitude toward the gospel. Harper continues, "When a culture once fails to respond to pioneer missionaries' first presentations of the gospel, no matter how socially incomprehensible and poorly enculturated the preaching may be, it draws to itself the label of resistant. Subsequently, resources and personnel will be channeled away from these people to more immediately promising groups" (1982, 208).

To avoid potential problems when discerning receptivity, the team needs to study prayerfully the people and then design its methods of engagement accordingly (methods are discussed further in chap. 25). This cultural exegesis project also demands that the members of the team be aware of their own cultures and where their worldviews and lifestyles may clash with those of the people; such awareness will help alleviate the possible problems noted by Harper and will assist them in discerning an effective communication strategy (see chap. 18).

Engel Scale

Several decades ago James Engel developed a scale (see fig. 19.2) to assist others in developing a better comprehension of where a people's understanding can be found and to better communicate the gospel to them. This scale became known as the Engel Scale and has been used by many researchers over the years. This scale assists the evangelist in knowing where best to begin when sharing the gospel with someone. While knowledge of the facts about the gospel does not always have a positive correlation with receptivity (e.g., someone can know much about the gospel and have a negative receptivity to it), the Engel Scale—as will be seen with the next tool—provides a valuable contribution to having a better understanding of a particular individual or people.

FIGURE 19.2: THE ENGEL SCALE

- –8 Awareness of a supreme being, but no effective knowledge of the gospel
- –7 Initial awareness of the gospel
- –6 Awareness of the fundamentals of the gospel
- –5 Grasp of the implications of the gospel
- –4 Positive attitude toward the gospel
- –3 Personal problem recognition
- –2 Decision to act
- –1 Repentance and faith in Christ
- 0 New believer
- +1 Post-decision evaluation
- +2 Incorporated into the body
- +3 A lifetime of conceptual and behavioral growth in Christ

We encourage you as you conduct your research to identify where the people or population segment among whom you are working can be found on this scale. It should be recognized that people do not generally progress linearly through each step over a period of time moving toward zero. Sometimes they seem to skip numbers, for the Lord can bring a people from no awareness of the gospel to repentance and faith in one gospel presentation. The Engel Scale is a tool to help the strategist know how to develop strategy and methods to reach the people.

Søgaard Scale

Viggo Søgaard developed a two-dimensional scale that attempts to wed together the cognitive and the affective characteristics of a people. A variation of his scale is found in figure 19.3. Søgaard eventually combined the two previously mentioned scales to produce a tool through which he attempted to portray *both* receptivity (Receptivity-Resistance Scale) and knowledge of the gospel (Engel Scale). The result was the Søgaard Scale (fig. 19.3). This tool is valuable because it assists strategists in recognizing that just because someone may know much about the gospel does not mean that that person will have a favorable attitude.

FIGURE 19.3: SØGAARD SCALE

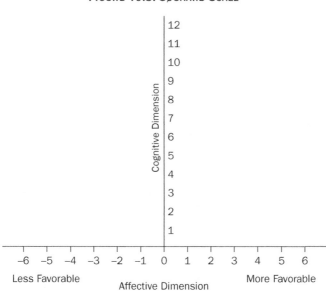

The cognitive (vertical) axis reveals the estimated general knowledge of the people when it comes to the gospel. The higher the number, the greater the knowledge. After developing a thorough understanding of the people (see chap. 17), strategists should estimate the approximate value on the cognitive axis, keeping in mind that such is a subjective experience.

In addition to plotting the gospel knowledge of the people, the strategist should also estimate the attitude of the people to the gospel and plot this on the horizontal axis. The end result is a single plot representing the general knowledge and affections toward the gospel.

Dayton and Fraser offer a helpful commentary on the use of this tool that reveals the practical outworking of Søgaard's work. They write:

> On the basis of research, we can locate individuals and even groups of people on this graph. Differences of awareness and attitude can then become the basis for selecting various sorts of methods and approaches. If the task is to raise the

---

Sidebar 19.1
Assessing Receptivity in Your Area

The following activity is designed to assist you and your team to better understand the receptivity levels in the general community where you live or among a particular people. Use the following questions as a guide to assist in your strategy and method development.

1. Draw a Resistance-Receptivity Scale for the people. Where do they fall on the scale? How will this location affect your strategy and methods of evangelism?
2. Estimate the general location of the people on the Engel Scale. How does their level of knowledge affect your strategy?
3. Chart the location of the people in your setting on the Søgaard Scale.

After completing 1–3, consider the following:

1. What can you and your team do to help move your people from their present understanding of the gospel to a full knowledge of the truth of the gospel? What needs to happen before such movement will take place? What are three methods that are the most likely to result in the accomplishment of such movement?
2. What can you and your team do to help move your people from their present attitude toward the gospel to a more positive attitude toward the gospel? What are three methods worth undertaking to accomplish such movement?

---

awareness of a people who know next to nothing about Christ and the gospel, then a method that stresses the conveying of the gospel information is strategic. If the task is to change a negative or indifferent attitude among people who know the basics of the gospel, then a method that focuses on attitude change is strategic. (1990, 116)

Discerning Receptivity

McGavran has written, "An essential task is to discern receptivity and—when this is seen—to adjust methods, institutions, and personnel until the receptive are becoming Christians and reaching out to win their fellows to eternal life" (cited in Dayton and Fraser 1990, 232). Therefore, the obvious question for the strategist is, "How does one determine whether an individual or a people is receptive?" The simple answer to this question is to share the gospel with them in a contextualized way and note their response. McGavran elaborates:

Are groups of persons becoming Christians? As Jesus Christ is proclaimed to this population and His obedient servants witness to Him, do individuals, families, and chains of families come to faith in Him? Are churches being formed? Is any denomination working in similar peoples planting self-propagating congregations? If the answers are in the affirmative, the homogeneous unit concerned is receptive. (cited in Dayton and Fraser 1990, 228)

So while there is no computer program that can tell strategists where the receptive people are found, general assumptions based on field research can be made. As Rick Warren notes, people tend to be more receptive when they are under tension and in transition (1995). Although these are very broad categories, they include times when people experience persecution, government oppression, famine, war, death, marriage, birth, migration, a change of employment, moving to college, and illness. If the opportunity will allow for the development of a partnership with churches in the area, then such believers should be consulted for wisdom related to receptivity levels among the people group.

Wagner adds that the common, working-class people and the poor tend to be more receptive to the gospel (1989, 84). Robert E. Logan and Neil Cole note that receptive people tend to fall into six categories:

- Bad people (Luke 5:32)
- Those in poverty (James 2:5)
- Young people (Matt. 18:3)
- Those searching for God through the occult and other religions (Matt. 7:7)
- The uneducated and the powerless (1 Cor. 1:27)
- Those seen as insignificant and discriminated against (1 Cor. 1:28–29) (2005, 47)

Dayton and Fraser attribute the receptivity level of a people to several variables:

1. The degree to which a people is satisfied with its present fate in life
2. The degree to which the rest of the people's lives are changing
3. The cultural sensitivity of the gospel presentation
4. The agent of the good news
5. The relative fit between the gospel and the cultural patterns that are presently dominant in a social group (1990, 179)

THE PRACTICAL IMPORTANCE OF THE PRINCIPLE

Earlier we wrote that among the highly receptive almost any method will work to bring people into the kingdom—even methods that lack healthy contextualization. And we noted that among the most resistant, even the most contextualized methods will not work well. Teams that are called to serve in one of these two settings generally have a very clear understanding of the challenges of the task set before them. The strategy development process is less complicated for them.

The discerning of receptivity is more important for a team that is not working among a people found at A or E on the Resistant-Receptivity Scale (fig. 19.1). When receptivity levels fall in this range, the Engel Scale and the Søgaard Scale become even more helpful. Commenting on this matter, Dayton and Fraser write:

> It is in the middle range that strategy differences can make substantial differences in the results. With good strategy, a large hearing for the gospel is possible whereas a poor or weak strategy simply will not break through the indifference or neutrality to stir up the desire for a better way of life. A difference in approach, or in the agent who attempts evangelization, or in the tradition of Christian piety, can produce either a large, virile Church or a small, struggling body. (1990, 180)

CONCLUSION

McGavran writes,

> The receptivity or responsiveness of individuals waxes and wanes. No one person is equally ready at all times to follow "the Way." . . . Peoples and societies also vary in responsiveness. Whole segments of mankind resist the Gospel for periods—often very long periods—and then ripen to the Good News. . . . One thing is clear, receptivity wanes as often as it waxes. Like the tide, it comes in and goes out. Unlike the tide, no one can guarantee when it goes out that it will soon come back again. (1970, 216–18)

The church is called to preach the gospel to all peoples, regardless of their receptivity to the message. Strategy must not block the gospel from being presented to anyone. However, strategy does enable the church to be a wise steward with the limited resources at its disposal and helps us to ask, "Where is the tide already coming in so that we will know where to begin?" *Therefore, unless a team is specifically called by God to a resistant people, it should begin where the Holy Spirit has been working to ripen the field for the harvest.*

CASE STUDY: GUJARATI HINDUS IN THE UNITED KINGDOM

In the following account David J. Reynolds shares from his experience of ascertaining receptivity among a certain Hindu group in the United Kingdom.

What work has been done so far among the Gujaratis has been almost exclusively among the majority Hindu population. This almost certainly is due to the fact that the Hindu is more outgoing than the Muslim.

Generally the Hindu is quite prepared to make friends and to invite others into his house. Friendship is certainly the start. Language workers have a particular entrée, which gives them a privileged position as well as a special responsibility.

Experience over the past six years shows, however, that the receptivity of the average Gujarati Hindu adult is zero. They have little or no awareness of Christianity, and among those who have, few other than the youngsters have any knowledge of the fundamentals of the gospel. Many equate the lower moral standards and crime prevalent today with "Christian" England and are obviously reluctant to associate with this.

Receptivity among youngsters is greater. There is the natural rebellion of youth against parental standards. Even today, however, the pressures are for youngsters to conform to the established social pattern. For a teenager to become a Christian can mean being thrown out of the house and totally cut off by the parents. For a younger person it can mean being kept indoors, or being forced to Hindu temple worship. Naturally if a "friendship" contact has already been initiated with the parents, they are more likely to allow their children to attend Sunday school, youth clubs, etc.

Over the next few years the biggest problem to be faced concerning receptivity is the question of race relations. The National Front is undoubtedly causing grave concern to all coloured immigrant groups and as a result they are becoming more inward looking and less receptive to "outsiders." (1978, 135–36)

REFLECTION AND DISCUSSION

- If you were serving among the Gujarati in England and Wales, what approaches would you use to connect with them and share the gospel?
- Why do you think there is a higher receptivity level among the younger generations?
- What social factors could cause this level to increase or decrease?

20

Discerning Need

It is important for strategists to think in terms of both receptivity and need. Together they provide a more accurate picture of reality and assist in making wise strategic decisions. Examining receptivity alone could result in sending teams into areas where there are already numerous vibrant and faithful churches, while gospel-barren fields remain without seed. However, only taking need into consideration could result in valuable resources being poured into hostile areas, while highly receptive areas go untouched with the gospel.

MISSIOLOGICAL TRIAGE IS NECESSARY FOR STRATEGY DEVELOPMENT

Anywhere people are without Jesus is a needy place for the gospel. But the world is a big place. So where do teams begin? Just as an emergency room has a system of triage to determine prioritization of treatment, understanding receptivity and need enables us to perform a metaphorical "missiological triage." In this chapter we address the importance of the principle of need and then show the relationship of both receptivity and need to strategy development while offering a set of guidelines to determine priority.

Evangelical Concentrations

The first matter that relates to need is the percentage of evangelicals found among the people. While there are devoted followers of Jesus who do not consider themselves to be evangelicals (and also evangelicals who are not followers of Jesus), missiologists have often used evangelicals as a benchmark to determine the number of followers of Jesus among a people. Since the accepted definition of an evangelical clearly includes one who has experienced a regenerative work of the Spirit, we advocate continuing this practice for the sake of estimation. With seven billion people in the world, a benchmark is needed. Strategists should seek to determine the number and percentage of

---

SIDEBAR 20.1
WHY 20 PERCENT?

In the following excerpt, Dayton and Fraser share (1) the definition of an unreached people group commonly held in the late 1970s and (2) why they advocate that 10 to 20 percent of the people need to be practicing Christians.

> What is an *unreached* people? The Strategy Working Group defines it as follows: "An unreached people is a group that is less than 20 percent *practicing* Christians."
> What do we mean by "practicing Christians"? How Christians will work out their religion in different places of the world will differ tremendously. The gospel has a marvelous ability to impregnate a culture and modify its Christian expression. Committed Christians within a particular group will know quite easily who are the practicing Christians and who are not.
> Why 20 percent? Why not 50 percent or 3 percent? The answer lies in our understanding of the diffusion of new ideas within a group. Because the group we are describing has internal consistency, it can be assumed that once an idea has taken hold in a major portion of the group,

the group has the ability to diffuse the idea within itself. Observation and research has shown that when approximately 10 or 20 percent of the people within a group have accepted an idea or a new religion, they have the ability to evangelize the rest of the group. When there are no Christians within a group, someone from the outside—a missionary—must enter the group with the Good News. Initially the number of outsiders will increase, but as the group grows, the number of outsiders should decrease. When the number of practicing Christians reaches 20 percent, these outsiders are no longer needed to reach the group. (1980, 38)

REFLECTION AND DISCUSSION

- Do you agree with this definition of an unreached people group? Why or why not?
- Why do you think most mission societies and agencies today subscribe to a much lower percentage (i.e., 2 percent) than the originally suggested 10 to 20 percent?

evangelicals living among the people or population segment they are attempting to reach. Some denominations and groups have already collected this information. However, some teams may have to conduct their own research to get an estimated number (see chap. 16). Whenever possible, it is best to partner with local believers to determine the field-based evangelical realities in the area.

But what constitutes an appropriate evangelical concentration? In other words, when is a people or population segment considered "reached"? It must be noted that all such numbers have no biblical support. Again, as long as there are individuals who are not followers of Jesus, there is a need for evangelism to take place in that area. Yet in light of the billions of people who do not know Jesus, there must be some guideline to assist in developing global strategies.

The Strategy Working Group that was developed following the International Congress on World Evangelization (Lausanne, 1974) provided a statistical definition of an unreached people as "a group that is less than 20 percent *practicing* Christians" (Dayton and Fraser 1980, 38). Later, less emphasis was placed on 20 percent and more on the people group having a viable church that could carry out the work of the Great Commission. Of course, the logical question should then be, "Why 20 percent?" To answer that question, we must turn our attention to the research of Everett M. Rogers.

In his renowned work *Diffusion of Innovations* (2003), Rogers explains that when a new idea, product, or concept is introduced into a society, the spread, or diffusion, of that knowledge occurs rapidly and throughout the society when 10 to 20 percent of the population has embraced it. Although Rogers's initial work was conducted in the field of agriculture, missiologists in the 1970s and 1980s applied his findings to the dissemination of the gospel across a people group.

Over time missiologists lowered this percentage. Most recently, missiologists consider a people *reached* whenever the evangelical percentage is at 2 percent, with at least 5 percent of the overall population considering themselves Christian. This has impacted agency thinking, as seen, for example, in the International Mission Board. It considers an *unreached* people group as having an evangelical population of less than 2 percent, without any consideration given to the percentage of those in the overall population who claim to be adherents to Christianity (http://imb.org/globalresearch/sge_terms.asp).

It must be clearly noted, once again, *that such numbers do not rely on biblical support.* The Spirit of the Lord is *not limited to percentages* of evangelicals among a people. When we think about making disciples of all the peoples of the world, it is helpful to have a goal in mind to assist in our kingdom labors. While we clearly recognize that in certain parts of the world even a 2 percent evangelical population is a lofty goal, the diffusion of innovation theory may offer strategists a helpful target for consideration. For this reason we conclude that a 10 percent evangelical concentration should be taken into consideration with strategy development.

Church-to-Population Ratios

Another factor to assist in determining the neediness of a people or area is the ratio of evangelical churches to the overall population, with the churches being understood as those that are intentionally engaged in reaching and teaching others the truth of God's Word. This matter of concern involves both the accessibility of the gospel to the unreached people and their knowledge of the gospel message. The more churches present, the greater the possibility that unbelievers have ready access to a proper biblical understanding of truth.

Again, having been influenced by Rogers's research on the diffusion of information across a people, the following points are offered as guides when developing mission strategy to reach an area. The Discipling a Whole Nation Movement (DAWN) advocates at least one intentionally evangelistic church for every 1,000 to 1,500 people in urban contexts and one such church for every 400 to 600 people in rural areas (Montgomery 1989, 77). To keep matters simple, the ratio we suggest here is one evangelical church for every 1,000 people in the urban environments, with each church ideally having 100 members. In rural contexts the ratio should consist of one evangelical church for every 500 people, with each church consisting of fifty members. Again, while we clearly recognize that in certain parts of the world such figures will be difficult to consider strategically, we offer these as guidelines.

RECEPTIVITY-NEED ANALYSIS GUIDELINE

Throughout the previous chapter and this one, we have emphasized that both receptivity and need should be considered in strategic planning. In my (J. D.) book *Discovering Church Planting: An Introduction to the Whats, Whys, and Hows of Global Church Planting*, I developed the following guideline to assist in developing strategy.

Strategists should consider giving priority to begin their work in areas and among people that can be categorized in quadrant A, followed by quadrant B. Quadrant A consists of peoples or areas that have a high receptivity to the gospel, a very low percentage of evangelicals, *and* few faithful evangelical churches. Quadrant B is composed of peoples or areas where there are few evangelicals and such churches *and* the receptivity is not very high. In Quadrant C a strategist would find a high percentage of evangelicals and churches *and* a high receptivity to the gospel. This area received a tertiary priority ranking

FIGURE 20.1: RECEPTIVITY-NEED ANALYSIS GUIDELINE

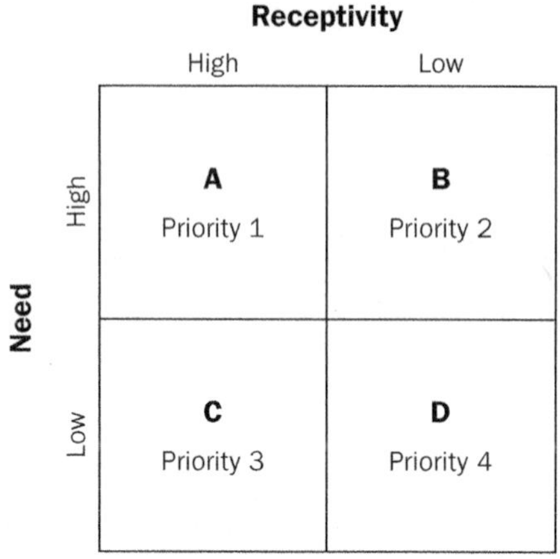

Receptivity

	High	Low
High	**A** Priority 1	**B** Priority 2
Low	**C** Priority 3	**D** Priority 4

(Vertical axis label: **Need**)

because the large numbers of evangelicals are already present. Though many people are highly receptive to the gospel, this quadrant already has a sufficient number of evangelical churches present to reach and teach the people coming into the kingdom. Quadrant D represents the lowest people or area of priority. Here one would find a large number of evangelicals and churches *and* a low level of receptivity to the gospel. If the people's receptivity increased, there would already be enough evangelical churches present to reach them.

It should also be noted that each quadrant is a broad generalization of a people, city, village, or society. Thus, within each quadrant there is a *range of receptivity levels* and *areas of need* (which includes the people's access to and knowledge of the gospel). Therefore, regardless of the quadrant in which the team labors, it would be wise to apply the Resistant-Receptivity Scale, the Engel Scale, and the Søgaard Scale—as discussed in chapter 19—to the different peoples and population segments across the quadrant.

For example, while Quadrant B is an area of high need but low receptivity, the team should not assume that all peoples in such an area are of the same receptivity level and have the same amount of need and equivalent knowledge about the gospel. A team developing a strategy to reach such an area should seek to discern settings where there are the people who are *more* receptive to the gospel than average as well as those with the greatest need.

GUIDELINES FOR KNOWING WHERE TO BEGIN

We conclude this chapter with three important starting points for developing mission strategy.

Great Commission

First, a team must assume the Great Commission. Jesus gave his followers this great mandate. While the account in Matthew 28:18–20 is generally the most popular version, variations are given in Luke (24:45–47), John (20:21–23), Acts (1:8), and in the disputed section of Mark (16:15). The command to make disciples comes with the expectation that the church will evangelize people, baptize them, and teach others to obey the commands of Jesus. Like all commands it comes with the expectation that there will be results. As a result the *general* response of mission teams should be to develop strategies that seek to reach the largest number of people in the shortest possible time, while remaining *absolutely* faithful to the biblical principles for healthy evangelism and discipleship.

Calling

The second guideline the team members must consider is that of God's calling on their lives. Some people have a very clear and distinct call to a particular people and place. For example, we read of such callings in the Scriptures when we look at the lives of Abram, Jonah, Jeremiah, and the other prophets. Our Lord does call some to the hard and nonreceptive soils. Some people *must* be called to serve as the Ezekiels, Jeremiahs, Adoniram Judsons, and William Careys, leaving behind few disciples at the conclusion of their ministries. If missionaries have received a call to a hard soil, then they *must* be faithful to God's calling on their lives. For them to avoid the call to the nonreceptive area and venture to the most receptive, resulting in a great ingathering into the kingdom, is a sinful thing and should be avoided. *The calling to a nonreceptive soil is just as legitimate, honorable, and important as the calling to serve among a highly receptive people.* Therefore, we must emphasize that the church should *never* discourage people from going to the nonreceptive people but should always challenge its members to go and to look for the most needy and most receptive even among the least receptive.

Think Receptivity and Need

If the team has not received a specific calling to a hard-soil area, then we suggest that it consider beginning to plan its mission strategy among Quadrant A in figure 20.1. Its labor would be among those peoples and population segments that are very receptive to the gospel but where few evangelical churches are found.

CONCLUSION

The world is a big place with a large number of people. While the size of the planet will not increase, its population is expected to grow. Knowing where to begin missionary ministry is important. In these two chapters we have provided guidelines to assist strategists in knowing where to start. By ascertaining both receptivity and need through research, one is able to better focus and not become too overwhelmed with this big world and its large quantity of people.

When the principles of receptivity and need are considered in conjunction with God's calling, the focus becomes even clearer. Whether the strategy needs to be developed for a very receptive area or for a hostile context, the team should now recognize the value of applying the various scales learned in the last chapter in order to know how to craft its methods in its place of service.

21

Visioning for the Future

N ot too long ago I (J. D.) had lunch with a student who was on his way to New England to serve as a church planter. As we discussed matters related to his future work, he commented, "But what happens when I get to the field and things do not go as expected?" His question revealed much wisdom: things will not occur in the field as pictured in one's mind. Henry Mintzberg correctly writes, "Smart strategists appreciate that they cannot always be smart enough to think through everything in advance" (1987, 69). This lack of definitive knowledge about the future by no means prevents the strategist from attempting to prayerfully discern the mental picture that the Lord would have him visualize as a future target to work toward, as Proverbs notes, "The wisdom of the prudent is to give thought to their ways" (14:8).

So while wise strategists know that they cannot think through everything, they can think about some things. They must discern their ways. Such discernment involves thinking about their vision for the future. Working in partnership with majority world believers in the area will help provide a more comprehensive perspective related to vision.

Richard Tanner Pascale and Anthony G. Athos believe so strongly in vision that they write: "Man is limited not so much by his tools as by his vision" (1981, 19). Illustrating this point they note:

> Long before the century of Columbus, man had developed the skills of seaman-ship and sailcraft. When the sailors of that time looked out upon the seas, what they *saw* was a flat surface and not surprisingly, when cartographers ran out of known world before they ran out of parchment, they inscribed the words "Here Be Dragons" on the ominous blankness. Then came Columbus. As he watched sailing ships disappear over the horizon, he noticed that they didn't just "disappear," but that the hull always disappeared first, then the sails, and finally the tip of the mast. In very pragmatic, operational terms, Columbus *saw* the oceans differently. (1981, 19)

What Is Visioning?

Visioning is the process of obtaining a vision. It is about considering the possibilities of the future. Strategists seeking to obtain a vision in essence are asking themselves, "What do we believe that the Lord desires us to work toward in our ministry?" This process is founded on the belief that we make our plans, but our ways are directed by the Lord (Prov. 16:9).

A vision is unique to a team and its context. Aubrey Malphurs defines vision as "a clear, challenging picture of the future of the ministry, as you believe that it can and must be" (2005, 151). While the purposes of God and his mission for the team are universals, the vision provided is unique to the moment in time. A vision is what the team believes the Lord desires to be accomplished in the future through its efforts. Vision is so critical to strategy development that Malphurs describes it as "of utmost importance to leaders and their ministry" (2005, 146). Without a vision of the future, the team members will not know what it is they are to accomplish.

In this chapter we first address the process of obtaining a vision. Second, we provide twelve reasons why vision is important. Finally, we conclude this chapter with discussion of casting vision before others.

Obtaining a Vision

A vision is not usually obtained overnight. Although the Lord can easily pro-vide the vision in a very short period of time, he may grow and mature it in the team through an extended process. In essence obtaining a vision involves (1) prayer and fasting; (2) understanding the context; (3) understanding the team; and (4) being aware of the resources available for the task. Figure 21.1 illustrates the process of obtaining a vision.

FIGURE 21.1: OBTAINING A VISION

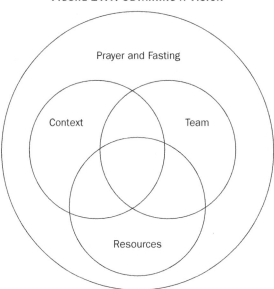

Prayer and Fasting

Obtaining a vision for what needs to be accomplished is not a mystical or arduous process but rather involves spending much time with the Lord; consideration of the context, team, and available resources is required. Prayer and fasting are to be a part of the entire process. Like all of life, the visioning process requires that one pray without ceasing (1 Thess. 5:17). Time alone with the Father is to precede and be sustained throughout the process. If the vision is to come from the Lord, then much time must be given to seeking his will on this matter. Ongoing prayer for wisdom and discernment is necessary to obtain the proper focus.

Know the Context

Knowledge of the context gained through studying it is extremely valuable to the process of obtaining a vision. It is difficult to obtain a picture of future possibilities without knowledge of the present realities. And without knowledge of the present realities, it is difficult to set wise goals and make healthy decisions about appropriate action steps to accomplish those goals.

Strategists must become students of the people they intend to serve. They must see both national believers and unbelievers as their cultural instructors. Knowledge of the natural and the human-made barriers in communities affects the way people live and interact. Strategists must be familiar with the demographics of the people. Information on the numbers of married people, education levels, ages, and incomes helps us obtain a better picture of the community. It is also important to understand the general cultural framing of the people. What are their ideals, their fears, and their hopes? Strategists need to know the spiritual context as well. Knowledge of the religions, sects, and cults helps provide a better understanding of the way people see and understand their world.

It is also important to study a people historically. The history of a people and area affects their present and future. The wise strategist also seeks to understand the people's political orientations. If the area has a large immigrant population, it is important to know the peoples' political views held while in their countries of birth. It is also wise to understand a community linguistically. Language provides an open door to its world. As noted previously, knowledge of the heart language and colloquialisms helps one to better understand a community.

Know the Team

A failure to have a good understanding of oneself and the team causes problems in obtaining a vision. While the Lord is able to accomplish more than we could ask or imagine (Eph. 3:20), he works through his people's callings, gifts, talents, idiosyncrasies, limitations, personalities, life experiences, and passions. A failure to understand how everyone on the team is molded and designed poses problems for healthy visioning.

For example, a team that has a strong calling and passion together with experience in ministry with adults will have a difficult time handling a five-year immersion in children's ministry. A strategist without such knowledge of the team could very likely have a vision to establish a well-developed children's ministry in the next year. While the vision may be present, the makeup of the team will hinder the outworking of that vision. Healthy visioning takes knowledge of the team into consideration.

When developing teams with nationals, patience and the allowance of extra time is an absolute necessity. Mistakes will be made, but the more time the team members spend with one another and in face-to-face communication, the easier it will be to work together. Teams formed from one church and sent to the field as church planters are likely to have a better understanding of one another than teams that have developed over long distances and are composed of different nationalities. Different team compositions will bring about different sets of challenges to the visioning process.

Know the Resources

While it is true that the Lord owns the cattle on a thousand hills (Ps. 50:10), the reality is that we do not. It is true that whenever God calls someone to a task, he also provides all the necessary resources to accomplish that task. Yet even with these matters in mind, we should also realize that the Lord sometimes wants to use our five loaves of bread and two fish to accomplish the miraculous, rather than give us enough food for the five thousand from the very beginning.

The wise strategist knows what resources are available in the present. These resources can include people to serve, money for expenses, time available for ministry, and other material blessings. Visioning takes into account the present reality of available resources, recognizing that additional resources may come in the future or may never arrive. When working with a team composed of national believers, one must take care to ensure that they are also contributing resources and that the Western missionaries are not creating a codependent relationship. Much prayer, wisdom, and consultation with all members of the team is important in such a situation. Missions history is filled with unhealthy stories where the use of Western resources resulted in partnerships that were engulfed by paternalism.

It should be noted that few available resources does not mean that the strategist should avoid dreaming big kingdom dreams. However, it should influence the visioning process, assuming that God has called one to the task and God has provided only a few resources. We must remember that the economy of the kingdom is not the economy of this world. A grandiose vision in our minds may be the opposite of what the Lord desires at the moment. While a small vision in our minds may not be trendy or cool, it may be exactly what the Lord wants, and he helps to lead us to such a vision with our few resources. To be fair we must also note the possibility that the Lord will provide a grandiose vision and few resources to accomplish that vision. If such is the case, then the wise strategist recognizes that few resources may require a longer time line for the implementation of all the action steps necessary to see the fulfillment of the vision.

IMPORTANCE OF VISION

Many of the reasons for the benefit for having a vision are the same reasons for having a strategy.

Malphurs's Seven Reasons

Malphurs has written much on the topic of strategy and vision development. In *Advanced Strategic Planning*, he provides seven reasons why a vision is so important (2005, 146–49). While some of these reasons are more important than others, each of them shows the value that vision provides to the ministry.

VISION CREATES A CAUSE

Vision helps people understand how they fit into God's plan for the out-working of his redemption across a people. Vision helps move people from where they are to where they need to be in using their gifts and talents for kingdom work. A vision helps the team understand its marching orders in light of the Great Commission.

VISION LEGITIMIZES LEADERSHIP

Leaders without a vision are leaders to be questioned. By their very nature leaders must lead, and lead toward the visions in their hearts. Having a vision helps others see the legitimacy of the leader for the task. Knowing the vision also helps others discern whether such a vision is from the Lord, and whether they should follow such a leader.

VISION ENERGIZES LEADERSHIP

Having a vision helps motivate leaders to the task. Malphurs recognizes this as "God-given passion" and a "fire" in the "bones" of the leader (2005, 148). I (J. D.) have often heard of runners, exhausted from the race, obtaining their second wind when they have a vision of the distance to the finish line and their position in the race. Vision keeps leaders moving.

VISION PROVIDES ENERGY

Vision inspires people to great things. Just as a vision energizes leaders, Malphurs notes that visions "are exciting and they energize people" (2005, 146). They help stir up zeal for the task at hand. He comments, "When your vision resonates with your values and mission, it generates the energy that fuels the accomplishment of the ministry task" (147).

VISION FOSTERS RISK TAKING

Just because someone postulates a vision to be realized does not mean that success is guaranteed. Mission strategy is often about going against the status quo. Strategy involves change and requires vision to move beyond the comfort zone. A vision requires taking risks, and working toward a vision requires faith.

VISION MOTIVATES PARTNERS

Malphurs titles this point as "Motivates Giving" (2005, 149). However, since wise strategists desire more than simply donors, we have expanded this to focus

198

on partners on a multitude of levels. A vision helps partners understand the calling and direction of the mission strategy. And the more compelling the vision, the more likely they will become involved in the work by praying and going to serve, as well as giving material and financial resources.

VISION SUSTAINS MINISTRY

The challenges that come with missionary labors are significant. Spiritual opposition comes from a variety of angles and in a variety of expressions. Vision helps provide sustenance for the God-given task. When people know that along with their callings God has provided their visions for the future, they are able to walk through the dark valleys, knowing that he is with them (Ps. 23:4).

Additional Reasons

To Malphurs's seven reasons on the importance of vision, we add five others. Our hope is that together these twelve different reasons will assist you in understanding the importance of having a vision for your strategy.

VISION CREATES OWNERSHIP

Whenever the visioning process involves everyone on the team, the resulting vision is owned by the group. Everyone buys into the process and is likely to own the vision for himself or herself. A clearly articulated vision also assists possible future partners. Whenever they understand that the team is moving toward an end vision and not haphazardly working together, they are more likely to own the vision as well.

VISION UNIFIES THE TEAM

A vision also helps establish a united effort among the team members. The team knows what it is working toward. It is not difficult to embrace goals when everyone understands the vision. A clear vision alleviates confusion. Team members better understand the methods they are applying when they are able to see the big picture.

Imagine a team wanting to climb a mountain but not knowing what mountain it was going to climb. Some team members may think they are going to the Himalayas to climb Everest. Others may be thinking Mount Kilimanjaro in Africa. Some may have in mind Clingman's Dome in the Smokey Mountains of Appalachia. There are stark differences between the challenges offered by each. Each mountain requires unique climbing gear. Each demands its own methods for ascent and descent. A missionary team without a vision is similar to a group of climbers knowing they need to climb a mountain but not agreeing on or even knowing which they will tackle.

SIDEBAR 21.1
THE IMPORTANCE OF CREDIBILITY

Malphurs notes that a vision must have credibility in the minds of those who will be working toward the completion of that vision. People will not make a commitment to a vision if they do not believe in it. Here Malphurs shares some thoughts on three elements contributing to a credible vision that is likely to be accepted by others.

THE CONTENT OF THE VISION. At issue is whether or not the vision is based on Scripture. When visionaries are able to point to a particular biblical principle in support of their dream, they catch the attention of those in the Christian community who have a high view of the Scripture. . . .

Content credibility, however, also depends on a solid relationship between the vision and some untapped opportunity. A vision that is highly sensitive to some obvious spiritual opportunity elicits believability. . . .

THE VISIONARY LEADER'S PERFORMANCE. People want to know the track record of the visionary leader. This consists of such characteristics as God's evident blessing on a person's life and ministry, prior success, gifts and abilities, strong communication skills, personal dedication, and a commitment to biblical values. Does the leader show extraordinary ability in any or most of these factors?

When it becomes evident God is uniquely blessing leaders' lives and ministries, they gain extraordinary credibility in the eyes of their followers and even the general public. Sometimes God grants special favor in that person's ministry in such a way that former

---

VISION IMPROVES COMMUNICATION

Communication breakdown is always possible in a conversation between two people. Add more people and the likelihood for confusion multiplies in the communication process. A vision, however, assists the development and maintenance of healthy communication between team members and any additional partners.

To return to the example of the climbers, imagine that their leader simply told them to bring their gear and supplies for the climb without telling them what mountain they were going to climb. Some would simply bring a good pair of hiking shoes, while others would bring sleeping bags for subzero temperatures. Depending on the location of the climb, some would possibly die from exposure to the elements, while others may overpack, weighing themselves down for the journey. Vision assists the team in understanding the end toward which it is moving. Knowing the vision up front assists in communication both before and throughout the process of finishing the task.

obstacles are removed and doors that normally are closed are opened.

Prior ministry experience powerfully communicates credibility in Christian circles, as does the presence of strong gifts or abilities, especially in the area of Christian leadership. There is a great need today for men and women with leadership experience who can direct ministries with sustained excellence, especially in preaching. . . .

Of course, the leader's personal dedication to the cause is an absolute must in creating trustworthiness for the vision. Generally, the perception is the greater the self-sacrifice or personal risk of the leader, the greater the trustworthiness of the cause.

THE VISIONARY LEADER'S INTEGRITY. Leaders who display integrity and trustworthiness are given high credibility by those within and outside the ministry community. Actually, the Christian community is directed to assign credibility on the basis of character. This is clearly spelled out in various passages such as 1 Timothy 3:1–13 and Titus 1:5–9. . . .

Character is the foundation of Christian leadership. A person's entire ministry and leadership rest on his or her character. If the character is flawed in some way, the ministry will be flawed proportionately. This is demonstrated time after time as leaders fall and take their ministries with them. (2007, 189–90)

REFLECTION AND DISCUSSION

- Do you agree with Malphurs on the importance of the credibility of the vision? If so, please explain your response.
- Of the three matters that contribute to a vision's credibility, which one do you think is the most important to you? To your team? Why?
- Can you think of any other matters that Malphurs does not mention?

VISION OFFERS FOCUS

I (J. D.) am extremely nearsighted. Without contacts or glasses I cannot see the big *E* at the top of the vision chart! Provide me with the correct prescription, however, and my vision becomes 20/20. What is my problem? Focus. My natural eyes cannot focus properly.

A lack of vision results in confusion among those laboring at the missionary task. Team members will be pulling in different directions. Partners will have no idea about what the team is planning to accomplish. Vision, like using glasses to correct my myopia, helps bring things into focus. Without a vision there is no clarity about what the Lord desires. Goals become fuzzy and unclear. And action steps to obtain the vision are taken with uncertainty.

VISION PROVIDES ALIGNMENT

Wind resistance is a terrible thing for auto racers. The drag of the wind against a car slows the vehicle down, sometimes even costing the race. Engineers, attempting to alleviate the effects of the wind, design cars that are more aerodynamically sleek, offering the least amount of resistance. Such vehicles have an alignment that requires a tighter and smoother construction, without large mirrors that jut out, cavities that trap air, and ninety-degree angles.

Vision is like the design of a high-performance race car. It helps pull missionaries together into an alignment that eliminates as much drag as possible. George Labovitz and Victor Rosansky describe alignment as a "force" that "coalesces and focuses an organization and moves it forward" (1997, 6). Vision helps provide a streamlined approach to accomplishing a task.

STEPS TO CASTING A VISION

The writer of Proverbs declares, "The purposes of a person's heart are deep waters, but one who has insight draws them out" (20:5). In mission strategy it is not sufficient for a vision to be locked within someone's heart; it must be communicated to others. Therefore, the wise steward is able to draw out that which is locked away from the world.

This process of communicating a vision is more art than science. The vision-casting process involves the ability to paint both prayerfully and patiently what the Spirit has been doing among the people and what he can do through a mission strategy. The art involved in the process is being able to paint the picture with enough detail so that others will be drawn to and energized by such a vision, but at the same time the picture cannot be so detailed that others would believe it impossible to accomplish such a vision.

Kandinsky, Still Life, and Monet

To continue with the painting analogy, strategists should be encouraged to consider vision casting as one would a work by Monet as opposed to Kandinsky or a still-life artist. Kandinsky painted some abstract works. In fact, I (J. D.) have a copy of a Kandinsky on my wall, and I have no clue as to what it represents. It looks like chaos. If a leader casts a vision in much the same way that the abstract artist communicates to the world, then he or she will find that most people will have no desire to follow such a vision, simply because they have no idea what is locked in the heart of the leader.

A still-life work of art, however, is a highly detailed painting. A bowl of fruit is clearly a bowl of fruit. The lines and shadowing are perfect and very realistic. When someone approaches casting a vision in much the same way that a still-life painter approaches painting, he or she can easily overwhelm others with too much detail. The vision is so grandiose that people will not believe such a feat is worth attempting, for they think that failure is the only possibility.

A Monet work, however, is an impressionistic piece of art. From a distance trees look like trees and a barn looks like a barn. Up close, though, it is evident that what gave the impression of actual objects was really broad and narrow brush strokes on a canvas—a few definite lines but mainly smudges and streaks. The style nonetheless allows for the picture to be completed in the minds of the observers, by stimulating their minds and personalities. Effective vision casting involves providing enough details of the vision so that people can "see" the possibility and recognize where their personalities, gifts, talents, and skills can fit into it.

Pray

After a vision has been developed, much prayer should be involved in the vision-casting process. Pray for God to be glorified throughout the process. Pray for the people to understand the vision and the need. Pray that no ungodly conflicts arise during the process.

Pray for patience as you share with others. It should be remembered that the Lord has been gracious with you in the visioning process. You have had the time to meditate on the vision and give it much consideration. Do not expect others to immediately agree with your vision. Be patient with them; allow them time to discuss, reflect on, and pray about the vision set before them.

Understand What Communicates with Your People

In casting a vision to one's team or organization, you must remember that you need to understand your people first and then work with them to understand your vision. How do they process information best? What are their educational levels? What are their likes and dislikes? Knowing that a group processes and assimilates information better in an informal discussion, rather than a lecture, should affect how you communicate your vision to them.

Communicate the Vision Redundantly

Rick Warren recommends restating the vision every twenty-six days (1995, 111). Keep the vision before the people. Talk about it. Blog about it. Write about it. Find ways to communicate over and over the vision on which the mission strategy will be based. Begin such communication with any leaders and then with the rest of the people. Develop as many creative ways as possible (that work in your context) to share the vision with those involved in the task.

SIDEBAR 21.2
LEGACY BY VISION

In the following excerpt, Gordon Coulter draws attention to Bill Bright's legacy that started with a vision for reaching others with the gospel. Here Coulter notes the importance of recognizing the seriousness of one's vision and the potential that a vision has to change the world:

> To further unpack the notion of vision, some have described it as *foresight*. It means seeing that which is yet to be and putting a plan together to make it a reality. Joel Hunter talks about how most of us deal with getting a group focused, but sometimes the focus is on the wrong things. He states, "Vision is critical to any ministry. Ministry without vision is like a ship without a compass, a surgeon without a scalpel, a writer without a pen."
>
> God is calling out leaders to fulfill the great "mission" as well as to implement visions that will bring this mission to reality. One of the greatest leaders of recent history was Dr. Bill Bright. In a recent *Christianity Today* article, Josh McDowell, Dave Hannah, and Rick Warren wrote of Dr. Bright's legacy. McDowell met Dr. Bright at Wheaton College in 1961. After Dr. Bright spoke in chapel, McDowell and a few other students met with him in the coffee shop. During that time, Dr. Bright shared his vision of how to be filled with the Holy Spirit by faith as well as his passion for evangelism. Dr. Bright had a passion for evangelism, and he was so "captivated by his calling to reach others for Christ that it became contagious. You simply couldn't be around Bill without walking away with a greater desire to share Christ.

> To Bill, evangelism was just a way of life."
>
> Warren comments that Billy Graham is gifted to speak to hundreds of thousands at one time, but Bill Bright spoke to hundreds of thousands one at a time—two different visions of carrying out the same mission. Warren states that Campus Crusade for Christ is the largest ministry in the world, yet the legacy of Bill Bright is the millions he either personally or corporately led to faith in Jesus Christ. Dr. Bright's vision for evangelism led him to develop the Four Spiritual Laws, the most widely distributed religious pamphlet in history. It has been translated into two hundred languages and read by an estimated two and one-half billion people. Bill Bright's vision started as a personal one—to reach the unreached—and developed into one of the most significant Christian ministries of all time. This tool, among many developed by Bright, was his vision for accomplishing God's mission of the Great Commission. . . .
>
> Imagine what would happen if every ministry would take their vision seriously and give all they had to accomplish that vision. Infuse your vision with passion and commit to staying with it. What if each one of us at the local ministries or worldwide mission organization level would keep on visioning the impossible biblical mandate to reach out to every living person on earth starting with our own neighborhoods? Nothing could stop such a movement. (2005, 64–65)

CONCLUSION

In this chapter we have addressed the important aspect of visioning as related to strategy development. Vision is critical for strategic development and implementation. Without knowing where the team is headed, its members are likely to wander aimlessly and be poor stewards with the opportunities and resources that the Lord has provided for the advancement of the gospel.

The art of vision casting involves painting a picture of future possibilities that is not so detailed that others believe you are a micromanaging taskmaster or so abstract that others believe you lack focus. Rather, it should provide an impression of the possibilities whereby others can understand how they can serve in the strategy.

22

Forming a Team

The use of a team is foundational to the development and implementation of missionary strategy. The Scriptures remind us of the value of partnerships in such passages as "victory is won through many advisers" (Prov. 11:14) and "plans fail for lack of counsel, but with many advisers they succeed" (Prov. 15:22). The writer of Ecclesiastes also points to the value of companions:

> Two are better than one,
>   because they have a good return for their labor:
> If either of them falls down,
>   one can help the other up.
> But pity anyone who falls
>   and has no one to help them up.
> Also, if two lie down together, they will keep warm.
>   But how can one keep warm alone?
> Though one may be overpowered,
>   two can defend themselves.
> A cord of three strands is not quickly broken. (Eccles. 4:9–12)

We begin this chapter by addressing the definition of a team. Next, by noting the strengths and limitations of teams, we show the value of them to missionary strategy. Finally, we conclude the chapter with guidelines to team development.

WHAT IS A TEAM?

A team should consist of a group that is few in number. Strategy development requires intimate interaction on a variety of topics. A large group makes this a cumbersome process at best. Jon R. Katzenbach and Douglas K. Smith correctly note, "Large numbers of people usually cannot develop the common purpose, goals, approach, and mutual accountability of a real team. And when they try to do so, they usually produce only superficial 'missions' and well-meaning intentions" (1993, 47). With this in mind, they offer the following as a definition of a team: "A team is a small number of people with complementary skills who are committed to a common purpose, performance goals, and approach for which they hold themselves mutually accountable" (1993, 45).

It is important to note the various components in this definition. First, as already mentioned, a team should be small in number. Two to six people should be sufficient. Whenever a team increases to eight, ten, or more people, the concerns noted by Katzenbach and Smith begin to arise.

Second, the team should have complementary skills. This does not mean that the members of the team should have the same gifts/talents/skills. While such uniformity would allow them to excel in a few areas, they would find themselves with several limitations. A complementary mix allows for both uniformity and diversity, with the latter helping to overcome the limitations of any one team member.

Third, the team must be committed to its common purpose, goals, and methods. Here uniformity is necessary. When developing a team with national believers, an extended period of time may be necessary to develop the team. There must be a healthy alignment of the hearts and minds of the members. In order for the team to execute the strategy, its members must be moving in the same direction. Failure to focus on these matters is similar to playing tug-of-war; each member holds the rope, but everyone pulls the rest in a direction they do not wish to go.

Fourth, team members hold one another accountable for a multitude of matters. A team provides accountability for accomplishing goals, action steps, and the end vision. This accountability helps the team avoid constantly redesigning its plans, especially when what is needed is commitment to the implementation of the original plan. A team should function as its own system of checks and balances for accomplishing what it sets out to accomplish.

While Katzenbach and Smith do not refer to mutual edification in their definition, we would add that a team must also be concerned with the welfare of the other team members. A healthy team is like a healthy body; all the systems need to be functioning in proper relation to the other systems. Of course, this element of mutual concern should not surprise us as we consider the apostle Paul's teaching on the body of Christ and the love we should have for one another. When one part of the body suffers, we all suffer. All the parts are needed and must work in harmony together. The result is a group of individuals who are not lone rangers but recognize that if one team member suffers, everyone suffers.

BIBLICAL EXAMPLE

One of the strongest arguments for a team approach to any ministry, whether or not such ministry involves strategy development and implementation, is that the biblical evidence favors a team approach to service. Throughout the Scriptures a team approach to ministry is advocated in various locations, with various people, and at various times. Jesus called followers to himself. He sent the Seventy-Two out in pairs (Luke 10:1). The missionary work of the apostle Paul continued this pattern of teamwork. Even when Paul was alone, such as in Athens, it was only for a short period of time (Acts 17:16). Although Paul and Barnabas went separate ways, Luke notes that both men immediately found other men to serve with them (Acts 15:36–41). We also observe that the local churches had a plurality of elders (Acts 14:23) to provide the necessary leadership.

THE RELATION OF TEAM TO MISSION STRATEGY

Although I (J. D.) remember seeing only occasional reruns of *The Lone Ranger*, I'm quite aware that the philosophy behind the television series has carried over into much of American life. The thought of being a rugged and mysterious individual, answering to no one, is a romantic notion. Unfortunately, this concept has influenced the church for many years as well. The notion of being a "lone ranger" for Jesus, unconnected to anyone else, appeals to the individualism of many people. However, kingdom service is not about an individualistic lifestyle. It is a team effort of the body of Christ laboring together for the Lord.

Just as ministry in general is not to be accomplished through a lone-ranger approach, the development of mission strategy is not to be done alone and in isolation. Strategy development is a team affair. Diverse perspectives, passions, gifts, and talents are needed not only for strategic planning but also for the implementation of the strategy.

STRENGTHS OF TEAMS

Though our bias for the use of teams is evident throughout this book, it is helpful to provide a brief list of the strengths of teams. This list is not exhaustive, though it includes what we consider to be the more beneficial aspects of team ministry, particularly related to the development and implementation of missionary strategy.

Shared Leadership

While most teams have a leader who is understood to be a "first among equals," the team provides for a dispersion of the responsibilities. No one is responsible for everything. If a team consists of individuals with complementary talents/gifts/passions, then the distribution of responsibilities is likely to be an easier task.

Encouragement

Missionary ministry, including the development and implementation of strategy, involves times of discouragement. Team members can edify one another during these difficult times. When plans do not go as expected, the members are able to draw from one another's support.

Diversity

Healthy diversity provides a team with different viewpoints, experiences in life, and, of course, gifts, talents, and passions. All these elements aid in the strategic planning process, when fresh perspectives are needed to know how to respond in certain situations. Team members can complement one another and still maintain diversity. Complete uniformity among the members is not recommended (we address team commonalities later in this chapter).

Strength in Numbers

The old adage about strength being found in numbers is very true when it comes to a team. For example, Labovitz and Rosansky observe the strength of the collaborative effort of several individuals working together when they write, "Great strategy is the product of *enrichment*, where many good thinkers come together and share ideas" (1997, 89). While an individual may often

209

question his or her decision-making process, a team with consensus can provide the necessary commendation that strengthens the conviction of the decision maker, helping facilitate the proper execution of action steps. When a team is being questioned by outsiders about its decision making, a unified team is able to take a stand on what it believes to be wise strategic planning.

Wisdom

Proverbs notes that "plans are established by seeking advice" (20:18) and "surely you need guidance to wage war, and victory is won through many advisers" (24:6). Collective wisdom allows a team to discern things that the natural mind is unable to visualize. Wisdom provides insight into that which is supernaturally discerned. The Lord works through the team to provide the necessary guidance for the multitude of decisions that must be made in strategic planning. The wisdom found among team members is extremely valuable for developing missionary strategy.

LIMITATIONS OF TEAMS

Of course, teams also have limitations. As long as sinful people are working together, there will be problematic matters. While such limitations are a part of our world, we still believe that the strengths of having a team to assist with developing and implementing missionary strategy far outweigh the limitations.

Length of Time to Make Decisions

Whenever more people are present, there are more opinions. More individuals have to consider and internally process the matter at hand. The end result is that it takes more time to make decisions as opposed to the time needed for a lone individual to plan strategy. With more people come additional phone calls, emails, and meetings to make decisions.

Conflict

Conflict is inevitable. All teams will experience it—and international teams will experience more of it than homogeneous teams (see, e.g., Roembke 2000). As long as there are diverse views and people present, conflict will arise (see Elmer 1993). While such does not necessarily denote that sin is present, conflict slows down the strategic planning process. Teams should be aware of this reality and plan ahead for how they will address conflict to ensure that the planning process moves forward.

DEVELOPING TEAMS

In the book *Leading Teams,* Anne Donnellon notes that teams move through four phases on their way to effectively implementing their strategies. These can be observed in table 22.1.

TABLE 22.1
PHASES OF TEAM DEVELOPMENT
(DONNELLON 2006, 31)

Phase	Responses
Team Forming	excitement, high expectations, establishing roles and rules
Team Conflict	competition among team members, confusion about roles and tasks, discouragement, conflict
Team Normalization	team routines settled, teamwork forms, trust evolves
Team Performance	hopefulness, productiveness, shared leadership

We present Donnellon's phases of team development here as a reminder that most teams move through a series of stages in the process of their members becoming effective in working together. Such movement should be understood not necessarily as a hindrance to the task of strategy development and implementation but rather as a curing process to best prepare the team for better work in the future. The time for any given team to progress through these phases will vary according to the context and the individuals involved. Different groups will progress through these phases at different rates.

In the first phase the team members come together to begin the process of getting to know one another. People are excited and have high hopes for the future. The second phase begins with the arrival of team conflict. If a team is not focused on its members' welfare, then it will be easy for the members to begin competing with one another. The third phase involves a routinization of ongoing activities and the development of trust. Teams that successfully navigate these three phases are more likely to enter a fourth phase, in which the team is highly productive.

KNOWING THE PEOPLE

It is not sufficient to simply have people together to work on developing and implementing a strategy. To develop a healthy team, the team leader must understand each member of the team. It is important to know the people who are serving on the team and how they can best use their passions, talents, gifts, and interests in the process. Different individuals will serve best in roles where their characteristics best complement the tasks. Part of understanding where

---

SIDEBAR 22.1
THE TEAM OF INDIVIDUAL(-ISM)

The following excerpt provides some good insight into the ironic situation that all teams are comprised of individuals who are not always team players.

> New teams—and even mature teams at times—tend to struggle as they grow. Issues related to how the work is performed and how team members relate to each other come quickly to the forefront.
>
> A *Business Week* magazine article discussed steps that were being taken by the Los Angeles Unified School District to overhaul its teaching process and introduce team concepts. In this article, a comment was made that gives us a clue as to why we struggle with teamwork. The district's assistant superintendent stated, "In the business world, sharing responsibility for a project is called teamwork. In classrooms, the way we teach today, it's called cheating."
>
> Most people in the workplace were reared in a school system that rewarded individual accomplishment. When they entered the workplace, the resulting learned behaviors were reinforced by a similar system of individual rewards such as promotions, merit raises, and forced rankings. Little emphasis was placed on collaboration and teamwork. This system led to behaviors that focused on the self and one's personal accomplishments. When team concepts were introduced into the organizational fabric, different behaviors and skills were required. Such a change brings with it difficulty and discomfort.
>
> Imagine a singer who has sung solo his entire career being asked to participate in a quartet. The singer must now learn new techniques, harmonize with the others, respect their needs, and communicate extensively. A different set of skills is needed that may initially generate feelings of inadequacy, insecurity, and sometimes, incompetence. The accompanying discomfort is real. (Blanchard, Randolph, and Grazier 2005, 46–47)

REFLECTION AND DISCUSSION

- Do you see any similar problems caused by individualism when it comes to missionary teams? If so, list them.

- Are there elements in your own life that would lead you to operate more from individualism to the detriment of your team? If so, what can you do now to make healthy changes?

---

people can best serve is to recognize that there are unifying matters that all potential team members should share in common.

Common Calling

Teams need to have a common calling from the Lord to the task and to the team. Sometimes this calling will be the only thing that keeps the team together and moving forward.

Common Philosophy

Teams should share a common philosophy toward ministry in general and strategy in particular. Without such a common thread, the team members may eventually find themselves at odds with one another over secondary matters.

Common Vision

Drawing from the previous chapter, the leader should ask if the team has a common vision to reach the population segment or people group in the area. Does this group of individuals have a perspective on what needs to be accomplished that is unifying and similar? Of course, as a team works together in the visioning process, the vision will become clearer. But before the team comes together, the question needs to be asked, "Do we share a common perspective to see the multiplication of disciples, leaders, and churches throughout this people?"

Common Theology

A team that works together must be a team that has theological harmony. The team must determine up front the nonnegotiables on which all team members must agree. While there should be some freedom with some secondary and tertiary matters, before beginning the journey together, team members must know where they will not compromise.

Common Missiology

As with theology it is impossible for a group of individuals to begin by clearly articulating all the finite details of their missiologies. However, it should be determined in advance where the group stands on certain issues. For example, what if some of the team members believe that their mission strategy is to establish C5 churches while others are adamantly opposed? For starters discussions should involve matters related to contextualization, church multiplication, and leadership development.

Common Connection

In order for team members to work well together, a common bond needs to be established. A team needs to "click" (see, e.g., Gladwell 2005). It needs a common chemistry whereby each member knows that he or she is a kindred spirit with the others in the group. While this common connection is a highly subjective matter, people have a sense of when it is present. The team members need to be friends with one another and get along well. The greater the diversity of the team, however, the greater may be the challenge of developing this sense of connection.

213

MANIFESTING THE BARNABAS FACTORS

In *The Barnabas Factors: Eight Essential Practices of Church Planting Team Members*, I (J. D.) address eight healthy practices found in the life of Barnabas that greatly assisted with kingdom expansion (Payne 2008, 10). While in the book I make the application to church-planting teams, these eight characteristics should be present in any team. Therefore, in addition to those commonalities we have already mentioned, potential team members should manifest the Barnabas Factors as well. These eight practices are *outward* manifestations of an *inward* character.

Walks with the Lord

This is the heart and foundation for the rest of the factors. Individuals who fail to walk with the Lord should not be involved in the development of mission strategies. Since such labors are supernatural tasks, individuals who do not maintain close fellowship with the Father should not be on the team. It is out of a healthy walk with the Lord that the team members will know

FIGURE 22.1: THE BARNABAS FACTORS

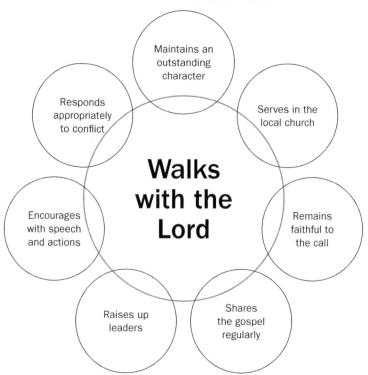

how to live in relation to God, one another, and those outside the kingdom and how to develop healthy strategy.

Maintains an Outstanding Character

Outstanding character is derived from a person's walk with the Lord. While no potential team member is perfect, character flaws hidden today will manifest themselves in the pressures of actual ministry later and will affect missionary strategy. Team members will continue their growth in Christ, leading to improvements in character. However, a high level of maturity should be expected of everyone at the time he or she joins the team.

Serves in the Local Church

If an individual does not have a history of faithful commitment to a local church, then he or she should not be considered for the team. An exception to this matter would be if the individual recently came to faith in Christ. It is difficult for someone to assist in the development of missionary strategy working toward the multiplication of healthy churches when he or she is not faithful to the Lord's commands for service in his body. A historic lack of value and love for local churches in someone's life is a sure sign that such disregard will continue into the future.

Remains Faithful to the Call

As mentioned in chapter 20, the matter of calling is critical to team development. Just as Barnabas was faithful to his calling in the face of persecution and team conflict, contemporary missionary teams also must consist of those faithful to the calling.

Shares the Gospel Regularly

We should not assume that missionaries regularly share the gospel. Team members must have both an evangelistic past and an evangelistic present. This reveals not only the health of their walk with the Lord but the health of their missionary calling and their attitude toward making disciples—all of which dynamically affect missionary strategy.

Raises Up Leaders

Team members need to have a vision and lifestyle that reflect the important responsibility they have to multiply leaders. Potential team members who have

215

little or no interest in multiplying leaders are very likely to have a negative impact on missionary strategy development.

Encourages with Speech and Actions

Teams need individuals who offer encouragement to other team members. The missionary team will experience great challenges, difficulties, and frustrations. The spiritual opposition against which it must fight will be draining. Team members need to encourage one another. When the action steps involved in the strategy are not playing out as desired, when the goals are not being accomplished within the appropriate time, and when the resources are few, team members need to rely on one another for verbal and practical encouragement. The Spirit is able to do great things through team members who love to encourage one another. A team of encouragers who speak and act in a manner that reflects the work of the indwelling Holy Spirit is a team that is better prepared for the struggles ahead.

Responds Appropriately to Conflict

Conflict was noted above as one of the limitations to team ministry. It will come, so teams need to be prepared. Healthy teams consist of members who know how to respond appropriately to conflict. Such members recognize that in responding to conflict, everything must be done (1) out of love (Rom. 12:10); (2) for the sake of the kingdom; (3) as a witness for the Lord; (4) out of a spirit of humility and servanthood; and (5) in seeking the best for the other members (Gal. 6:10).

TEAM ALIGNMENT

The manifestation of the above-mentioned commonalities and the Barnabas Factors help to create and maintain team alignment. Without healthy alignment according to a team's purpose and goals, it will be difficult—if not impossible—to develop and implement healthy strategies. Labovitz and Rosansky describe the importance of alignment in *The Power of Alignment*. Though they refer to organizations, consider the following points adapted from their book and applied to teams:

- The main thing for a team as a whole must be a common and unifying concept to which every member can contribute.
- The team must be able to see a direct relationship between what it does and this common and unifying concept.

- The main thing must be clear, easy to understand, consistent with the strategy of the team, and actionable by every member. (1997, 43–44)

Alignment provides a laser-like focus for the group to accomplish the purpose for its existence. Alignment helps the group to be a better steward of its resources. It also assists the group in being more efficient in its service. Without proper alignment, the team members

- Will lose focus
- Will wonder if the goals are being accomplished
- Will question the relevancy of the goals to the purpose and end vision
- Will not work in harmony with one another and instead become lone rangers

---

SIDEBAR 22.2
THE CONTRACT OF STRATEGY

In the following excerpt taken from the article "What Mission Strategy Is and Does," Gordon MacDonald describes strategy as a contract.

Strategy—something like the football player's game plan, centers on principles of ministry. Some of these are unchangeable because of their doctrinal base. Others are in a constant state of flux because they are related to the changing characteristics of the mission, the culture of the field, and the development of tools to do the job. Determining the difference between the changeable and the unchangeable is a matter of current debate in church and missionary renewal. By definition, a missionary strategy is a long- and short-range plan for evangelizing a given area of the world: the planting of the church or the carrying on of support activity to other missions. It is a "contract" under which a group of people agree to work. Until it is changed, it is the highest authority to which each member of the group can appeal. In that strategy, one will find the definition of activities to be done, the geographical boundaries, the necessary personnel descriptions, what the level of success and failure is, and finally who directs the effort and determines when it is completed. A copy of the strategy should be in the hands of everyone connected with the mission board's task. (1971, 1)

REFLECTION AND DISCUSSION

- Do you agree or disagree that a strategy should function as a "contract" among team members? Why?
- How does the fact that strategies will often need adjustment as the team implements its action steps affect the notion of the strategy as a contract?

CONCLUSION

Healthy teams are essential to the development and implementation of strategies. While every team has limitations, the strengths found working with aligned team members far outweigh any potential drawbacks. Wise team leaders will take the necessary time to consider prayerfully the individuals to invite to participate on the team. In addition to considering the Barnabas Factors when selecting team members, the team leader should also keep in mind the commonalities discussed in this chapter.

23

Assessing the Resources

One of the necessary components for the implementation of a strategy is the resources. Different strategies require different quantities—and qualities—of resources. A strategy that involves beginning a Bible study group in a community will obviously require fewer resources than a city-reaching strategy that involves starting medical and dental clinics. The resources necessary to most strategies can be categorized into three areas: people, time, and money. In this chapter we assist the strategist in assessing his or her necessary resources in these areas.

While all the cattle on a thousand hills belong to the Lord (Ps. 50:10), the reality is that they do not belong to you or me. Teams will have limited resources and often believe that they do not have enough resources. While some teams will have more than others, we want to encourage missionaries to recognize that if the Lord has called you and your team to a task, then he will provide the necessary resources for the strategy.

Therefore, assessing the resources available to the team is a very important part of the strategy development process. It is a matter of being good stewards with the Lord's resources (Matt. 25:14–30). While the Lord can take the few loaves of bread and fish and feed a multitude, he still expects our faithfulness (Matt. 14:13–21). Foolishness with resources will not result in the Lord's blessings, whether our resources are few or many.

PEOPLE

People are the most valuable resource for the implementation of the strategy. Without the right people doing the right things, it will be very difficult to experience long-term, effective execution of the action steps to accomplish the primary and secondary goals.

Numbers

While a team should consist of just a few people, most strategists can come up with other ways in which additional people can serve. These may include the use of short-term mission teams, summer missionaries, and interns. How many people do you think will be necessary to execute the action steps during the first year? Will these people be volunteers? Will they be required to raise their own funds in order to assist in the strategy? Where will you find these people? Will they come from other churches in other countries? Will they come from local believers? If you are not able to obtain the necessary number of people to assist, then it will be necessary to revise the strategy.

Skills/Abilities

What skills and abilities will such people need? While you and your team develop the action steps, make certain that you are able to obtain the right people for the tasks. If your strategy involves communication in a different language, will the people need to be fluent in the language? Will they need to know how to teach the Bible in a large gathering, small gathering, or both?

Churches

The use of local churches is very important in implementing many mission strategies. Congregations generally have a wealth of resources that the team does not have. Connect with the leaders of these churches, share your vision, and invite them to consider partnering with your team in the strategy. But in the process of developing your vision, ensure that you do not overlook churches in the setting where you serve—they may be able to provide the most valuable resources of all in terms of knowing the local context and historical factors that newcomers are likely to overlook.

TIME

Time is another commodity that absolutely must be taken into account when considering resources related to strategy. For some people time is more valuable

---

SIDEBAR 23.1
CONSIDERING THE OLD AND THE NEW

In an article for *Evangelical Missions Quarterly*, John Allen shares his concerns regarding beginning missionary work in new areas and the potential impact it can have on established work.

As we have seen, strategies to reach the unreached typically demand a heavier investment of time and patience than we are used to. One of the most difficult questions in formulating a strategy for the unreached is to work out how you can reach new targets without fatally diminishing the resources available for reaching existing ones. Most of us are over-committed already, and the evangelical individualism that makes us stubbornly determined to do it all by ourselves doesn't help either.

We could well find areas where, in order to make a contribution, we need to act in partnership with other evangelical causes. Ministering to the unreached is liable to expose us to all sorts of strange new configurations and alliances, some of which may not yield us much glory. (1989, 134)

REFLECTION AND DISCUSSION

- What are some possible ways that teams may begin to work in new areas without hindering their already established work by using resources for the new work?
- How does having a limited amount of resources help a team stay focused?
- Should teams consider other Great Commission Christians as resources available to them—even if these other groups come from other denominations, networks, and churches? If so, what are the strengths found in such alliances as mentioned by Allen? What are the limitations of such resources?

---

than money. In chapter 24 we note that goals need an expiration date. The team needs to set a date when it believes the goal will be accomplished. Goals may not be accomplished with the desired precision, but a time-oriented approach will help the team to stay focused and moving forward.

With the goals that your team has established, how much time does the team have to accomplish them? Is it a reasonable amount of time? What circumstances will affect the amount of time the team has to accomplish the goals? Are any of the team members bivocational or have another ministry role that will compete for their time?

MONEY

While money is not the primary resource for a strategy, it is important in implementing many strategies. If a team has developed a strategy that requires a great amount of money, but such money is not available and does not appear to be coming anytime soon, the team will need to revise its strategy. Although this is simply good common sense, over the years we have observed individuals concluding that if the money was not present, then God was not involved in the strategy. While that may be the ultimate explanation, it is more likely that the strategy was in need of revision and that God's calling had not changed for the missionaries.

A team should develop a financial budget for its strategy. This document should show how much money the team estimates that it will need in the first year and how it will spend the money. In addition to asking questions about the amount and use of the money, a team needs to ask, "Where will we obtain the money?" While some organizations may already have a set amount of money available for mission strategy, others do not. If a team decides to solicit funds from established churches and individuals, then the team will have to weigh the amount of time necessary for such partnership development in light of

---

SIDEBAR 23.2
RESOURCES NEEDED

The following account describes a portion of the strategy supporting the video project *More than Dreams*, to reach Muslims with the gospel and encourage ministry partners across the world.

For decades, a well-documented phenomenon has been occurring in the Muslim world—men and women who, without knowledge of the gospel, or contact among Christians in their community, have experienced dreams and visions of Jesus Christ. The reports of these supernatural occurrences often come from "closed countries" where there is no preaching of the good news and where converting to Christianity can invoke the death sentence. . . .

Beginning in 2002, a group of people interested in this phenomenon took initial steps in bringing it to the attention of a worldwide audience through a series of video programs. Numerous on-site interviews were conducted with former Muslims who

had experienced a dream or vision of Jesus resulting in their conversion to Christianity. From the outset, the producers endeavored to represent a global cross-section of Islam in the series, and for that reason, stories were sought in Arabic-speaking countries, Muslim areas throughout Africa and Asia and the secular Muslim nation of Turkey. (*More than Dreams* 2007)

REFLECTION AND DISCUSSION

- What do you think were the most important resources needed to implement this strategy?
- For each of the most important resources you listed, estimate the amount of those resources using the categories "high," "medium," and "low." For example, if you believe only a few people were needed, then you would estimate the people resource number to be low.

the time required for its strategy. Also, some agencies have policies that do not allow teams to do fund-raising from donors who already give to the agency. Teams connected to an agency will need to be familiar with such policies.

OTHER CONSIDERATIONS

Because some churches and individuals are not always quick to give money to missionary strategy, it would be worth the effort for a team to consider the tangible items it intends to purchase with the money and then ask others to provide such resources. Bibles, books, outreach supplies, transportation assistance, and photocopies are just some examples of things that a team may need for its strategy. Making a request for such miscellaneous assistance allows some groups to participate in the missionary work in a tangible manner that helps them to know exactly how their money is being used.

CONCLUSION

The amount of resources that a team is blessed with is not the determining indication of whether God has called it to the particular task at hand. It is unwise for a team to assume that just because it does not have all the people, time, and money desired to implement its strategy, it has misunderstood the leading of the Spirit. An examination of the Scriptures reveals that the apostle Paul had few resources—by most contemporary standards—but he was able to accomplish great things for the kingdom. A lack of the desired resources requires the team to reevaluate its strategy. While important, resources are not the ultimate issue in the development and implementation of strategy.

24

Setting Goals

uthor C. Peter Wagner notes, "A thorough understanding of missionary goals is the first step toward the formulation of an effective strategy" (1971, 17). Without goals a team is like a group of people wandering around aimlessly. Members may know that they are supposed to be doing something for the kingdom but are not completely certain what that something is. Or they may know their purpose, but without goals they find themselves randomly attempting to complete tasks, hoping they may accomplish their purpose.

Goals are designed to move a strategy from theory toward reality. While goals are not sufficient alone to accomplish the vision (action steps are needed; see chap. 25), they push the team in the direction of completion. For this reason and others listed below, it is necessary to spend a chapter addressing priorities and goals.

Few individuals today have written as much on missionary strategy and goal setting as Edward R. Dayton and Ted W. Engstrom. Although this chapter is not a summary of their work, we do quote liberally from their writings, believing much wisdom can be found in their thoughts. According to Dayton and Engstrom, goal setting is a cyclical process: "Goals need priorities; prioritized goals require planning; good planning helps us to live effective lives; effective living will help us set new and better goals" (1976, 22).

While their words are related to life in general, much here can be applied to the process of developing healthy goals for missionary strategy. In this chapter we discuss the cyclical process of working through priorities, planning, and goal setting.

Connection between Goals and Planning

There is an obvious and intimate connection between goals and planning. As Eric S. Fife and Arthur F. Glasser point out, "Unless field leadership is able to keep ultimate goals rigidly in view, planning tends to degenerate, permitting every man to do what appears right in his own eyes" (1961, 86). Planning involves attempting to meet goals, and goals cannot be accomplished without planning. Or to envision it another way, plans and goals are like the stones that made up ancient archways. The overall arch was only possible as the stones pressed on one another for support. If one of the stones were removed, the arch would collapse. Similarly, the strategic plan and goals exist because of one another. Dayton and Engstrom compare the connection to nautical terminology: "Goals are what motivate us toward the future; but goals without plans are like a ship with a destination, but without a rudder. You may be moving, but you will have very little control over your direction. Good goals deserve good *planning*" (1976, 22).

What Are Goals?

A goal is something yet to be accomplished that is a step in the process toward completing one's strategy. Therefore, a goal is a step that moves the team forward to achieving the end vision. While the path of strategic planning is filled with several significant goals, each of these consists of several smaller goals to be achieved first. A goal must be time sensitive, measurable, require ownership by someone, and achievable.

Time Sensitive

Goals need an expiration date. Teams establishing goals need to set dates to accomplish the goals. Even though some may not be accomplished in the lifetime of the team, a completion date for each goal is needed on the calendar. Teams that fail to establish such dates are likely to continue a great deal of activity that is not working toward the completion of their goals. A goal such as "We will have made initial contact with the people in location X by October 1, 2015" shows that the team is considering its goals in a time-sensitive manner. While the time-sensitive characteristic of a goal also requires sensitivity to the

Spirit's leading, allowing for some flexibility, establishing deadlines helps the team to stay focused, motivated, and united.

Measurable

If a team is unable to measure its goals, then it will not be able to determine whether it has met them. A goal such as "to have ten believers before we start two small-group Bible studies" shows that the team is thinking in terms of measurability. It has decided that it will not start the desired group Bible studies until it has ten believers.

Requires Ownership

Healthy goals are owned by a particular individual or individuals connected to the team. Goals without an owner are like automobiles without wheels; they may be nice to look at, but they are going nowhere. Without someone embracing and stepping out in the lead to accomplish a goal, it is unlikely that the goal will be reached. Numerous matters vie for a team's attention. Without a definitive commitment to accomplishing the goal, everyone on the team may believe that someone else is working toward it. Commitment brings the necessary accountability for the establishment of healthy goals.

Achievable

Dayton and Fraser make an excellent point when they note, "We set goals for results because we believe it is God's will that some results occur rather than others. By faith we want to set forth what we think God wants *accomplished* in this generation" (1990, 240). Goal setting is not an attempt to undermine God's will. Rather, his will is to be sought in this process, knowing that he desires his church to achieve certain standards.

The team must believe it can accomplish the goals it establishes. Such does not negate faith or the power of the Spirit. Zechariah reminds us that God uses his power, and not our abilities, to accomplish his plans (Zech. 4:6). While some trust in horses and chariots, strategists must trust in the name of the Lord our God (Ps. 20:7). And while such is the declaration of the psalmist, in the same chapter he writes, "May he grant you your heart's desire and fulfill all your plans!" (Ps. 20:4 ESV). The writer of Proverbs reveals, "The horse is made ready for the day of battle, but the victory belongs to the Lord" (21:31 ESV). The team that heeds these words is wise. While it has goals to accomplish to prepare for "battle," the outcome is placed in the Lord's hands. Stewardship requires that those who establish goals have faith that if God has revealed the goals to the team, then in the power of his Spirit and with the resources he has provided, the team will be able to accomplish his goals.

Great Commission Oriented

By definition mission strategy should be oriented toward the glorification of our Lord by making disciples of all nations, baptizing them, and teaching them to obey the commands of Jesus (Matt. 28:18–20). Like the compass needle designed to point north, so mission strategy is designed to relate to the multiplication of disciples, leaders, and churches. Dayton and Fraser help strategists keep this in mind by noting, "Our final goal is a cluster of congregations with enough Christians and resources necessary to complete evangelization in their own people group" (1990, 238). To this, Wagner adds, "Not only will strategy based on biblical priorities seek the ultimate goal of making disciples, but it will also attempt to make the maximum *number* of disciples possible" (1971, 28, emphasis in original). While there are numerous goals that teams could develop to accomplish numerous tasks, mission strategy—and the goals that support such strategy—is always oriented toward the Great Commission.

GOAL SETTING IS ABOUT GOOD STEWARDSHIP

The establishment of goals assists the team in maintaining a healthy stewardship with its resources of time, money, and people in particular. Goals hold team members accountable to one another as well as to those who support the team's ministry. Once a team has established goals, it creates a set of mile markers on the road of the journey toward the end vision. From time to time the team members need to ask one another if they are approaching those mile markers. Others who support the team's ministry share this obligation as well.

GOALS IN THREE LEVELS

Mission strategists should think in terms of establishing immediate, short-range, and long-range goals. Immediate goals are those that must be accomplished as soon as possible. They are the most urgent and most pressing. We will label these as goals to be accomplished before the team enters the field through the first year. Short-range goals are usually those for the first through third years, and long-range goals are those for three years and beyond. All the goals that a team establishes need to build on one another. There is a purpose for each goal and an interconnectivity among them. Over the course of time the goals work together to accomplish the vision (see fig. 24.1).

FIGURE 24.1: GOALS IN THREE LEVELS
(ADAPTED FROM DAYTON AND ENGSTROM 1979, 60)

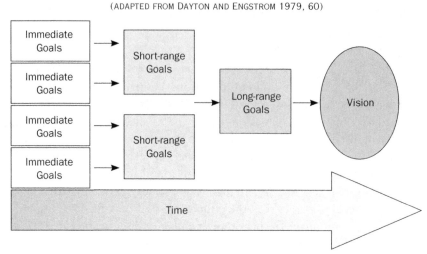

THE INTERCONNECTIVITY OF GOALS

Goals are critical components of the journey toward achieving the vision. Prior to the fulfillment of the vision several major accomplishments generally need to be completed, which we call major goals. And in order for these major goals to be completed, several minor accomplishments need to be completed, referred to as minor goals.

Using the analogy of taking a journey in an automobile, we can say that our major goals would be the most significant turns we would have to make on our drive—a left turn to exit our community, a right turn to enter the freeway. The need to take exit ramp 101, followed by a right turn onto Fourth Street would be major accomplishments on our drive. Without them we would not arrive at our destination.

Dayton and Engstrom assert, "In any organization there is (or should be) a relationship between all of the goals" (1979, 58). In light of our driving analogy, it is important for the strategist to realize that major goals are interconnected and can be achieved only by the completion of a series of smaller goals, such as passing three mile markers before exit ramp 101, dodging the large obstruction in the road on Fourth Street, and slowing down in the construction zone.

In essence the accomplishment of significant goals is based on the accomplishment of lesser goals, stacked on the accomplishment of even lesser (tertiary) goals. For the sake of brevity and clarity, we will concentrate on major and minor goals in this book. After you read this chapter, we are confident that you will be able to see the interconnectivity of the goals and will be able to understand even the tertiary goals supporting your minor goals.

To use another analogy, a mission strategy may be seen as a set of stairs, with each step moving the team closer to achieving the vision (see fig. 24.2). We recognize that the application of strategy in the field does not always happen in such a linear fashion, but we use this analogy for heuristic purposes to illustrate that our end goals are reached only through a series of sequential accomplishments. Patience and good communication among team members are necessary if there is a mixture of linear and nonlinear thinkers, a situation that is very likely to exist when Western and majority world believers are serving together.

The accomplishment of each goal along the journey to achieving the vision consists not of one single step but rather of a series of related components of both major and minor goals (fig. 24.2).

FIGURE 24.2: THE RELATIONSHIP OF MINOR AND MAJOR GOALS

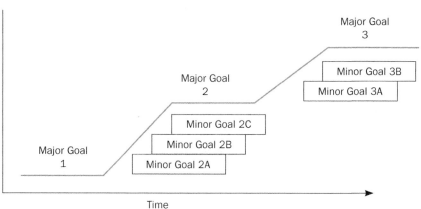

GUIDELINES TO SETTING GOALS

When we combine figures 24.1 and 24.2, the resulting model behind goal setting appears in figure 24.3.

Now that we recognize the big picture behind the process of setting goals, it is time to address the practical components involved in setting those goals related to mission strategy. The following are guidelines to assist in the development of a contextualized strategy. It will be evident that these components were addressed in other chapters throughout this book. Therefore, if clarification is needed, we suggest returning to the corresponding chapter for review.

FIGURE 24.3: INTERCONNECTIVITY OF GOALS

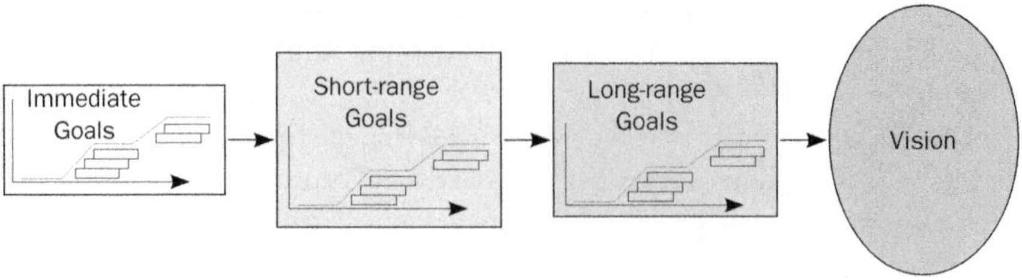

Know Your Purpose

The development of goals related to mission strategy is intimately connected to the purpose of the team that is implementing the strategy. A team must not lose sight of its purpose. A failure at this level will result in multiple deviations from the original vision, likely leading the team down a multitude of paths not directed toward the fulfillment of the end vision. The purpose for the team's existence must be related to the goals developed by the team. As Dayton and Engstrom write, "Just as purposes without goals can be discouraging, goals without purposes can be hopeless. There must be some ultimate purpose toward which the Christian organization is moving" (1979, 54).

Know Your Context

In order to set wise goals, a team needs a healthy knowledge of the people among whom it is called to serve. While this does not require that the team members become sociologists or anthropologists, they do need to have at least a basic understanding of the demographics, culture(s), spirituality, history, geography, politics, and language of the people.

Know Your Team

Knowledge of the team members' gifts, passions, talents, abilities, and life experiences is critical to helping the team establish goals. Goals that are too challenging for the present team are certain to remain unaccomplished. If the team has ownership in the development process of goal setting, it is more likely to develop goals that it is equipped to accomplish and share ownership of those goals.

Visualize the Big Picture

Robert H. Hayes offers a unique perspective on strategic planning in "Strategic Planning—Forward in Reverse?" (1985, 115). Although his model was originally applied to the business world, some of his ideas are helpful for developing mission strategy. We often visualize most forms of strategic planning as a series of large strategic leaps, illustrated in figure 24.4.

While it is important to visualize the overarching process, the notion of large leaps is sometimes daunting to the strategist. Hayes writes, "Because each step is so big and so visible, whoever proposes the change takes on an enormous risk in return for the chance to reap huge rewards. Success creates heroes; failure brings severe consequences" (1985, 115). Rather, Hayes advocates a paradigm that offers progress through a series of incremental, small steps, as portrayed in figure 24.5.

FIGURE 24.4: STRATEGIC LEAPS TOWARD THE VISION

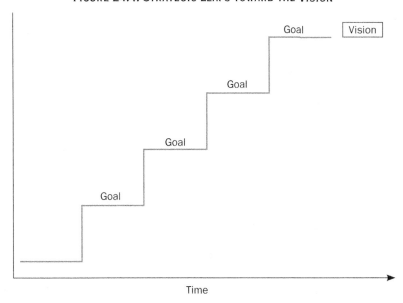

In our model of strategic planning, keep in mind the image from figure 24.5, but recognize that it is only a big-picture version of figure 24.2. In other words, if we magnified the line of progress in figure 24.5 to show the details, we would see figure 24.2, and not figure 24.4, showing its interconnected goals and steps. Considering strategic planning from this perspective helps us to understand that the risks involved as we progress from one goal to the next do not have to be overwhelming. If we consider strategic planning as making incremental achievements, then we are more likely to be better prepared for the necessary long-term approach. The development of mission strategy is more like the mental and emotional preparation for a marathon than that

Figure 24.5: Small Steps toward the Vision

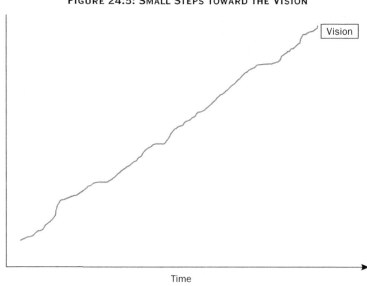

for a sprint. If we conceptualize our strategy as a series of Spirit-guided steps of progress toward accomplishing the vision, then we can better understand where we are in the strategy and how we fit in it at that location. It also helps us recognize that—depending on our vision—we may not experience the end vision in our tenures or even lifetimes.

Sidebar 24.1
On Writing Goals

The following template (adapted from Dayton and Fraser 1990, 300) is designed to help you and your team develop well-written goals. If you need assistance in filling in the blanks, reread the sections in this chapter titled "What Are Goals?" and "Avoid Unclear Goals."

    Goal name: _____
    Is this a major or minor goal? _____
    Goal number: ____
    Purpose of goal: _____
    We plan to accomplish this goal by
        this date: _____

We will know that we have accomplished this goal because: __
_____
We plan to take these steps to accomplish this goal: _____
These are the people who are responsible for accomplishing this goal: _____
The resources needed to accomplish this goal are:
Cost: _____
People: _____
Time: _____
Other: _____

Know Your Vision

The other day I (J. D.) watched the cartoon *Alice in Wonderland* with my children. At one point in Alice's journey, she encounters the Cheshire Cat, who informs her that as long as she does not know where she is going, any path she takes will get her to her destination. It illustrates why a team must have its destination in mind before establishing its goals. This end vision will assist teams in making certain that both major and minor goals point in the proper direction.

SIDEBAR 24.2
GOAL SETTING AS A TEAM

The following excerpt provides insight into the importance of developing goals as a team:

As this example suggests, team goals are important because they engage team members and team leaders in dialogue that not only establishes the goals but also helps build the team as a unit. Most people have had far more experience with individual goals than with team goals as work has tended to be built around individual responsibility. By asking team members to focus on their team's performance and determine where performance improvement goals should be set, team leaders gain valuable insight from many sets of eyes, rather than just their own. At this stage of the change process, it is appropriate to ask teams to think of ways they can better contribute to working more efficiently and effectively. Now that the teams have access to critical organizational information, clearer goals can be set.

As a team sets goals, it is critical to create goals that are truly useful, meaningful, and motivating. To work well for a team, the goals need to be POWER goals—that is, goals that provide answers to five key questions:

Pinpointed: "What exactly are we trying to accomplish?"

Owned: "What's in it for us, and can we buy into this responsibility?"

Well-defined: "How can we assess and measure our progress?"

Energizing: "Is this goal realistic yet challenging?"

Resourced: "Are we clear on the resources available to us for this task?" (Blanchard, Randolph, and Grazier 2005, 68–69)

REFLECTION AND DISCUSSION

- Do you foresee any challenges arising for your team if most members are more familiar with individual goals? If so, what challenges do you anticipate and how will you help to overcome them?

- As a leader, do you find it difficult to work with others in setting goals? Would you rather determine the goals and tell everyone to support those goals, or develop a collaborative effort among the team to determine the goals?

- What are the strengths and limitations of a team working together to establish its goals?

SIDEBAR 24.3
EVANGELIZATION PRIORITIES

The Strategy Working Group of the Lausanne Movement developed the following priorities as related to world evangelization (adapted from "Evangelization Priorities for the Coming Decade"):

1. To initiate church planting among the unengaged, unreached people groups that currently have no access to the gospel
2. To provide Scriptures for the 2,251 language groups that don't have Scriptures

3. To reach the 60 percent of the world's people who are "oral learners"
4. To encourage revolutionary approaches toward Muslims, Hindus, and Buddhists—nearly half the world's population
5. To seek renewal and reformation in the church
6. To integrate the global prayer movements with world evangelization
7. To work together more intentionally and inclusively, through alliances, networks, and partnerships—sharing contacts, information, and resources;

Pray

The process of goal setting, as with all strategy development, requires the leadership of the Spirit. Godly wisdom is absolutely necessary. Just as Solomon could discern a path to solving the case of the two prostitutes (1 Kings 3:16–28), similarly teams need the wisdom to be able to set the goals that the Lord would desire.

Prioritize

Though we may develop a multitude of goals, not all are appropriate. McGavran has noted that "Christian missions must cease being an enterprise in which all kinds of activities are ranked as about equal in importance. Christian missions must become the kind of a job in which priorities are put into force" (1955, 117). Teams are more likely to stay focused and discern the best route to take when they first understand their priorities. Dayton and Engstrom write, "Purposes and goals point direction. Priorities help us to choose which goals are most important" (1979, 77).

As much as possible we must set major goals in order, recognizing that the implementation of strategy does not always happen in such a linear and chronological fashion. The same is true of the prioritization of the minor goals. It is important to determine which major goals must be reached first, second, third, and so on, and which minor goals must be achieved in this fashion to accomplish the major goals. This prioritization assists teams in to demonstrate unity with one another as evidence of the deity of Christ and his love for the world

8. To increase our demonstration of compassion and reach out to the neglected of society

9. To seek to use media and technology, and other creative means, more effectively to spread the gospel among the masses

10. To train and equip pastors and the laity from every language group and culture

11. To empower and provide training in evangelism, discipleship, and church planting for younger leaders as well as laymen and laywomen

12. To encourage extensive and innovative initiatives to reach and disciple children and young people in each new generation

13. To allocate a much larger portion of our resources toward the least-reached areas of the world

REFLECTION AND DISCUSSION

• If you were going to set goals that were measurable, achievable, and time sensitive for some of these priorities, what would those goals look like?

• Why is it important for a team to know its priorities before setting goals?

reverse thinking, beginning with their vision and working backward to their first necessary step on that path.

Ask Good Questions

The team needs to ponder and discuss matters related to the implementation of its strategy. It needs to ask good questions about what it believes are the goals that the Spirit is leading it to establish.

Avoid Unclear Goals

One of the challenges facing strategists today in setting goals is ensuring that such goals are clear. Fuzzy goals emphasize activity, while clear goals communicate results. Table 24.1 will help you compare and contrast well-written goals with poorly written goals, enabling you to develop a better understanding of how to state the goals that your team hopes to accomplish.

Constantly Evaluate

Goals need to be evaluated in light of the end vision, purpose, context, and the team. Since matters related to the context and team may change over time, the team needs to constantly evaluate the goals it establishes. This is not a license to constantly change the goals, but it does offer the freedom to make revisions as the team progresses toward its end vision. Since missionary strategy involves humans in a changing environment, goals sometimes need to

235

TABLE 24.1
WELL-WRITTEN AND POORLY WRITTEN GOALS
(ADAPTED FROM DAYTON AND ENGSTROM 1979, 62)

Well-Written Goals	Poorly Written Goals
Stated as past events	Emphasize doing activities
To be accomplished in a definite time	No definite understanding of when they will be accomplished
Clear expectations	Unclear expectations
Practical and doable	Theoretical
Precise	Too brief or too long
One goal per statement	Two or more goals per statement

change. A team must be willing to make adjustments to its goals as the Spirit reveals the need. However, it should be noted that if the team is constantly changing its goals, there may be a problem with its strategic planning.

CONCLUSION

Missionary strategy consists of immediate, short-range, and long-range goals. Goals are to be not an end unto themselves but rather accomplishments on the journey toward the achievement of the vision. Wise strategists are able to see the overarching picture and the interconnectivity of their major and minor goals. Goals help unite the team and keep everyone moving forward in the same direction.

It is important that a team celebrate its accomplishments on the way toward achieving the vision. As goals are achieved, times of thanksgiving, rest, and fun should occur. The celebration that occurs whenever a goal is accomplished strengthens team camaraderie, encourages the individual(s) primarily responsible for its accomplishment, and allows the team members to play together, instead of always being consumed with goal-oriented activity.

25

Choosing Appropriate Methods

I n order for any team to move from the theoretical development of its major and minor goals toward the accomplishment of those goals, it must choose the methods it will use. In this chapter we define methods as action steps, or the means to accomplish a task. Methods are the "how-to" components of strategy. Without methods there will be no actions. And without action steps, strategies will not be accomplished.

Although it is possible to write of method as being a philosophy of doing something, such as "my method of reaching the world with the gospel is through telecommunications," in this chapter we focus on the practical steps. So to continue with this example, while the philosophical method is telecommunications, the practical method (i.e., the action step) is sharing the gospel through Facebook by discussing John 3:5 with interested friends.

Action steps are the practical tasks necessary—the means—to accomplish the minor, and thus eventually the major, goals in the mission strategy. Without action steps a strategy is simply a theory in the mind of the strategist. Action steps move the team from the theoretical foundation to the practical field. Luecke notes that "once specific, measurable, achievable, realistic, and time-bound goals have been assigned at the unit level, the question is: How will we achieve these goals? The answer is through *action steps*. Action steps are the 'who,' 'what,' and 'when' of carrying out a strategic initiative and achieving assigned goals. The sum of these steps should complete the job" (2005, 84).

This chapter builds on the assumption that the strategist has already established the minor and major goals that make up immediate, short-range, and long-range goals and has a good understanding of the context and the personalities of the team members (see previous chapters).

We write this chapter to provide assistance in the process of moving to the implementation, or execution, stage of mission strategy found in the next chapter.

REFLECTION AND DISCUSSION

Before a team begins developing methods to accomplish its goals, several questions are worth considering. The following is a list of six important questions to ask. They will generate conversation among team members as they work toward a consensus on the methods to be used.

Are the Methods Biblically Grounded?

While methods are culturally defined, missionary methods must be rooted in the Scriptures. The methods cannot be practices that extend beyond the biblical parameters for appropriate missionary action. The methods cannot diminish or augment the gospel and what it means to be a follower of Jesus. The methods must do everything to communicate the truth of the Scriptures to others, whether directly or indirectly.

Are the Methods Ethical?

The methods used cannot advocate any unethical practices. While we believe that ethical matters would indeed fall under the category of methods needing to be biblically grounded, for the sake of emphasis we have included this parallel question here. The history of the church includes numerous examples of unethical missionary practices done in the name of Jesus. An examination of how some people sought to evangelize certain Muslim groups and Native Americans provides sufficient evidence of unethical methods. Coercion, threats, and manipulation have no place in missionary methodology.

Do the Methods Avoid Unhealthy Pragmatism and Paternalism?

Closely related to the notion of the ethicality of missionary methods are the issues of pragmatism and paternalism. Pragmatism is the philosophy that whatever works to accomplish one's goal is appropriate methodology. Granted, all teams should be pragmatic (practical) to some degree. We desire to know what is working and not working to reach people with the gospel. However, taken too far, an "anything goes" approach to missionary methods becomes the justified reality in the name of Jesus. Pragmatism advocates that the end (e.g., goal) justifies the means (i.e., method). Just because people have come to Christ and churches have been planted, however, does not mean that the missionaries used healthy methods to reach the people. Just because we healed the sick and clothed the naked does not mean that our strategy was faithful to the God of compassion.

Paternalism is the philosophy that assumes that the missionaries know what is best for the people to whom they are called. This belief generally results in the use of methods that cause the people to become dependent on the missionaries for everything. The resulting churches are not truly indigenous because they have been planted using methods derived from a philosophy of paternalism. In modern times strategic imperialism can exist in the same way that political imperialism existed in the past.

Will the Methods Allow for the Gospel to Connect with the People?

The methods used must take into consideration where the people can generally be found on the Resistance-Receptivity and Søgaard scales (see chap. 19). The cultural expression of the methods used must not interfere with the people hearing the truth of Jesus. A method that is ineffective among a particularly resistant people may work very well among a more receptive people. The team needs to have a good understanding of the people being served as it shares the gospel.

Methods are not universal. They are contextually developed in time. And unlike principles, they do not always translate effectively from context to context. Methods that worked well in one context may be disastrous in a different context. Teams must make certain that their methods are not irrelevant. They also must keep in mind that the only offense to the people they are trying to reach is the message of the cross (Gal. 5:11), and not the methods used to communicate the message of the cross.

Are the Methods Highly Reproducible among the People?

While the context and strategy will require that some methods used to implement certain action steps will be very complex, caution should be used here. If the vision involves the multiplication of disciples, leaders, and churches, then the team must make sure that it is modeling methods before the people that they will in turn be able to adjust and reproduce within their context. If the methods selected are too technical and complex for the people to manage after coming to faith, then the team is likely creating a paternalistic situation. As we noted in chapter 5 and show in the Reproducibility-Potential Guide (see fig. 5.1), there is generally an inverse relationship between the reproducibility and the complexity of any given method.

The resources used need to be kept in check and remain within the means of the people. A failure to think about reproducibility at the level of methods is likely to result in stagnant growth.

Does the Team Have the Resources Necessary to Use the Methods?

Methods selected must be in line with the resources that the Lord has already granted to the team. While the Lord requires the team to walk by faith, he also grants wisdom and expects his people to be good stewards with the means they presently have. Although he may lead a team to develop methods beyond the resources he has presently provided as a test of faith, normally the methods used by the team must come from what it has received. On a related note, if the resources that the team desires are difficult for them to obtain, then the team is probably not guided by a missiology embracing multiplication—for the local believers are unlikely to be able to obtain those resources.

METHODOLOGICAL MATTERS

Before addressing the guidelines for developing methods, it is important to consider several factors related to methods in general. These five principles will assist the team in making wise decisions about the methods it uses. While this list is not exhaustive, it is a starting point.

Methods Must Be Held Loosely

Methods that work well today may not be as effective at a later time. G. W. Peters notes:

> A method which may be very effective at one time, at one place, among one people, may not be effective at another time, another place, another people. In fact, it may prove disadvantageous if not disastrous. Therefore, a method-bound movement cannot become an effective *world* movement. Neither can it last very long. It will soon be relegated to the outdated and the outworn. We do not need a renewal of the Gospel, but we do need continuous renewal of methodology to communicate the age-old Gospel in an intelligible, meaningful, and purposeful manner. (1975, 181)

Methods that lead to the planting of churches among a particular people may not work well when applied to a different people. A particular Bible storying tool that worked well in one part of the country may not be an effective communication tool in another part of the country. Recognizing that individuals, peoples, and societies change with time, wise strategists do not get locked into using one particular method but know how to adjust as circumstances change.

SIDEBAR 25.1
METHODS IN ALBANIA

Tom Steffen offers a helpful case study in understanding the effect of our methods on others:

> A young Albanian woman training at the Los Angeles Intercultural Urban Internship told me that Albanians see religion, including Christianity, as political and manipulative. She recounted the time when Islam entered Albania forcibly. "We became Muslims on the outside so we could remain Albanians on the inside," she said. "We did whatever was required by the Islamic government so that we could maintain our culture. And we were basically successful!"
>
> Today, as Islam pours much-needed money into this destitute country, Albanians again recognize political manipulation in spite of their desperate need for outside finances. They wonder again, "Are we being duped?"
>
> This Albanian woman noted the success that church planters were having among young people in the cities— so much success that some mission agencies have decided not to send additional personnel.
>
> But her parents were not impressed with this "so-called" successful church planting. They saw these newly planted churches as cults. Her parents told her they could never attend such churches.

> "They're not Albanian!" they said. And her parents are not alone.
>
> She then told why her parents felt so adamant about the new churches. The church planters are young, single missionaries, providing young people with fun things to do. The adults find it hard to take the young missionaries seriously. They go from house to house like the cults. There's no church building. They pray and sing in English. They teach a new religion with no historical tradition. Unlike the rich heritage and long religious traditions of the Greek Orthodox in the south, the Roman Catholics in the north, or the courting Muslims, this cult begins with the more recent Jesus. (1998, 432–33)

REFLECTION AND DISCUSSION

- Knowing what you know now, what are some of the methods you and your team would attempt to apply in this part of Albania? Why these?
- What different action steps could the church planters have used to show that the way of Jesus was not a new religion?
- How much of the methodology used by the church planters communicated a poor Christian theology to the Albanians? What does this case study reveal about the "truths" we communicate to others by the methods we use to reach them?

Methods Will Exclude People

Everyone will not be reached by the same method. The use of education to reach some people will exclude those who cannot go to school. The means of printed literature will exclude those who cannot read. With this in mind, teams must realize that it will take many different methods to reach people in their areas with the gospel.

Methods Are Not the Same

Strategists must understand that though there are different ways to accomplish certain goals, not all of them are the best for accomplishing the vision. Just because a team is able to accomplish a goal with a particular method does not mean that the method it uses is best for the situation. A person can drive a nail into a board with a saw, but how much better, and more effective, is it when he or she uses a hammer? Discernment should be used and team counsel should be sought in deciding which action steps to take to accomplish each goal. Regarding this matter, Dayton and Fraser write: "The means chosen to achieve goals make a significant difference in the outcomes that result as action is taken. Some methods are better means to our ends than others, given the mix of people who will be doing the evangelizing, the theological structure which we bring to bear on our understanding of the nature of the task and our goals, and the context within which we will be evangelizing" (1980, 282).

Clearly, determining the appropriateness of a particular method is a somewhat subjective matter. Such involves wisdom and discernment to determine whether the means selected to accomplish the team's task is the best route to be pursued.

Methods Are Often Developed on Location

It is very likely that a team will have to develop action steps through trial and error. Again, Dayton and Fraser's comments are most helpful: "We will have to do far more than simply sensitize ourselves to the cultural dimensions so that we can know how best to plug in our standardized solutions. Completely novel approaches which have never been taught in seminary or college and which are not written up in any missiological journal may have to be devised. We need to be ready and flexible to do just that" (1980, 294). Necessary innovation is likely to be especially true in the rapidly changing urban contexts of the world.

Such innovation in mission strategy is not a highly complicated matter. In the book of Acts, the innovation—to overcome significant barriers to gospel advancement—was a matter of following the leadership of the Spirit of mission (e.g., Acts 10: the reception of the gospel and Spirit by the God-fearers in Cornelius's house; Acts 11: the birth of the church in Antioch; Acts 16: the birth of the church in Philippi). In each situation the believers were required to change their general way of functioning and thinking. However, once the adjustments were made—sometimes with great reservation and sometimes by force—the gospel continued to expand beyond the sociocultural barriers.

Methods Must Be Kept in Check

Although missionaries should not embrace pragmatism, they must use a contextual discernment when it comes to their methods. If they are not seeing people come to faith and mature in Jesus and churches being planted, and if they are not observing the accomplishment of their goals, then it is very possible they need to change their methods.

While the methods used must be kept in check with reality, caution is required. There is also the possibility that the lack of results is not a methodological issue. If the team is working among people who are resistant to the gospel, then it is very unlikely that any method used would result in people becoming disciples. (The reverse is also generally true: almost any method will be effective among a highly receptive people.)

Therefore, the team must constantly be walking in step with the Spirit regarding its labors. The team members need to be students of their contexts. They need to discern if a methodological shift is necessary, or if they are to continue along their present path. If the team finds itself laboring among a resistant people, then it should use methods that will assist in moving the people toward a more favorable understanding of the gospel.

DEVELOPING METHODS

Before entering into the implementation (e.g., execution) stage of missionary strategy (covered in the next chapter), the team must develop methods to accomplish its major and minor goals. Methods related to the immediate and short-term goals are the most urgent and are likely to be developed the fastest. It is not uncommon for teams to struggle when trying to develop methods to accomplish long-term goals. Generally, the more immediate the goal is to the team's present activities, the easier it is for the team to conceptualize and develop the corresponding methods. While long-term goals may be a challenge for now, it is still important for teams to develop at least a rough notion of the methods it will use to accomplish two or three of its long-term goals. The following points are offered to guide teams through the process of developing those methods necessary for the immediate, the short-term, and the long-term periods.

Pray

As noted throughout this book, prayer must consume the life of the mission strategist. The practice of praying without ceasing (1 Thess. 5:17) should also be applied to the development of methods. Wisdom and discernment are needed in the process of determining the best course of action for the team.

Look to Biblical Examples

Although the debate continues about what is descriptive and prescriptive in the Scriptures, we should allow the first-century believers a great deal of latitude with respect to the model they offer us today for what the church should be doing in the world. Roland Allen—when referring to the apostle Paul—provides a similar exhortation:

> Unless we are prepared to drag down St. Paul from his high position as the great Apostle of the Gentiles, we must allow to his methods a certain character of universality. . . . But, important as I believe it to be in the very early stages of our missions to follow the apostolic practice, which manifestly and undeniably conduced to his astounding success, yet it is of comparably greater importance that we should endeavor to appreciate the principles in which the Apostle's practice was rooted, and to learn the spirit which made their application both possible and fruitful. (1962, 147–48).

Also addressing this issue, while also referencing the apostle, Hesselgrave writes:

> As we have said, there seems to be little to indicate that the Holy Spirit expects us to slavishly follow every Pauline procedure in our evangelistic outreach. On the other hand, there is explicit teaching in the Epistles which directs us to carry on the same activities in a similar way—namely, to go where people are, preach the gospel, gain converts, gather them into churches, instruct them in the faith, choose leaders, and commend believers to the grace of God. And where would we find a pattern for these activities that is less likely to lead us into blind alleys than is the apostle Paul's missionary work? . . .
>
> We conclude, then, that Paul's message was absolutely normative, and that his manner of life and missionary methodology were less normative. It is a

matter of degree. There is room for adaptation in each case, but less in the case of his message and more in the cases of his lifestyle and methodology. (1980, 57)

Missionary teams should not attempt to re-create a first-century context but need to discern between the timeless principles and the contextualized methods used in the Scriptures. Even the biblical examples provide much guidance in the area of methodology.

Look to Other Kingdom Citizens

If there are other teams and churches in the area that are observing growth through conversions and the development of healthy churches, then new teams should seek to better understand what methods the Lord is using to reach people in the area. However, teams should not limit their observations to those serving nearby or among the same people. Who else has been able to accomplish similar goals as those of the team, regardless of context? It is very likely that there is much to learn from their methods. Strategists should not feel as if they have to reinvent the wheel. There is great wisdom in looking toward others. Such investigations may reveal methods that the team needs to embrace but may also reveal methods that the team should avoid.

Prioritize

As discussed in the previous chapter, a team is faced with a multitude of possibilities for action. A team must know its priorities when setting goals. The same principle applies to developing methods. Certain goals need to be accomplished before other goals can be accomplished; therefore, prioritization is necessary at the methodological level.

Know the Goal

In order to begin developing action steps, strategists must know the goal that they desire to achieve. A significant connection exists between the goal and the action required to accomplish it. For if someone does not know the goal to be achieved, how will he or she devise a series of tasks to accomplish it? The goal provides the focus; the action step provides the means to accomplish the task. Luecke's questions help clarify this relationship to assist in determining the action steps:

> In approaching a goal, ask this question: What are all the steps that must be taken to accomplish our goal? Once you have the answer, ask this question for each step you've identified: Can this step be broken down into sub-steps? By asking

that same question over and over for each step and its component sub-steps, you will eventually reach a point where steps can no longer be subdivided. At that point you will have identified every action step. (2005, 84)

Evaluate Resources

Before a team can develop healthy action steps, it must examine the resources that the Lord has provided for it to accomplish its task. Time, money, and people involved must be taken into account. While grandiose action steps may be supported by the statement, "We'll trust the Lord to provide all these resources," teams must recognize that sometimes the Lord chooses to glorify himself through only five loaves and two fish.

Brainstorm

The concept of brainstorming has been around for some time. It is the activity of a group gathered with one purpose: to postulate a multitude of possibilities for action, no matter how simple or complex they may appear.

With the goal in mind, the team should consider a variety of possible means to accomplish this goal. Consider writing down all the team's thoughts no matter how lofty or simple. Brainstorming is not the time to critique the random thoughts tossed out by team members. Rather, allow all the team members to share, making sure that everyone's suggestions are noted. At the conclusion of this activity, the team should have generated a variety of possible steps to take.

Use Discernment

Although brainstorming will yield several possible courses of action, some will be better than others. A great deal of discernment is needed to choose the wisest action steps. While the brainstorming activity is designed to include all possible options for action, discernment is now needed to select the best route for the team.

Make Sure the Steps Are Measurable

For a team to know when the action steps have been implemented, such steps must be measured in some manner. If a team has decided that major goal X will be accomplished whenever minor goals X1, X2, and X3 are accomplished, the team must determine how it will know when these minor goals are accomplished. What are the steps required to bring them to fulfillment? How does the team know when it has taken the steps toward completion of the minor goals? The team should be able to measure its progress by comparing where it was in relation to its vision before the methods were used and where it is afterward.

Assign Responsibility

An individual or individuals must be responsible for carrying out the methods. The action steps must be owned by someone; responsibility must be assigned. If someone does not take responsibility for the action, it is unlikely the goal will be accomplished.

The individual or individuals responsible should be passionate about the required action and capable of carrying out the method. Of course, such zeal is more likely to be found among those who were able to assist in the development of the strategy. They will have had ownership in the entire process up to this point.

Be Time Sensitive

Just as goals are to be time bound, methods must also be implemented in a predetermined amount of time. This time sensitivity means that the action must happen in the future. Dates of accomplishment should be set but not written in stone. Since all mission strategy involves flexibility, the dates when action steps are to be accomplished are not definitive but rather somewhat tentative. Teams should set dates in their calendars to accomplish the tasks but must recognize that schedules sometimes require adjustment, since they are working with dynamic individuals and not attempting to market a corporation's product.

While such flexibility is important, it must not be abused. Teams should not be lackadaisical in their planning or in executing their action steps. The habitual recalibration of a team's calendar may be a sign of poor planning or simply laziness. Malphurs reminds strategists of the temptation that comes when putting off actions until later: "The temptation for leaders is to wait for exactly the right time and ideal conditions to act. That is the theoretical world. In the real world, however, there is no exactly right time or ideal conditions. At some point you have got to take the plunge, you have got to move, or you will miss the God-given opportunities" (2005, 281).

Just Do It

After the team believes it has done what needed to be accomplished in each of the aforementioned categories, the team has to take action. It needs to act based on all its previous work. The time has come to apply all the labor

247

leading up to this point in the process of taking the action steps. It is here that the theory and planning become reality.

CONCLUSION

In any given context there are usually many different ways to accomplish a given goal. In spite of this plethora of potential options, not all methods are the most advantageous to the overall strategy. The selection of appropriate methods is an important matter for strategists to keep in mind. Without such action steps, goals will not be achieved and visions will go unfulfilled.

26

Execution

A failure to execute a strategy is typically a failure at implementation. Without execution strategic planning remains theory. Teams can spend a great deal of time researching a people or an area and developing their plan and yet fail to accomplish what they had planned to do. They dream big dreams and have excellent intentions, but at the end of the day many of their desires may remain unfulfilled. Larry Bossidy and Ram Charan refer to execution as the "missing link between aspirations and results" (2002, 19). They also note, "Execution is fundamental to strategy and has to shape it. No worthwhile strategy can be planned without taking into account the organization's ability to execute it" (21). In this chapter we address the components involved in the implementation, or execution, of a strategy.

In the process of planning we attempt to determine the future. While only the Lord has control over the future, we recognize that the decisions we make have an effect on the future. For example, if I fail to pay my electric bill, the electric company will shut off my electricity. If I fail to put gas in my automobile, eventually it will stop. Dayton and Fraser offer a wonderful description: "Planning is an attempt to produce surprise-free futures, to anticipate as much as possible what the future is likely to hold and how we will respond to it" (1990, 294). While we know we cannot predict the future within our God-given means, we can work diligently as good stewards of the kingdom to serve the Lord to the fullest. Good execution of a plan involves discernment, decision making, and action steps to accomplish what we believe the Lord would have us do.

PRAY

Successful execution must involve prayer as a major stage in the implementation process. Although teams should not be fearful of execution, they should be cautious and discerning. The writer of Proverbs warns, "Whoever makes haste with his feet misses his way" (19:2 ESV), and "The plans of the diligent lead surely to abundance, but everyone who is hasty comes only to poverty" (21:5 ESV).

Just as the team has made prayer a significant component of the strategy development process, it must continue in this pattern. Rushing into a matter is a sure way to ignore the warnings from Proverbs. The team needs divine leadership throughout the execution process.

KNOW YOUR VISION AND GOALS

The proper execution of a strategy requires that a team clearly understand the vision toward which it is working and the goals that support that vision. A loss of focus and a failure to work toward healthy goals are sure ways to implement the wrong plans. Healthy execution of the action steps requires avoiding distractions while keeping the main thing the main thing.

KNOW YOUR RESOURCES

What has the Lord provided for the team to execute the strategy? While the team may desire to accomplish a particular strategy, the Lord may not have provided the resources needed to accomplish a certain set of action steps. The execution of a strategy requires that the team recognizes its available resources and uses them accordingly.

GET THE RIGHT PEOPLE DOING THE RIGHT THINGS

Having team members do activities for which their gifts best suit them is vitally important. People have different abilities, passions, gifts, personalities, life experiences, and talents. While such diversity can be good in many situations, it is not always conducive to the execution of a strategy. Generally, individuals are most efficient, energized, and willing to follow through on their commitments to an action step when they are operating from their passions and spiritual gifts.

Having the right people in the right places doing the right actions is somewhat of an art in and of itself. The wise team leader will get to know his or her team long before the team begins to attempt to implement a strategy. On those rare times when this is not possible, the leader should expect that challenges will hinder the plan's execution and be ready to make the necessary changes in action step assignments.

KEEP IT SIMPLE

The action steps need to be broken down into bite-size pieces. Encouragement and excitement come whenever a team is able to experience progress at a rapid rate. Generally, grand accomplishments do not occur overnight. By breaking down each piece of each action step into smaller tasks, the team can recognize its progress toward accomplishing the vision.

If an action step appears too daunting, a team may become paralyzed by its analysis of the situation. Execution becomes more doable in the minds of team members when they realize that progress will be made bit by bit, step by step. As teams manage to keep their actions simple, they will also receive the blessing of empowerment that comes from steady advancement.

In his best-selling book *Good to Great: Why Some Companies Make the Leap and Others Don't*, Jim Collins comments on this connection between the team and keeping matters simple: "What do the right people want more than almost anything else? They want to be part of a winning team. They want to contribute to producing visible, tangible results. They want to feel the excitement of being involved in something *that just flat-out works*. When the right people see a simple plan born of confronting the brutal facts—a plan developed from understanding, not bravado—they are likely to say, 'That'll work. Count me in'" (2001, 177).

The challenges set before missionaries are daunting. Whether in dense urban contexts or remote rural villages, the challenges can appear to be both overwhelming and paralyzing. The need to keep matters simple often seems to contradict the complexity of the challenges surrounding the team. However, it should be remembered that throughout the Scriptures, the Lord shows himself both faithful and powerful as he works through the simple matters in his kingdom to reach into the complexities of the kingdom of darkness.

PROBLEM SOLVE AS YOU GO

Strategy is mainly developed in a somewhat sterile laboratory and is adjusted on location. While planning is necessary, the strategist must recognize that unforeseen problems will arise during the execution of the strategy. The strategist must anticipate the obstacles and barriers to the implementation of the strategy. Part of being a strategist involves the role of problem solver. Dayton and Engstrom are aware of this reality: "There is a close relationship between planning and problem solving. When we plan, we identify the goal we are attempting to meet. In problem solving, we decide what stands between us and the goal, so we can try to overcome the obstacle" (1979, 78). Some of the challenges to execution will be small while others will be great. Regardless, the strategist must overcome them.

Dayton and Engstrom offer excellent counsel regarding the role of a problem solver. In *Strategy for Leadership: Planning, Activating, Motivating, Elevating*, they outline seven basic steps to overcoming obstacles (1979, 96). Although

---

SIDEBAR 26.1
ANTICIPATING PROBABLE OUTCOMES

In the following account John D. Robb recalls the importance of thinking carefully about implementing one's plans *before* actually executing them:

> Several years ago, while serving in Malaysia, I gave my time and involvement, along with other Christian leaders, to a mass media evangelistic campaign. It was reported to have been highly successful in other cities so we decided to lend it our support. Many pastors and churches were involved and gave heavily of their time, energy, and money.
>
> The campaign appealed to a certain segment of the population—English-educated young people—and there were many "decisions" from among this group. However, very few became disciples and were integrated into the churches. On top of that, 50 percent of the population, the Muslims, were incensed by this culturally insensitive approach.
>
> If we pastors and missionaries had thought strategically and exercised

foresight in visualizing the probable impact of the campaign, as far as the likely number of disciples that would be made and the adverse reaction by the Malay Muslims, we would not have employed this standard, pre-packaged approach to our unique, culturally diverse city. We would have developed long-range evangelistic strategies for each of the distinct social and cultural groups that took into account their uniqueness as groups. (1994, 38–39)

REFLECTION AND DISCUSSION

- Why do you think Robb and those working in the city did not consider the probable impact beforehand?
- What are the challenges to considering the different probable outcomes of an executed strategy?
- Have you and your team considered the probable outcomes of your strategy? If so, do you think any adjustments are necessary at this time?

many of these steps are common knowledge, they offer teams a simple linear approach to responding to challenges that threaten to erect roadblocks on the path toward fulfilling the vision.

Understand What Needs to Be Done

The first step in the problem-solving process is not only understanding the problem but recognizing what needs to be done to remove it. If someone has a roof that leaks whenever it rains, then the roof needs to be repaired. If a fungus is damaging a farmer's crops, then the fungus needs to be destroyed or otherwise removed as a threat to the crops. While this is an obvious first step, it is all-important that the team clearly focus on the problem and the desired outcome.

Compare the Task to a Known Problem

Since there is nothing new under the sun, the team needs to understand how others have responded to the same or a similar problem. Knowing how to problem solve comes from learning from the experiences of others. It is also possible to learn from others who have responded inappropriately to their problems.

Devise an Overall Strategy or Approach

As problems arise, teams will have to develop strategies to respond to them. These strategies within the larger overall strategy can be thought of as "mini-strategies" on the path toward accomplishing the end vision.

Make a Plan to Solve the Problem

The problem-solving strategy now must move from the theoretical to the practical. This step involves developing action steps to resolve the matter at hand.

Gather Resources to Carry Out the Plan

What people, time, finances, and so forth are needed to solve the problem? While most problems that a team faces will require only a small amount of time or other resources to resolve, some issues will require much greater resources.

Carry Out the Plan

The team needs to implement the strategy to solve the problem. Throughout this process it must be careful to keep in line with its overall strategy to accomplish the end vision. And while overcoming the roadblock to accomplishing that desired end, it must make certain that it quickly returns to the proper course of action.

Use the Results

Teams rarely forget previous roadblocks, but they must also remember what they did to overcome, bypass, or fix them. The results of the problem-solving process should be used to assist the team in solving future problems. Results from solving major problems should be communicated to others who are involved in supporting the work of the team.

REFOCUS ON THE PRIORITIES

A team will face many situations that will challenge it to compromise its convictions. While such compromises may even foster a faster path toward the vision, the team must make sure that it does not lose sight of its priorities. From time to time the team members will need to gather together to remind one another of the biblical and missiological priorities that drive them to execute the strategy. These times for refocusing are healthy and necessary as the team members urge one another on to good works.

READJUST TO REALITY

In *Planning Strategies for World Evangelization*, Dayton and Fraser remind us that "plans need constant revision. The further plans stretch into the future, the less likely they are to describe what will really happen" (1990, 299). A team will need to readjust goals, action steps, and other elements of the strategy to changing realities. Such readjustment is not only necessary for the team to remain on the proper course to the fulfillment of the end vision, but it also helps the team to stay motivated. Distractions can result in a loss of focus, leading to a sense of discouragement and decreased motivation. It is unwise to ignore the brutal facts of reality when matters do not go as expected. Ignorance is not bliss. And people will begin to question leadership if they believe the situation on the field has shifted but their leaders apparently remain oblivious to such changes.

Sometimes the need for readjusting to reality can come from team successes. Effectiveness can lead the team to become nearsighted and lose focus. Another comment by Dayton and Engstrom is helpful at this point:

> Surprisingly, a major reason for failure can be success! Many times an organization which was successful in achieving its initial purpose comes to believe

that it has done everything right and that the way it has done things in the past will therefore be exactly the way to do things in the future. But times do change, and it is vitally important that organizations change with them. (1979, 48–49)

Past successes can become future problems. An ongoing readjustment is not only necessary but also healthy for a team. Also, teams should be aware of changing contextual realities. What works well for the team in one part of a city may not work well in a different location or with different people.

CONCLUSION

Because the world in which missionary strategy is implemented is composed of social beings, it is always changing. Change is one thing that a strategist can count on when developing strategy. While the details of change can rarely be predicted, strategists who prayerfully stay focused, keep the strategy simple and flexible, and expect to problem solve as they implement the strategy are more likely to reach their goals when on location.

All leaders and teams make mistakes. But wise team members serve the Lord with all their hearts, minds, and abilities, trusting his will to be done on earth as it is in heaven. How the team responds to its mistakes makes a great deal of difference.

27

Evaluation

While the strategy development process concludes with evaluation, the reality is that evaluation must permeate everything the team does. It is not simply something to be done after a task or project has been completed or the vision has been achieved. It is a means to monitor the progress and focus of the team according to its purpose and vision.

To better understand the process of evaluating mission strategy, it helps to know that it is not a contemporary creation. Malphurs notes that evaluation is found in several locations throughout the New Testament. He observes:

> While no examples exist in the New Testament of a church passing out some kind of performance appraisal, that does not mean that they did not appraise their people and ministries, nor does it mean that we do not have the freedom to do so. Luke regularly supplies us with progress reports and church updates in Acts 2:41, 47; 4:4; 5:14; 6:1, 7; 9:31, 35, 42; 11:21, 24; 14:1, 21; 16:5; 17:12. In 1 Timothy 3:1–13 Paul gives the qualifications for deacons and elders. That means that some kind of evaluation was made, or such qualifications would not have made sense. In 1 Corinthians 11:28 Paul preached healthy self-examination to the members of the church at Corinth. He encouraged them to examine themselves before taking the Lord's Supper. This would result in the proper proclaiming of the Lord's death (v. 26) and preclude judgment (vv. 29–32). Again, in 2 Corinthians 13:5–6 he tells the people of the church to examine and test

themselves to see whether they are in the faith. To fail such a test would have been a calamity. But he seems to indicate that not to test oneself would be an even greater calamity. Then in Revelation 2–3 God evaluates six of his churches, looking for what they are doing well and not so well. (2005, 296)

EVALUATION LEADS TO BETTER STEWARDSHIP

Honest evaluation challenges the team to consider its stewardship of what the Lord has provided for it. It serves as a time to evaluate what it is doing in light of the billions of people on the planet who are not followers of Jesus. Almost every year I (J. D.) get an eye exam. As noted in chapter 21, I am extremely nearsighted. According to my doctor, my vision is fine; the problem is my ability to focus. Periodically my prescription changes, and I need stronger lenses to help my eyes focus properly. Ongoing evaluation is similar to getting a new prescription. It allows the team to refocus on the task in light of any changes that may have occurred.

EVALUATION REVEALS WHAT NEEDS TO CHANGE

Change is inevitable, especially when it comes to implementing a mission strategy. It should be understood not as a distraction but as a part of the journey. Regular, ongoing evaluation assists the team in discerning what needs to be changed in its strategy in light of its end vision. Healthy necessary changes come from a proper assessment of the present realities.

EVALUATION LEADS TO OVERALL IMPROVEMENT

By recognizing what needs to be changed, the team is better positioned to make the necessary adjustments in its overall strategy. Evaluations may reveal that not only is change necessary at the team level but also that specific team members may need to make personal adjustments. While individual changes are often necessary, team members should not view such evaluations as infringing on their personalities, character, or style. Strategy evaluation is not an opportunity to foster the development of critical attitudes. Rather, a team must understand that both corporate and individual change are part of the process of moving the team toward completing the vision.

Sometimes evaluation reveals that improvement will be achieved when new goals are established. Sometimes methods will need to be adjusted in light of evaluation. Like a diagnostic check on an automobile, an evaluation of strategy will assist the team in understanding what needs to be improved for the kingdom.

EVALUATION REVEALS WHAT IS IMPORTANT

Evaluation makes a statement about a team's priorities. Malphurs is correct when he notes that "what gets evaluated gets done. We evaluate some things and do not evaluate others. What we choose to evaluate sends a message to our people. It says this is important; whereas something else is not as important, because it isn't evaluated" (2005, 297–98).

While there will be certain aspects of the strategy implementation process that will deserve more scrutiny than others, the team must make certain that evaluation permeates the entire strategy development process. A failure to saturate everything with intentional, regular, and ongoing evaluation can

---

SIDEBAR 27.1
THE VALUE OF EVALUATION

Greg W. Burch, Andy Sexton, and Angela Murray share the importance of evaluation in their article "Strategic Impact: Multiplying Our Effectiveness with Children at Risk." Drawing from their research and experience of serving children, they remind strategists of the importance of taking time to evaluate.

Monitoring and evaluation are key components to being strategic in our care of children at risk. Monitoring is making sure that the activities in your strategic plan are being done, and budgeting. Evaluation is making sure those activities are having the desired impact . . . that your vision and objectives are being met. This is an essential part of being strategic. If you don't evaluate, you can never celebrate! Evaluation can also be useful in that it can highlight the potential unintended negative impacts our work may be having. Take, as an example, a prevention project in Guatemala, which sought to reduce the number of children taking to life on the streets. The organization worked in some of the poorest communities on the outskirts of Guatemala City. An in-depth evaluation of the work demonstrated that the children involved in the scheme benefited greatly from the project and were much less likely to migrate to the streets. However, the evaluation also revealed that other families in the community who were not part of the scheme felt alienated and marginalized by the work. While they appreciated that the organization was attempting to offer help to the most vulnerable, the community felt they should be involved in the decisions regarding who receives help in the future. These findings enabled the organization to refine its mode of working and allowed much stronger community links to be formed. (2009, 479)

REFLECTION AND DISCUSSION

- What do you think is meant by the statement, "If you don't evaluate, you can never celebrate!"?
- How did the evaluation process help the team make future improvements? What do you think it added/changed based on its findings?

258

create confusion among team members and partners who are left wondering why some aspects of the strategy are important and others are not so important. In the section titled "Specifics on Evaluation," we have listed what we believe are specific elements that—when evaluated regularly—assist the team with saturating the strategy development and implementation processes with healthy evaluation.

EVALUATION HELPS ENCOURAGE THE TEAM

While evaluation does help the team to know what needs to be changed, it is also designed to provide the team with encouragement. Just as a team needs to recognize what it must do to improve, it also needs to know what is being done well. The evaluation process is not simply about making changes; it also creates opportunities for celebration. Teams should take encouragement in their evaluation processes. By knowing what is working well, the team can concentrate on its strengths in the future.

DEVELOPING A PHILOSOPHY OF EVALUATION

Even before a team is developed, it is important for each potential member to recognize that healthy teams embrace a philosophy of evaluation that will influence all that they do in the field. The following four elements are presented to assist potential teams with understanding and supporting an approach to missionary strategy that involves regular and intentional evaluation.

An Atmosphere of Evaluation

Strategists and teams need to create a healthy atmosphere that makes evaluation an expected ongoing process. This process must continually occur throughout the team's ministry. The team must always be evaluating, before, during, and after implementing its methods. As Luecke notes, "No action plan can foresee the many obstacles and changing conditions that people will face over the weeks and months it takes to implement a strategy. Thus, midcourse adjustments and management intervention are inevitable and necessary" (2005, 96). By maintaining a perennial approach to evaluation, any necessary midcourse adjustments can be discerned and implemented.

Ongoing self-evaluations should be encouraged. Team members need to develop the habit of keeping their hearts in check with their callings. Frequently, team members need to examine whether they are following through on their commitments. Such self-evaluations are a reminder to each team member of the great trust that has been extended to him or her for missionary work. If

259

all team members know that they are to evaluate themselves, then the findings revealed through biannual evaluations by the team leader should come as no surprise.

A Healthy Discontent

Teams are wise to embrace an attitude of "healthy discontent" with their missionary labors. This attitude comes from the recognition that there is always room for improvement, both as a team and as individuals. Knowing that nothing is accomplished to perfection, teams should understand that there is always room for growth. Such an attitude will prevent team members from developing a spirit of criticism toward one another, themselves, and the unbelievers around them. A healthy discontent recognizes that the individual and the team do their best but are growing in the process of their kingdom service. The refrain, "What could I/we have done better, if I/we could do it again?" is a question that should constantly echo in the minds of team members.

Expectations Must Be Tempered by Reality

It is rare that a strategy is executed exactly as it is written down on paper or conceived in someone's mind. It is difficult to find a team that was able to accomplish its desired goals exactly as it had planned. Implementing mission strategy is not like implementing a strategy for the assembly line, where there is much more predictability with inanimate objects. Mission strategy focuses on sentient beings and must address spiritual opposition. The realities on location cannot be predicted with high levels of precision.

Though the team must walk by faith, its expectations should be tempered by reality. Although the Lord will often work miracles where we serve, he also will often allow the team's realities to be shaped without obvious divine intervention. Teams must learn to keep high expectations but recognize that the implementation of mission strategy is more art than science. Experience will come over time, but even with much experience, situations are so fluid that the team must prepare itself accordingly. Foremost, the team must also recognize that the Spirit's plans and leading *must always* supersede the expectations of the team (e.g., Acts 16:6–10).

Biannual Evaluation

While teams should constantly evaluate everything they do, they need to designate a time every six months to focus on prayer and evaluation. During such meetings the team should pray for wisdom to discern what it needs to change in light of the upcoming year. It needs to ask, "What did we learn from the previous six months that will lead to more faithful service for the upcoming year?" and "What is not working so well?" (A few resources to consider are Dayton and Fraser 1990, 320–27; Malphurs 2005, 295–309; and Harvard Business School 2005, 95–108 and 140.)

During such an evaluation time, the team is likely to become aware of practices it needs to drop and avoid in the future. Action steps that resulted in faux pas and communication breakdowns with the people are to be discarded. Teams will also recall the parts of the strategy that were implemented well, leading to the advancement of the gospel and churches planted.

The biannual evaluation should also be a time when the team leader is able to spend time with each member of the team. This time of personal evaluation should be an occasion to assist team members in their ministries and help them prepare for the rest of the year. As much as possible, a team should be self-evaluating. The members need to keep one another in check, encouraging and exhorting one another to good works.

This assessment process is especially important when it comes to evaluating the team leader. A healthy team includes evaluation for everyone, including the first among equals. Each individual should be evaluated based on his or her strengths and limitations, personality, overall connection with the team, quality of and faithfulness to the ministry, character, and productivity. It is unfortunate when a team member must be released from ministry with the team after an evaluation. However, an atmosphere of positive evaluation and healthy discontent among team members, which allow for addressing small problems before they become major issues, helps avoid an acrimonious departure. It is easier to stop a leak than a raging flood.

A portion of the biannual evaluation should be devoted to celebrating and praising the Lord for the wonderful things he has allowed the team to accomplish. It should be a time to look back in rejoicing. Teams must make sure that while they have a healthy discontent with their kingdom labors, they must also incorporate an attitude of gratitude for all that has occurred to advance the gospel among the people and work toward the multiplication of disciples, leaders, and churches.

SPECIFICS ON EVALUATION

The evaluation of a strategy should examine as many aspects of it as possible. We have listed seven components as specifics for evaluation. It should be obvious at this point that our list is basically a rough outline of the contents of this book.

Vision

The team should remind itself of the vision at least once per month. During the evaluation process the team members need to ask: "Do we all still have the same end vision toward which we are working?" If everyone does not have the same vision in mind and heart, then the team needs to refocus.

Priorities

Are the team's priorities still the same, or has there been an addition or subtraction? While it is likely that the priorities of the team will not change very much, the team needs to make certain that it keeps these in mind. A failure to keep sight of the priorities will have devastating effects on the implementation of the strategy.

Goals

Here the team must keep both the minor and the major goals in mind. Reflection and discussion include: "Did we accomplish our minor and major goals?" and "Were our goals achieved on time?" If not, "Why not?"

Context

While most contexts will not change significantly from year to year, the team must constantly evaluate its contexts geographically, demographically, culturally, spiritually, and politically. For example, economic shifts, disasters, war, political turmoil, and migrations all affect communities. In most cases urban contexts will change faster than rural contexts. The main question asked should be, "How has the population segment or people group changed in the past several months, and does the change require a revision of our strategy?"

Team

It has already been mentioned that the team also needs to go through an evaluation process. Evaluation at this level should be regarded not with dread but rather as a means to grow as individuals and as a team in order to do a better job accomplishing the strategy.

Methods

The action steps used by a team must be evaluated in light of how well they communicate the gospel, move people toward a more favorable attitude toward the gospel, connect the people with the gospel, build up kingdom citizens through local churches, and foster the multiplication of disciples, leaders, and churches. Team members need to ask: "Did our methods lead to the accomplishment of our minor and major goals?" If not, then they should ask, "Why not?" and "What needs to be adjusted?"

Resources

Although most team members will always feel that they do not have enough resources, the resources available must be objectively evaluated. Did the team use its time, other people/churches, money, and so forth in the most efficient manner? Could it have done something differently with a better outcome?

CONCLUSION

Conducting evaluations is a challenging process. Team members must have the discipline to create an atmosphere of evaluation among themselves. Evaluation is a necessary habitual practice that will assist team members in staying focused and remaining good stewards of the opportunities made available to them. While evaluation is sometimes a convicting process, it is one that strengthens both the unity and the zeal of the team in its actions to advance the kingdom. Occasionally the team will need to bring in an outside evaluator in order to gain the perspective necessary for honest evaluation.

Appendix

People-Group Profile

GENERAL INFORMATION

Name of people group:

Description of people group:

_____

_____

Population:

Geographical area:

Primary language:

Primary religion:

LOCATION/ENVIRONMENT

Terrain and climate:

_____

_____

_____

Affect of the terrain and climate on the people group's lifestyle:

_____

_____

Any recurring natural disasters?

_____

_____

_____

_____

People reside mostly in:

☐ cities ☐ towns ☐ villages ☐ farms
☐ other:

_____

LANGUAGE/LITERACY

Primary language:

Secondary language:

Tertiary language:

Adult literacy percentage:

How is literacy defined?

_____

_____

_____

This profile was developed by Jim Slack based on his experiences as the church growth consultant for the International Mission Board. Our thanks to Jim for allowing us to reproduce this profile here.

ECONOMICS

Effect of geography on the economic situation:

Income sources:

Status of wealth distribution:

Products/crafts:

Economic status compared to the rest of the nation:

Modernization/utilities:

Principal occupations:

Economic trends:

LIVING CONDITIONS/COMMUNITY DEVELOPMENT

Food/nutrition:

Water (domestic/agricultural):

Shelter:

Energy/fuel/electricity:

Clothing:

Mass communication:

Health care:

Technological trends:

SOCIETY

Family structures:

Rule/authority/selection:

Neighbor relations:

Social habits/groupings:

_____

_____

Rate of adaptation to change:

☐ static ☐ slow ☐ medium ☐ rapid

Acculturation to national society:

☐ distant ☐ near ☐ intermediate

Self-image:

☐ threatened ☐ depressed
☐ prestigious/proud

Judicial system:

_____

Crisis/conflicts:

_____

Celebrations/recreation:

_____

Art forms:

_____

Media:

☐ radio ☐ TV ☐ newspapers ☐ films
☐ videos ☐ recordings ☐ online ☐ other:

CHILDREN/YOUTH

Education/type of schooling:

_____

Labor/tasks:

_____

Problems (morality/family/insurrection/etc.):

_____

Greatest needs:

_____

RELIGION

Primary religion:

Secondary religion:

Tertiary religion:

Religious practices/ceremonies:

_____

Redemptive analogies/"bridges":

_____

Spiritual climate/openness:

_____

Pastor/evangelists to the people group:

_____

Missionaries to the people group:

_____

Who is Jesus Christ to the people group?

Percent who believe Jesus is the Son of God:

Percent who believe Jesus is a prophet, teacher, a good man, but not God's son:

Percent who believe Jesus is myth:

Percent who have never heard of Jesus:

Total number of evangelicals:

Total number of evangelical churches:

Word of God translated into the language? Where is it available?

267

Literacy rate:

Forms of gospel presentations available:

☐ radio ☐ tape/CD ☐ literature ☐ films
☐ videos ☐ other:

_____

_____

Receptive to change and to Christianity?

_____

_____

Require outside (cross-cultural) assistance?

_____

_____

Recommended approaches for the gospel:

☐ Jesus video ☐ home Bible studies
☐ cell groups ☐ special recreation events
☐ music concerts ☐ other:

Items for Prayer

_____

_____

_____

_____

_____

_____

Bibliography

Agar, Michael. 1996. *The Professional Stranger: An Informal Introduction to Ethnography*. 2nd ed. Bingley, UK: Emerald Group.

Allen, John. 1989. "New Strategies for Winning Unreached Youth." *Evangelical Missions Quarterly* 26, no. 2 (April): 126–37.

Allen, Roland. 1962. *Missionary Methods: St. Paul's or Ours?* American ed. Grand Rapids: Eerdmans.

Anderson, Justice. 1998. "The Great Century and Beyond." In *Missiology: An Introduction to the Foundations, History, and Strategies of World Missions*, edited by John Mark Terry, Ebbie C. Smith, and Justice Anderson, 199–218. Nashville: Broadman & Holman.

Andrews, Kenneth. 1971. *The Concept of Corporate Strategy*. Homewood, IL: Dow Jones-Irwin.

Anonymous. 2004. "H Scale for Hindu Contextualization." *Evangelical Missions Quarterly* 40, no. 3 (July): 316–20.

Babcock, Rufus, ed. 1864. *Forty Years of Pioneer Life: Memoir of John Mason Peck, D.D.* Philadelphia: American Baptist Publication Society. Online: http://www.archive.org/stream /40yearspioneer00peckrich_djvu.txt [accessed 4 April 2011].

Baker, Robert. 1974. *The Southern Baptist Convention and Its People*. Nashville: Broadman Press.

Bardwick, Judith M. 1996. "Peacetime Management and Wartime Leadership." In *The Leader of the Future: New Visions, Strategies, and Practices for the Next Era*, edited by Frances Hesselbein, Marshall Goldsmith, and Richard Beckhard, 131–40. San Francisco: Jossey-Bass.

Beaver, R. Pierce, ed. 1967. *To Advance the Gospel: Selections from the Writings of Rufus Anderson*. Grand Rapids: Eerdmans.

Bettenson, Henry, ed. 1956. *The Early Christian Fathers*. New York: Oxford University Press.

Beyerhaus, Peter. 1964. "The Three Selves Formula." *International Review of Missions* 53:393–407.

Blanchard, Ken, Alan Randolph, and Peter Grazier. 2005. *Go Team! Take Your Team to the Next Level*. San Francisco: Berrett-Koehler.

Bossidy, Larry, and Ram Charan. 2002. *Execution: The Discipline of Getting Things Done*. New York: Crown Business.

Bowers, Paul. 1987. "Paul's Mission." *Journal of the Evangelical Theological Society* 30, no. 2 (June): 185–98.

Brown, Rick. 2006. "Contextualization without Syncretism." *International Journal of Frontier Missions* 23, no. 3 (Fall): 127–33.

———. 2007. "Brother Jacob and Master Isaac: How One Insider Movement Began." *International Journal of Frontier Missions* 24, no. 1 (Spring): 41–42.

Burch, Greg W., Andy Sexton, and Angela Murray. 2009. "Strategic Impact: Multiplying Our Effectiveness with Children at Risk." *Evangelical Missions Quarterly* 45, no. 4 (October): 476–82.

Burnett, David. 2002. *Clash of Worlds*. London: Monarch Books.

Cairns, Earle E. 1996. *Christianity through the Centuries*. Grand Rapids: Zondervan.

Carey, William. 1792. *An Enquiry into the Obligations of Christians to Use Means for the Conversion of the Heathens in which the Religious State of the Different Nations of the World, the Success of Former Undertakings, and the Practicability of Further Undertakings, Are Considered*. London: Baptist Missionary Society.

Carver, W. O. 1932. *The Course of Christian Missions*. New York: Fleming H. Revell.

Clutterbuck, Basil. 1957. "World Missionary Strategy." *London Quarterly and Holborn Review* 182 (January): 29–34.

Cohen, Eric. 1990. "The Missionary as Stranger: A Phenomenological Analysis of Christian Missionaries' Encounter with Folk Religions." *Review of Religious Research* 31, no. 4 (June): 337–50.

———. 1991. "Christianity and Buddhism in Thailand: The 'Battle of the Axes' and the 'Contest of Power.'" *Social Compass* 38, no. 2: 115–40.

Collins, Jim. 2001. *Good to Great: Why Some Companies Make the Leap and Others Don't*. New York: Harper Business.

Conner, R. Dwayne. 1971. "The Hierarchy and the Church's Mission in the First Five Centuries." ThD diss., Southern Baptist Theological Seminary.

Corwin, Gary. 2007. "A Humble Appeal to C5/Insider Movement Muslim Ministry Advocates." *International Journal of Frontier Missions* 24, no. 1 (Spring): 5–20.

Coulter, Gordon. 2005. "Building Mission and Vision." In *Management Essentials for Christian Ministries*, edited by Michael J. Anthony and James Estep Jr., 59–75. Nashville: Broadman & Holman.

Coupland, Douglas. 1991. *Generation X: Tales for an Accelerated Culture*. New York: St. Martin's Press.

Covell, Ralph. 2000. "Faith Missions." In *Evangelical Dictionary of World Missions*, edited by A. Scott Moreau. Grand Rapids: Baker Academic.

Cruse, Rick. 1999. "Measuring Fruitful Ministry." *Evangelical Missions Quarterly* 35, no. 1 (January): 50–53.

Davies, J. G. 1967. *The Early Christian Church*. Garden City, NY: Anchor Books.

Davis, Charlie. 1997. "What Church Planters Need to Know about Dancing in Venezuela." *Evangelical Missions Quarterly* 33, no. 1 (January): 50–57.

Dayton, Edward R. 1980a. "To Reach the Unreached." In *Unreached Peoples '79*, edited by C. Peter Wagner and Edward R. Dayton, 25–31. Elgin, IL: David C. Cook.

———. 1980b. *God's Purpose/Man's Plans*. Monrovia, CA: MARC.

———. 1981. "To Reach the Unreached." In *Perspectives on the World Christian Movement: A Reader*, edited by Ralph D. Winter and Steven C. Hawthorne, 581–96. Pasadena, CA: William Carey Library.

Dayton, Edward R., and Ted W. Engstrom. 1976. *Strategy for Living: How to Make the Best Use of Your Time and Abilities*. Glendale, CA: Regal Books.

———. 1979. *Strategy for Leadership: Planning, Activating, Motivating, Elevating*. Old Tappan, NJ: Fleming H. Revell.

Dayton, Edward R., and David A. Fraser. 1980. *Planning Strategies for World Evangelization*. Grand Rapids: Eerdmans.

———. 1990. *Planning Strategies for World Evangelization*. Rev. ed. Grand Rapids: Eerdmans.

DeNeui, Paul. 2002. "Contextualizing with Thai Folk Buddhists." http://www.agts.edu/syllabi/ce/summer2002/mthm639oleson_sum02_np_r2.pdf (accessed October 11, 2012).

Dixit, Avinash K., and Barry J. Nalebuff. 1993. *Thinking Strategically: The Competitive Edge in Business, Politics, and Everyday Life*. London: W. W. Norton.

Donnellon, Anne. 2006. *Leading Teams*. Boston: Harvard Business School.

Douglas, J. D., ed. 1975. *Let the Earth Hear His Voice: The Proceedings of the Lausanne Committee on World Evangelism*. Minneapolis: World Wide Publications.

Elmer, Duane. 1993. *Cross-Cultural Conflict*. Downers Grove, IL: InterVarsity.

Eshleman, Paul. 2007. "'A Northstar for Evangelization Strategy': Looking toward Cape Town 2010." *Lausanne World Pulse* (September). http://www.lausanneworldpulse.com/research.php/806/09-2007?pg=all (accessed April 26, 2011).

Eusebius of Caesarea. 1984. *Ecclesiastical History*. Translated by C. F. Cruse. Grand Rapids: Baker.

"Evangelization Priorities for the Coming Decade." Online: http://www.lausanne.org/all-documents/priorities.html [accessed 11 May 2011].

Feddes, David. 2007. "Reproducing Christians." *Evangelical Missions Quarterly* 43, no. 3 (July): 346–54.

Fetterman, David. 1998. *Ethnography: Step by Step*. 2nd ed. Thousand Oaks, CA: Sage.

Fife, Eric S., and Arthur F. Glasser. 1961. *Missions in Crisis: Rethinking Missionary Strategy*. Downers Grove, IL: InterVarsity.

Frend, W. H. C. 1976. *Religion Popular and Unpopular in the Early Christian Centuries*. London: Variorum Reprints.

———. 1982. *The Early Church*. Philadelphia: Fortress Press.

Galloway, Bryan K. 2006. *Traveling Down Their Road: A Workbook for Discovering a People's Worldview*. Singapore: privately published.

Garrison, David. 2004. *Church Planting Movements*. Midlothian, VA: WIGTake Resources.

Gilliland, Dean S. 1983. *Pauline Theology and Mission Practice*. Eugene, OR: Wipf & Stock.

Gladwell, Malcolm. 2005. *Blink: The Power of Thinking without Thinking*. New York: Little, Brown.

Glasser, Arthur F. 1968. "Confession, Church Growth, and Authentic Unity in Missionary Strategy." In *Protestant Crosscurrents in Mission: The Ecumenical-Conservative Encounter*, edited by Norman A. Horner, 178–221. Nashville: Abingdon.

Global Research Department of the International Mission Board. Online: http://public.imb.org/globalresearch/pages [accessed 11 April 2011].

Green, Michael. 1970. *Evangelism in the Early Church*. Grand Rapids: Eerdmans.

Greeson, Kevin. 2004. *Camel Training Manual*. Bangalore, India: WIGTake Resources.

———. 2007. *The Camel: How Muslims Are Coming to Faith in Christ*. Midlothian, VA: WIGTake Resources.

Guy, Laurie. 2004. *Introducing Early Christianity*. Downers Grove, IL: InterVarsity.

Harnack, Adolf von. 1908. *The Mission and Expansion of Christianity in the First Three Centuries*. 2 vols. Translated by James Moffatt. New York: G. P. Putnam's Sons.

Harper, George. 1982. "How Valid Is Receptivity in Determining Mission Strategy?" *Evangelical Missions Quarterly* 18, no. 4 (October): 204–9.

Hartford, Paul F. 2000. "Teams in Mission." In *Evangelical Dictionary of World Missions*, edited by A. Scott Moreau. Grand Rapids: Baker Academic.

Harvard Business School. 2005. *Strategy: Create and Implement the Best Strategy for Your Business*. Boston: Harvard Business School Press.

Hatch, Nathan, Mark Noll, and John Woodbridge. 1979. *The Gospel in America*. Grand Rapids: Zondervan.

Hayes, Robert H. 1985. "Strategic Planning—Forward in Reverse?" *Harvard Business Review* 85, no. 6 (November–December): 111–19.

Hedlund, Roger E. 1985. *The Mission of the Church in the World*. Grand Rapids: Baker.

Hesselgrave, David J. 1980. *Planting Churches Cross-Culturally: A Guide for Home and Foreign Missions*. Grand Rapids: Baker.

———. 1992. *Communicating Christ Cross-Culturally*. 2nd ed. Grand Rapids: Zondervan.

———. 1995. "Contextualization That Is Authentic and Relevant." *International Journal of Frontier Missions* 12, no. 3 (July): 115–19.

———. 2000. *Planting Churches Cross-Culturally*. 2nd ed. Grand Rapids: Baker Academic.

———. 2005. *Paradigms in Conflict*. Grand Rapids: Kregel.

271

———. 2011. "Kingdom Missions and the Evangelical Future." http://edstetzer.com/blog (accessed February 22, 2011).

Hesselgrave, David J., and Edward Rommen. 1989. *Contextualization: Meanings, Methods, and Models*. Pasadena, CA: William Carey Library.

Hiebert, Paul. 1987. "Critical Contextualization," *International Journal of Missionary Research* (July): 104–11.

———. 1994. *Anthropological Reflections on Missiological Issues*. Grand Rapids: Baker.

Higgins, Kevin. 2006. "Identity, Integrity and Insider Movements: A Brief Paper Inspired by Timothy C. Tennent's Critique of C-5 Thinking." *International Journal of Frontier Missions* 23, no. 3 (Fall): 117–23.

———. 2007. "Acts 15 and Insider Movements among Muslims: Questions, Process and Conclusions." *International Journal of Frontier Missions* 24, no. 1 (Spring): 29–40.

Hodges, Melvin L. [1953] 1976. *The Indigenous Church*. New enlarged ed. Springfield, MO: Gospel Publishing House.

———. 1968. "A Pentecostal's View of Mission Strategy." *International Review of Missions* 57, no. 227 (July): 304–10.

Hunsberger, George. 2000. "Accommodation." In *Evangelical Dictionary of World Missions*, edited by A. Scott Moreau. Grand Rapids: Baker Academic.

Hyde, Walter W. 1946. *Paganism to Christianity in the Roman Empire*. Philadelphia: University of Pennsylvania Press.

Isenberg, Daniel J. 1987. "The Tactics of Strategic Opportunism." *Harvard Business Review* 65, no. 2 (March–April): 92–97.

"John Mason Peck." Southern Baptist Historical Library and Archives. http://www.sbhla.org/bio_peck.htm (accessed March 31, 2011).

Judson, Edward. 1883. *Adoniram Judson, D. D.: His Life and Labours*. London: Hodder & Stoughton.

Kane, J. Herbert. 1975. *A Global View of Christian Missions*. Grand Rapids: Baker.

———. 1976. *Christian Missions in Biblical Perspective*. Grand Rapids: Baker.

———. 1982. *A Concise History of the Christian World Mission*. Grand Rapids: Baker.

Katzenbach, Jon R., and Douglas K. Smith. 1993. *The Wisdom of Teams: Creating the High-Performance Organization*. New York: Harper Business.

Kidd, B. J., ed. 1920. *Documents Illustrative of the History of the Church*. 3 vols. London: Society for Promoting Christian Knowledge.

Kim, W. Chan, and Renee Mauborgne. 2005. *Blue Ocean Strategy: How to Create Uncontested Market Space and Make the Competition Irrelevant*. Boston: Harvard Business Review Press.

King, Roberta. 2000. "Extent of Missionary Identification." In *Evangelical Dictionary of World Missions*, edited by A. Scott Moreau. Grand Rapids: Baker Academic.

Kraft, Charles. 1979. *Christianity in Culture: A Study in Dynamic Biblical Theologizing in Cross-Cultural Perspective*. Maryknoll, NY: Orbis.

Kwast, Lloyd. 1981. "Understanding Culture." In *Perspectives on the World Christian Movement*, edited by Ralph D. Winter and Stephen C. Hawthorne, 361–64. Pasadena, CA: William Carey Library.

Labovitz, George, and Victor Rosansky. 1997. *The Power of Alignment: How Great Companies Stay Centered and Accomplish Extraordinary Things*. New York: John Wiley & Sons.

Latourette, Kenneth Scott. 1937. *A History of the Expansion of Christianity*. Vol. 1: *The First Five Centuries*. New York: Harper & Brothers.

———. 1941. *A History of the Expansion of Christianity*. Vol. 4: *The Great Century, AD 1800–AD 1914; Europe and the United States of America*. London: Eyre & Spottiswoode.

———. 1953. "The Light of History on Current Missionary Methods." *International Review of Missions* 42, no. 166 (April): 137–43.

———. 1970. *A History of the Expansion of Christianity*. Vol. 6: *The Great Century: North Africa and Asia*. Grand Rapids: Zondervan.

Lewis, Rebecca. 2007. "Promoting Movements to Christ within Natural Communities." *International Journal of Frontier Missions* 24, no. 2 (Summer): 75–76.

———. 2009. "Insider Movements: Honoring God-Given Identity and Community." *International Journal of Frontier Missions* 26, no. 1 (Spring): 16–19.

———. 2011. "Possible Pitfalls of Jesus Movements." *Mission Frontiers* 33, no. 3 (May–June): 21–24.

Lindsell, Harold. 1971. "Faith Missions." In *Concise Dictionary of the Christian World Mission*, edited by Stephen Neill. Nashville: Abingdon.

Logan, Robert E., and Neil Cole. 2005. *Beyond Church Planting: Pathways for Emerging Churches*. St. Charles, IL: ChurchSmart Resources.

Luecke, Richard. 2005. *Strategy: Create and Implement the Best Strategy for Your Business*. Boston: Harvard Business School Press.

MacDonald, Gordon. 1971. "What Mission Strategy Is and Does." *Evangelical Missions Quarterly* 8, no. 4 (October): 1–6.

Malphurs, Aubrey. 2005. *Advanced Strategic Planning: A New Model for Church and Ministry Leaders*. 2nd ed. Grand Rapids: Baker Books.

———. 2007. "Communicating the Vision." In *Leadership Handbook of Management and Administration*, edited by James D. Berkley, 189–90. Grand Rapids: Baker Books.

Mandryk, Jason, ed. 2010. *Operation World*. Colorado Springs: Biblica.

McGavran, Donald A. 1955. *The Bridges of God: A Study in the Strategy of Missions*. New York: Friendship Press.

———. 1965. "Wrong Strategy: The Real Crisis in Missions." *International Review of Missions* 54: 451–61.

———. 1970. *Understanding Church Growth*. Grand Rapids: Eerdmans.

———. 1990. *Understanding Church Growth*. 3rd ed. Revised and edited by C. Peter Wagner. Grand Rapids: Eerdmans.

McQuilken, Robertson. 1997. Paper presented at the Southeastern Regional Meeting of the Evangelical Missions Society, Charlotte, NC.

Mintzberg, Henry. 1987. "Crafting Strategy." *Harvard Business Review* 65, no. 4 (July–August): 66–75.

———. 1994. *The Rise and Fall of Strategic Planning: Reconceiving Roles for Planning, Plans, Planners*. New York: Free Press.

———. 2007. *Tracking Strategies: Toward a General Theory*. New York: Oxford University Press.

Montgomery, Jim. 1989. *DAWN 2000: 7 Million Churches to Go*. Pasadena, CA: William Carey Library.

Moreau, A. Scott. 2012. *Contextualization in World Missions: Mapping and Assessing Evangelical Models*. Grand Rapids: Kregel.

"More than Dreams: Muslims Coming to Christ through Dreams and Visions." 2007. *Lausanne World Pulse*. http://www.lausanneworldpulse.com/worldreports/595/01-2007 (accessed May 12, 2011).

Neill, Stephen. 1986. *A History of Christian Missions*. London: Penguin Books.

Nevius, John L. 2003. *The Planting and Development of Missionary Churches*. Hancock, NH: Monadnock Press.

Nicholls, Bruce. 1962. *Missionary Strategy*. n.p.: Evangelical Missionary Alliance.

———. 1979. *Contextualization: A Theory of Gospel and Culture*. Exeter, UK: Inter-Varsity Press.

Parshall, Phil. 1980. *New Paths in Muslim Evangelism*. Grand Rapids: Baker.

———. 1998. "Danger! New Directions in Contextualization." *Evangelical Missions Quarterly* 34, no. 4 (October): 404–10.

Pascale, Richard Tanner, and Anthony G. Athos. 1981. *The Art of Japanese Management: Applications for American Executives*. New York: Simon & Schuster.

Patterson, George, and Richard Scoggins. 1993. *Church Multiplication Guide*. Pasadena, CA: William Carey Library.

Paulinus. 1952. *Life of St. Ambrose*. Translated by John Lacy. New York: Fathers of the Church, Inc.

Payne, J. D. 2008. *The Barnabas Factors: Eight Essential Practices of Church Planting Team Members*. Smyrna, DE: Missional Press.

———. 2009. *Discovering Church Planting: An Introduction to the Whats, Whys, and Hows of Global Church Planting*. Colorado Springs: Paternoster.

———. 2010. "From 35,000 Feet to 15,000 Feet: Evangelical Statistics in the U.S. and Canada." http://www.jdpayne.org/2010/01/14/from-35000-to-15000-feet-evangelical-statistics-in-the-u-s-and-canada/ (accessed May 23, 2011).

Peters, G. W. 1975. "Contemporary Practices of Evangelism." In *Let the Earth Hear His Voice: The Proceedings of the Lausanne Committee on World Evangelism*, edited by J. D. Douglas, 181–204. Minneapolis: World Wide Publications.

Read, William R. 1973. "Frontier Missions Needed for Brazil's Frontier Road System." In *The Gospel and Frontier Peoples: A Report of a Consultation December 1972*, edited by R. Pierce Beaver, 169–88. Pasadena, CA: William Carey Library.

Reapsome, Jim. "Nevius, John Livingstone." In *Evangelical Dictionary of World Missions*, edited by A. Scott Moreau. Grand Rapids: Baker Books, 2000, 676–77.

Reynolds, David J. 1978. "The Gujarati Indians of England and Wales." In *Unreached Peoples '79*, edited by C. Peter Wagner and Edward R. Dayton, 129–37. Elgin, IL: David C. Cook.

Robb, John D. 1994. *Focus: The Power of People Group Thinking; A Practical Manual for Planning Effective Strategies to Reach the Unreached*. Monrovia, CA: MARC.

Roberts, Alexander, and James Donaldson, eds. 1951. *The Ante-Nicene Fathers*. Vols. 1–4. Grand Rapids: Eerdmans.

Roembke, Liann. 2000. *Building Credible Multicultural Teams*. Pasadena, CA: William Carey Library.

Rogers, Everett M. 2003. *Diffusion of Innovations*. 5th ed. New York: Free Press.

Rudnick, Milton L. 1984. *Speaking the Gospel through the Ages*. St. Louis: Concordia.

Schnabel, Eckhard J. 2008. *Paul the Missionary: Realities, Strategies, and Methods*. Downers Grove, IL: InterVarsity.

Schwarz, Christian A. 1996. *Natural Church Growth*. Carol Stream, IL: ChurchSmart Resources.

Sills, M. David. *Reaching and Teaching*. Chicago: Moody Press, 2008.

Sire, James. 2004. *The Universe Next Door*. Downers Grove, IL: InterVarsity.

Smith, Alex G. 1977. *Strategy to Multiply Rural Churches: A Central Thailand Case Study*. Bangkok: OMF.

Smith, Donald K. 1992. *Creating Understanding*. Grand Rapids: Zondervan.

Smith, Ebbie C. 1994. "What's Right with Church Growth." Southwestern Baptist Theological Seminary. Unpublished paper.

Soper, Edmund Davison. 1943. *The Philosophy of the Christian World Mission*. Nashville: Abingdon-Cokesbury.

Speer, Robert E. 1902. *Missionary Principles and Practice: A Discussion of Christian Missions and of Some Criticisms upon Them*. New York: Fleming H. Revell.

Spradley, Joseph. 1979. *The Ethnographic Interview*. New York: Holt, Rinehart & Winston.

Stark, Rodney. 1996. *The Rise of Christianity*. Princeton, NJ: Princeton University Press.

Starkes, Thomas. 1984. *God's Commissioned People*. Nashville: Broadman.

Steffen, Tom. 1993. *Passing the Baton*. La Habra, CA: Center for Organizational & Ministry Development.

———. 1996. *Reconnecting God's Story to Ministry: Cross-cultural Storytelling at Home and Abroad*. Waynesboro, GA: Authentic Media.

———. 1998. "Flawed Evangelism and Church Planting." *Evangelical Missions Quarterly* 34, no. 4 (October): 428–35.

Steuernagel, Valdir. 2008. "A Mission Voice from Latin America: Partnering for World Mission." *Lausanne World Pulse* (April). http://www.lausanneworldpulse.com/themedarticles.php/927/04–2008?pg=all (accessed April 26, 2011).

"Strategy." 1983. In *The American Heritage Dictionary*. New York: Dell.

Swank, Gerald O. 1977. Frontier Peoples of Central Nigeria and a Strategy for Outreach. Pasadena, CA: William Carey Library.

Sweet, William Warren. 1944. *Revivalism in America*. Nashville: Abingdon.

———. 1950. *The Story of Religion in America*. New York: Harper & Brothers.

Tennent, Timothy C. 2006. "Followers of Jesus (Isa) in Islamic Mosques." *International Journal of Frontier Missions* 23, no. 3 (Fall): 101–13.

Terry, Bruce. 1975. "American Indian Evangelism." *Mission Strategy Bulletin*, n.s., 2, no. 5 (June 6). http://www.ovc.edu/missions/msb/indevang.htm (accessed May 13, 2011).

Terry, John Mark. 1994. *Evangelism: A Concise History*. Nashville: Broadman & Holman.

———. 2000. "Indigenous Churches." In *Evangelical Dictionary of World Missions*, edited by A. Scott Moreau. Grand Rapids: Baker Academic.

Tippett, Alan R. 1969. *Verdict Theology in Missionary Theory*. Lincoln, IL: Lincoln Christian College Press.

Travis, John. 1998a. "Must All Muslims Leave Islam to Follow Jesus?" *Evangelical Missions Quarterly* 34, no. 4 (October): 411–15.

———. 1998b. "The C1–C6 Spectrum." *Evangelical Missions Quarterly* 34, no. 4 (October): 407–8.

Tucker, Ruth A. 2004. *From Jerusalem to Irian Jaya: A Biographical History of Christian Missions*. 2nd ed. Grand Rapids: Zondervan.

Tzu, Sun. 2008. *The Art of War*. New York: Chartwell Books.

Wagner, C. Peter. 1971. *Frontiers in Missionary Strategy*. Chicago: Moody Press.

———. 1973. "'Church Growth': More than a Man, a Magazine, a School, a Book." *Christianity Today* (December): 11–14.

———. 1983. *On the Crest of the Wave: Becoming a World Christian*. Ventura, CA: Regal Books.

———. 1989. *Strategies for Church Growth: Tools for Effective Mission and Evangelism*. Ventura, CA: Regal Books.

———. 2000. "Church Growth Movement." In *Evangelical Dictionary of World Missions*, edited by A. Scott Moreau. Grand Rapids: Baker Academic.

Walker, Ken. 2010. "Out of Context." *Christianity Today* (April): 14–15.

Warren, Max, ed. 1971. *To Apply the Gospel: Selections from the Writings of Henry Venn*. Grand Rapids: Eerdmans.

Warren, Rick. 1995. *The Purpose Driven Church: Growth without Compromising Your Mission*. Grand Rapids: Zondervan.

Weinrich, William C. 1981. "Evangelism in the Early Church." *Concordia Theological Quarterly* 45 (January–April): 61–75.

Wells, Stuart. 1998. *Choosing the Future: The Power of Strategic Thinking*. Boston: Butterworth-Heinemann.

Whiteman, Darrell. 1997. "Contextualization: The Theory, the Gap, the Challenge." *International Bulletin of Missionary Research* 21 (January): 2–7.

Winter, Ralph D. 1975. "The Highest Priority: Cross-Cultural Evangelism." In *Let the Earth Hear His Voice: International Congress on World Evangelization Lausanne, Switzerland*, edited by J. D. Douglas, 213–25. Minneapolis: World Wide Publications.

———. 1981. "The New Macedonia." In *Perspectives on the World Christian Movement: A Reader*, edited by Ralph D. Winter and Steven C. Hawthorne, 293–311. Pasadena, CA: William Carey Library.

———. 1984. "Unreached Peoples: The Development of a Concept." In *Reaching the Unreached*, edited by Harvey Conn. Phillipsburg, NJ: Presbyterian & Reformed.

Winter, Ralph, and Bruce A. Koch. 2009. "Finishing the Task: The Unreached Peoples Challenge." In *Perspectives on the World Christian Movement: A Reader*, edited by Ralph D. Winter and Steven C. Hawthorne, 531–46. Pasadena, CA: William Carey Library.

Winter, Ralph D., and Steven C. Hawthorne, eds. 1981. *Perspectives on the World Christian Movement: A Reader*. Pasadena, CA: William Carey Library.

Wolcott, Henry F. 2008. *Ethnography: A Way of Seeing*. Lanham, MD: AltaMira Press.

Scripture Index

4:4 19, 26, 40, 55
6:10 216

Ephesians

1:3–14 40
1:7–10 25
2:5 175
2:19–22 6
3:9 40
3:10 19
3:20 196
4:30 15
6:12 2

Philippians

1:21–23 60
2:11 6

Colossians

1:13 6

1 Thessalonians

5:17 195, 244
5:19 15

1 Timothy

3:1–13 201, 256
3:6 133
6:15 41

2 Timothy

2:15 162
4:9–13 41

Titus

1:5 57
1:5–9 201

Philemon

2 63

James

2:5 183
4:13–14 27
4:13–16 3, 35
4:15 27, 42
5:16 19

1 Peter

2:9 6

2 Peter

3:13 35

Jude

3 26

Revelation

2–3 257
19:7 6

Subject Index

Printed in Great Britain
by Amazon

43984719R00169